WORKING UNDER DIFFERENT RULES

Working under Different Rules

Edited by

Richard B. Freeman

A National Bureau of Economic Research Project Report

RUSSELL SAGE FOUNDATION • **NEW YORK**

The Russell Sage Foundation

The Russell Sage Foundation, one of the oldest of America's general purpose foundations, was established in 1907 by Mrs. Margaret Olivia Sage for "the improvement of social and living conditions in the United States." The Foundation seeks to fulfill this mandate by fostering the development and dissemination of knowledge about the country's political, social, and economic problems. While the Foundation endeavors to assure the accuracy and objectivity of each book it publishes, the conclusions and interpretations in Russell Sage Foundation publications are those of the authors and not of the Foundation, its Trustees, or its staff. Publication by Russell Sage, therefore, does not imply Foundation endorsement.

Library of Congress Cataloging-in-Publication Data

Working under different rules / edited by Richard B. Freeman.
    p.   cm.
    ISBN 0-87154-276-5 : — ISBN 0-87154-277-3 (pbk.) :
    1. Labor—United States—Congresses. 2. Labor—Congresses.
  I. Freeman, Richard B. (Richard Barry), 1943– .
HD8057.W64 1993
331'.0973—dc30   93-23604
                                                                      CIP

RUSSELL SAGE FOUNDATION
112 East 64th Street, New York, New York 10021

10 9 8 7 6 5 4 3 2

Relation of the Directors to the Work and Publications
of the National Bureau of Economic Research

1. The object of the National Bureau of Economic Research is to ascertain and to present to the public important economic facts and their interpretation in a scientific and impartial manner. The Board of Directors is charged with the responsibility of ensuring that the work of the National Bureau is carried on in strict conformity with this object.

2. The President of the National Bureau shall submit to the Board of Directors, or to its Executive Committee, for their formal adoption all specific proposals for research to be instituted.

3. No research report shall be published by the National Bureau until the President has sent each member of the Board a notice that a manuscript is recommended for publication and that in the President's opinion it is suitable for publication in accordance with the principles of the National Bureau. Such notification will include an abstract or summary of the manuscript's content and a response form for use by those Directors who desire a copy of the manuscript for review. Each manuscript shall contain a summary drawing attention to the nature and treatment of the problem studied, the character of the data and their utilization in the report, and the main conclusions reached.

4. For each manuscript so submitted, a special committee of the Directors (including Directors Emeriti) shall be appointed by majority agreement of the President and Vice Presidents (or by the Executive Committee in case of inability to decide on the part of the President and Vice Presidents), consisting of three Directors selected as nearly as may be one from each general division of the Board. The names of the special manuscript committee shall be stated to each Director when notice of the proposed publication is submitted to him. It shall be the duty of each member of the special manuscript committee to read the manuscript. If each member of the manuscript committee signifies his approval within thirty days of the transmittal of the manuscript, the report may be published. If at the end of the period any member of the manuscript committee withholds his approval, the President shall then notify each member of the Board, requesting approval or disapproval of publication, and thirty days additional shall be granted for this purpose. The manuscript shall then not be published unless at least a majority of the entire Board who shall have voted on the proposal within the time fixed for the receipt of votes shall have approved.

5. No manuscript may be published, though approved by each member of the special manuscript committee, until forty-five days have elapsed from the transmittal of the report in manuscript form. The interval is allowed for the receipt of any memorandum of dissent or reservation, together with a brief statement of his reasons, that any member may wish to express; and such memorandum of dissent or reservation shall be published with the manuscript if he so desires. Publication does not, however, imply that each member of the Board has read the manuscript, or that either members of the Board in general or the special committee have passed on its validity in every detail.

6. Publications of the National Bureau issued for informational purposes concerning the work of the Bureau and its staff, or issued to inform the public of activities of Bureau staff, and volumes issued as a result of various conferences involving the National Bureau shall contain a specific disclaimer noting that such publication has not passed through the normal review procedures required in this resolution. The Executive Committee of the Board is charged with review of all such publications from time to time to ensure that they do not take on the character of formal research reports of the National Bureau, requiring formal Board approval.

7. Unless otherwise determined by the Board or exempted by the terms of paragraph 6, a copy of this resolution shall be printed in each National Bureau publication.

(Resolution adopted October 25, 1926, as revised through September 30, 1974)

CONTENTS

CONTRIBUTORS

Rebecca Blank is an associate professor of economics at Northwestern University and a member of the research faculty at NU's Center for Urban Affairs and Policy Research. She is also a research associate of the National Bureau of Economic Research. Her research focuses on the interaction between macroeconomic effects, labor market and social welfare programs, and the behavior and well-being of low-income families. Recent research includes a study of the dynamic patterns of participation in AFDC and Food Stamp programs, several studies of the relationship between economic growth and income distribution over the 1980s, and comparative work on social protection programs between the U.S. and other industrialized countries.

David Card is professor of economics at Princeton University. He is currently the co-editor of *Econometrica*, and a research associate of the National Bureau of Economic Research. His current research interests include: evaluating the benefits of school spending, analyzing the contributions of civil rights legislation and other factors in black-white wage differentials, and the labor market effects of minimum wages.

Richard B. Freeman holds the Herbert Ascherman Chair in Economics at Harvard University. He is also director of the Labor Studies Program at the National Bureau of Economic Research, and executive programme director of the Comparative Labour Market Institutions Programme at the London School of Economics' Centre for Economic Performance. He is currently a member of the Secretary of Labor and Commerce's Commission on The Future of Worker Management Relations. His research interests include youth labor market problems, trade unionism, high-skilled labor markets, crime, economic discrimination, philanthropic behavior, income distribution and equity in the marketplace, and labor in developing countries.

Lawrence F. Katz is Chief Economist of the U.S. Department of Labor. He is currently on leave from his positions as a professor of economics at Harvard University and a research associate of the National Bureau of Economic Research. His research interests include family income inequality, labor mobility and unemployment, changes in the structure of wages, theories of wage determination, the problems of disadvantaged youth, and regional economic growth. He is currently an editor of the *Quarterly Journal of Economics*.

Lisa M. Lynch is an associate professor of economics and international business and co-director of the Clayton Center for International Economic Affairs at the Fletcher School of Law and Diplomacy, Tufts University. She is an editor of the *Journal of Labor Economics*, associate editor for *Labour Economics: An International Journal*, and a research associate of the National Bureau of Economic Research. Her current research examines the impact of private sector training on workers' wages and firms' productivity, and the school to work transition of youths. She is the author of numerous papers in research volumes and journals and has lectured extensively in the United States, Canada, Europe, and Japan.

Joel Rogers is professor of law, political science, and sociology at the University of Wisconsin-Madison, where he also directs the Center on Wisconsin Strategy (COWS), a research and policy institute active in current debates on industrial upgrading. He is a consultant to the Labor and Human Resources Committee of the U.S. Senate. His research interests include normative democratic theory, political parties, labor organizations and other secondary associations, wage regulation, welfare administration, occupational and vocational training, and the linkage of human capital and technology policies in industrial upgrading.

Wolfgang Streeck is professor of sociology and industrial relations at the University of Wisconsin-Madison. He is presently a Fellow at the Wissenschaftskolleg zu Berlin. His research interests include comparative industrial relations in Western Europe, interest groups, and problems of European integration. He is presently finishing a book on the "social dimension" of the European common market, and is working on a study (with Ronald Dore) on the differences between Japanese, German, British, and American capitalism.

PREFACE

For American workers the 1980s, and to a lesser extent the 1970s, were a difficult time. Real earnings fell for many. Labor productivity grew slowly. The proportion of workers in sectors with high and increasing productivity, such as manufacturing, declined. Once the world leaders in reducing work time, Americans came to work more hours in a year than Europeans (though not as many as the Japanese). Employee representation in trade unions declined precipitously, creating a union-free environment in most of the economy.

While the United States still leads the developed world in productivity and real income per person (using purchasing power to put foreign currency on a dollar scale), and while the unemployment rate is lower in the United States than in Western Europe, the American way of organizing work and rewarding workers no longer guarantees hardworking citizens a piece of the American dream. The gap between higher paid and lower paid workers widened dramatically in the 1980s. Many young persons today see their economic position as falling short of that of their parents. Child poverty rates exceed those in most advanced countries. The homeless and the urban "underclass" seem to have become permanent fixtures in America.

Are deteriorating earnings, rising inequality, falling unionization, and increased child poverty common to advanced countries, or are these problems unique to the United States? How does the American labor market stack up against those of our major trading partners and competitors in the world? How do other advanced countries organize their workplaces; train, motivate, and pay workers; and support those at the bottom of the income distribution? What are the lessons from overseas for how we might improve our competitive position and the well-being of our workers?

To answer these questions, the National Bureau of Economic Research undertook a four-year project to compare labor markets in Western Europe, Canada, Japan, and Australia with the American labor market. The research was organized around four topics—changes in wages and wage differentials, training within firms, employee representation, and social programs and labor market flexibility—and one country-to-country comparison, between Canada and the United States. Researchers visited firms, training centers, government agencies, and unions and analyzed computerized data files on tens of thousands of workers in other advanced countries to determine how the labor institutions of those countries function and how they affect wages, working life, and ultimately productivity and living standards.

The leaders of each research group presented their major conclusions and some of the evidence underlying those conclusions at a conference in Washington, D.C., on May 7, 1993. This volume gives (revised) versions of the summary papers, along with an introduction and a concluding chapter on lessons for the United States. The detailed studies are being published by the University of Chicago Press for the National Bureau of Economic Research, in a new series entitled *Comparative Labor Markets*.

I am grateful to the many researchers who worked on this project, and to the project leaders, who organized and directed the work. All of those involved in the project are grateful to the government officials, managers, academics, and labor leaders in the various countries, who spent time helping us understand the way their country's institutions and labor markets operate.

The project also owes much to the Ford Foundation, which funded most of the research, and in particular to Franklin Thomas, president of the Foundation, for his interest in widening the perspective in which we view the problems facing American workers. Several other foundations in the United States and overseas also helped fund parts of specific projects. The Russell Sage Foundation supported the conference in Washington and the publication of this volume.

RICHARD B. FREEMAN
August 1993
Cambridge, Massachusetts

1

HOW LABOR FARES
IN ADVANCED ECONOMIES

Richard B. Freeman

In 1909 Samuel Gompers, a founder of the American labor movement and president of the American Federation of Labor, visited Europe to examine "from an American viewpoint . . . life and conditions of working men in Great Britain, France, Holland, Germany, Italy, etc." Gompers was struck by the poor living standard of Europeans compared with Americans: "Poverty such as exists in Belgium and Holland can hardly be conceived by the average dweller in an American city." Gompers noted many ways in which Europe could learn from the United States, ranging from provision of running water to efficient operation of railroads, areas in which Europe was "half a century behind time." But nowhere did he find lessons for the United States from Europe. On the union front, which concerned him most, "the national [labor] movement in no foreign country can compare with the American Federation of Labor."[1]

Throughout the twentieth century, economic and social developments broadly validated Gomper's "America first" view of the labor scene. Through two world wars and the recoveries that followed them, the United States led the world in productivity, real wages, and conditions at the workplace. During the cold war, American unions were preeminent defenders of free enterprise and supporters of independent unions overseas. American business dominated world markets and pioneered the consumer society.

The evidence in this book shows that at the approach of the

twenty-first century the situation for American labor is quite different. Labor productivity and living standards are high in the United States, but this country no longer dominates other advanced economies in providing good jobs at good wages. American work arrangements, modes of pay, training, and labor representation are not clearly superior to those in other countries. Low-paid workers in the United States earn so much less than the average that they have worse standards of living than comparable workers in Europe or Japan. Japanese firms that offer lifetime employment, job rotation, enterprise unions, and bonus payments outcompete American firms in many markets. German firms with apprenticeship programs, works councils, and workers on boards of directors, train workers better and empower them at the workplace in ways that American firms do not. Countries whose conditions horrified Gompers are among the most prosperous in the world, as any tourist to Belgium or Holland will attest. Productivity and real wages are increasing less rapidly in the United States than in Europe and Japan. The evidence of the falling position of American workers vis-à-vis those in other advanced countries motivates the analyses in the ensuing chapters of this book.

HOW THE UNITED STATES RATES ... IN EMPLOYMENT

I start with an area in which the American labor market has done well in comparison with other countries—the creation of jobs. From the mid-1970s through the early 1980s most West European countries suffered from slow economic growth and high or rising unemployment. While the United States was no exception, its employment record was markedly better than that of Western Europe. The United States added some 20 million jobs from 1975 to 1985, whereas employment fell slightly in Common Market countries and increased by just 2.5 million in all of the Organization for Economic Cooperation and Development (OECD) countries in Europe, even though Europe has a larger population than the United States.[2] The result was that a substantially larger proportion of the working-age population was employed in the United States throughout most of the 1980s and in the early 1990s than in Western Europe (Figure 1.1).

Because employed Americans work more hours than employed Europeans (though less than the Japanese) the difference in work activity between the United States and Europe is even greater when adjusted for hours worked. In most European countries annual

Figure 1.1   Percentage of Fifteen- to Sixty-four-year-olds Working in the United States and Western Europe, Adjusted for Hours.

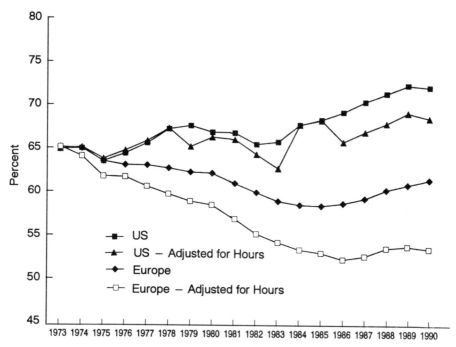

SOURCE: OECD, 1992b (Table 2.1), with hours adjusted from OECD, 1993b (Table B) and OECD, 1982 (Table 2.13). The figures for Europe are a weighted average of the countries using 1988 employment as weights for all years, and employment from OECD, 1990b.

hours worked fell in the 1970s and 1980s, in part because Europeans took longer vacations and in part because they reduced the hours worked per week. By contrast, in the United States the trend toward less work and more leisure essentially ended. In 1970 Americans worked fewer hours over the year than the Germans or the French. In 1992 Americans worked the equivalent of one month per year more than the Germans, French, or other Europeans.[3]

The difference in employment is not largely a matter of differences in the desire to work. Rates of unemployment in Europe, which were historically lower than in the United States, came to exceed those in the United States in the early 1980s (Figure 1.2). Exceptionally large proportions of European youths, in particular, sought jobs but could not find them from the early 1980s through the mid-1990s.

Figure 1.2   Unemployment Rates, 1973 to 1990.

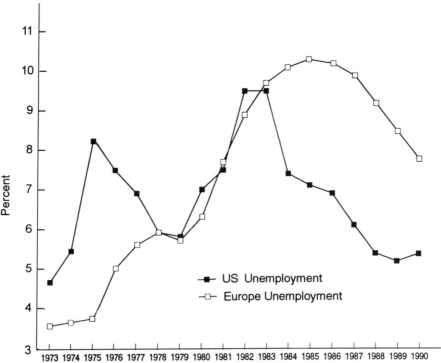

SOURCE: OECD, 1992b (Table 2.15) and OECD, 1982 (Table 2.14).

While the United States did well in providing employment, some aspects of the "great American jobs miracle" look less wondrous on close inspection. For one, the difference in hours worked is a two-edged sword. Having short vacations and relatively long weekly hours at work is nothing to trumpet to the world. Most people, even economists, regard leisure as good, and rate societies that provide more leisure for their citizens as doing better, all else being the same, than those that do not. The more rapid growth of employment in the United States also should not be viewed as a "fact of life." It occurred from the mid-1970s through the mid-1980s. From 1987 through 1991 employment grew more in the European Economic Community (EEC) than in the United States—representing an increase of 17 million jobs in the EEC compared with 8 million jobs in the United States, though this differential fell as Europe entered a recession thereafter.[4] In addition, much U.S. job growth occurred in low-wage service industries, where many women may have been "pushed" into the job market by the falling incomes of their husbands. Along virtually all dimensions during this period, the Japanese employment record surpassed that of the United States.

Still, as one of the few labor markets in the developed world that provided more employment for its working-age population in an economically troubled decade, the American labor market deserved the plaudits it received during the 1980s.

. . . IN FLEXIBILITY AND MOBILITY

Many European analysts and policymakers attribute U.S. job creation to America's flexible and relatively unregulated labor market. Virtually every indicator shows that the United States has a more mobile work force and allows management greater flexibility in hiring, firing, or altering work conditions than the managements have in most other advanced countries.

The greater flux in the job market in the United States (and Canada) than in other advanced countries can be seen in rates of geographic mobility (OECD, 1991, Table 2.14), in rates of job turnover (OECD, 1987, Table 4.1), and in accessions and separations in manufacturing (OECD, 1991, Table 2.13), all of which are higher in the United States than in Europe or Japan. It also shows up, most dramatically, in the duration of unemployment (Figure 1.3). In the United States, people move rapidly between unemployment and employment. Only a small proportion of unemployed Americans are out of work for more than one year, compared with nearly half the unemployed in Europe and nearly 20 percent of those in Japan.[5] In any month the proportion of Americans who leave unemployment far exceeds the proportion of Europeans who do so. In 1988, 46 percent of Americans unemployed in a given month were no longer unemployed the following month, whereas only 5 percent of Europeans unemployed in one month in 1988 left unemployment the following month.[6] At the same time, however, the chance of entering unemployment in a given month is also higher in the United States than in Europe or Japan. Two percent of Americans became unemployed in a month in 1988, compared with 0.4 percent of Japanese and Europeans.[7]

With respect to business flexibility, the EEC has asked European managers about factors that constrain their operations in the job

Figure 1.3   **Percentage of Unemployed Who Are Jobless One Year or More, 1991.**

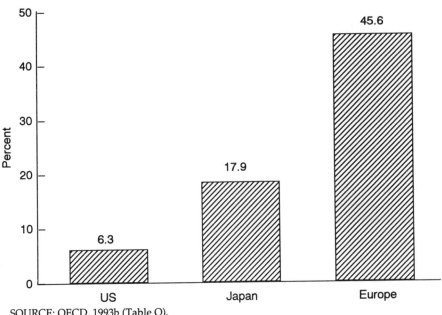

SOURCE: OECD, 1993b (Table Q).

market. In 1991, 27 percent reported that "insufficient flexibility in hiring and shedding labor" was a very important obstacle to employing more people. An additional 35 percent reported that it was an important obstacle. European firms in many countries must give laid off workers severance pay and lengthy advance notice, and may have to obtain the approval of works councils or government agencies before making large-scale dismissals. Only in the United Kingdom, where the labor market most resembles the American market, do most employers report that flexibility is not a barrier to increasing employment. In addition, 68 percent of European managers reported that nonwage labor costs were very important or important obstacles to increasing employment.[8] Mandated expenditures for employee benefits and payroll taxes are higher in many European countries than in the United States.

The concordance of high mobility and flexibility with growth of jobs in the United States convinced many European governments and analysts in the 1980s that "American-style" labor market flexibility was the route to full employment (OECD, 1990c). Some went a step further and advocated the reduction of state welfare programs that allegedly impede flexibility—an issue that Chapter 5 of this volume explores.

Whatever their virtues, high labor market mobility and flexibility are not logically necessary for a good employment performance. The proportion of the population with jobs or the proportion that is jobless depends on the *difference* between the rate of job finding and the rate of job losing. When economic conditions are good, firms with great flexibility in adjusting employment may hire more workers than firms with less flexibility, but they will also reduce employment more when conditions are bad. High rates of job loss and job gain produce short durations of joblessness and short periods of job tenure; they do not necessarily produce low rates of unemployment. The case in point is Japan, whose lifetime employment practices make it an outlier among developed countries in labor turnover, but which has the lowest unemployment rate of major economies.[9]

Even if high turnover were to reduce unemployment, moreover, it does so with a cost. Firms usually want low turnover, because finding and training new employees is expensive. And people don't like writing résumés, interviewing, and searching want ads, especially if they are unemployed. Turnover also impedes training. When turnover is high, firms will not provide as much workplace training as when turnover is low.[10] The high mobility of labor in the United States is one reason American firms provide only limited training for workers.

Whether high mobility and flexibility are a mixed bag with good and bad features, as I argue, or the unalloyed good that some believe them to be, the fact is that the American job market has higher mobility and flexibility than job markets in other advanced economies.

. . . IN PRODUCTIVITY AND LIVING STANDARDS

Much is made of faltering American productivity. Some believe that the Japanese or Germans have higher levels of productivity than Americans. It is true that the great American advantage in productivity and living standards that so impressed Gompers in 1909 was largely eroded in the 1980s. But properly measured,

American productivity is high, and the nation's average standard of living remains at the top of the world tables.

Comparing productivity or standards of living across countries is difficult. Transforming output or earnings in foreign currencies into U.S. dollars using exchange rates can be misleading. The value of currency on the foreign exchange market varies for reasons that have nothing to do with productivity or living standards, so that comparisons based on exchange rates can give an erroneous picture of how people fare in different countries.[11] For instance, in its annual report on the state of world economies the World Bank compares gross domestic product (GDP) per capita in countries around the world in U.S. dollars, obtained by transforming other national currencies into dollars using exchange rates. These statistics show that in 1991 a host of countries surpassed the United States in GDP per capita: Switzerland, where GDP per capita was an astounding 51 percent higher than in the United States; Japan, where it was 21 percent higher; Germany, 6 percent higher; and the Scandinavian countries, as well.[12] But as American tourists overseas in the early 1990s learned to their dismay, at prevailing exchange rates the prices of consumer goods in these (and many other) countries exceeded those in the United States, rendering invalid any contrast of output based on exchange rates.

A better way to compare productivity and living standards across countries is to use the purchasing power parity (PPP) of currencies. The PPP of a currency shows how much of that currency is needed to buy a given basket of goods, compared with how much that basket would cost in dollars. Table 1.1 shows how other advanced countries stack up against the United States in GDP per capita and labor productivity, in purchasing power units. The table measures the U.S. position as 100 and gives the position of other countries as percentages of the United States. Column 1 shows that in 1991, no country had a per capita GDP larger than that of the United States; the United States had the highest volume of goods and services produced per capita in the world.

But per capita GDP or output does not itself measure productivity. GDP per head is the multiplicand of productivity—output per worker or output per hour worked—and workers per capita or hours worked per capita. To see how productivity differs among countries, one must transform GDP per capita into GDP per employee or, better yet, GDP per hour worked. Since Europeans work

Table 1.1   Gross Domestic Product in Purchasing Power Parity Dollars in Advanced Countries, Relative to the United States

Country	GDP/Capita, 1991[a]	Productivity, GDP/ Employee[b]	GDP/Hours 1991[c]	GDP/Employee Projected to the Year 2000[d]
United States	100	100	100	100
Major Countries				
Japan	87	78	69	93
Germany	89	90	102	93
France	83	96	102	105
United Kingdom	74	76	—	80
Italy[e]	77	96	96	104
Canada	89	89	92	90
Smaller Countries				
Australia	74	76	92	74
Austria	81	82	—	84
Belgium	79	96	—	104
Denmark	81	75	—	76
Netherlands	76	81	101	76
Norway	78	76	96	83
Spain	57	82	76	93
Sweden	79	71	85	72
Switzerland	99	87	—	87

[a] Column 1 data calculated from GDP per capita estimates based on purchasing power parity, from OECD, 1992d (Table 2-5). The estimates are for 1990. I have updated them to 1991 by applying the growth of real GDP in each country from OECD, 1993a (Table 1.1) and growth of population from U.S. Bureau of the Census, 1993 (Table 1359).
[b] Column 2 data calculated by dividing column 1 by employment per person, with employment data from OECD, 1993 (Table 1.2) and population data from U.S. Bureau of the Census, 1993 (Table 1359).
[c] Column 3 data calculated by dividing column 2 by hours per person from OECD, 1993 (Table B).
[d] Column 4 projections were obtained by applying 1979–1990 growth rates from OECD, 1992b (GDP per capita in Table 3.2, and GDP per employee in Table 3.7).
[e] Italian figures for productivity are suspect due to the large underground economy.

fewer hours than Americans, European countries will look better in comparisons of productivity than in comparisons of GDP per capita. Since the Japanese work more hours than Americans, by contrast, they will look worse in productivity than in GDP per capita.

Columns 2 and 3 of Table 1.1 compare productivity across countries, scaled relative to the United States. The per worker GDP measured in column 2 show a smaller U.S. advantage over European countries. For instance, output per employee in 1991 was 4 percent lower in Belgium than in the United States, whereas output per person was 21 percent lower. Some of the government statistics that underlie the table may be erroneous: for instance, Italian productivity is probably overstated, due to the failure to count workers in Italy's large and vibrant underground economy. But the data give a valid picture of the overall position of the United States compared with other countries. Column 3 of the table shows, further, that much of the remaining U.S. advantage over European countries is due to differences in hours worked over the year. These data indicate that hourly productivity is quite similar among advanced countries, save for Japan and Spain.[13] Because productivity is growing less rapidly in the United States than in other countries, however, the U.S. position is likely to worsen by the year 2000 (column 4).[14] At the beginning of the twenty-first century America will no longer lead the world in labor productivity—a far cry from where it stood at the beginning of the twentieth century.

... IN PAY AND POVERTY

The well-being of wage and salary workers depends on their rate of pay, which is related to, but not identical with, labor productivity. In his 1909 survey, Gompers reported low rates of pay for workers in Europe, which he transformed into dollars using the exchange rates of that era. Column 1 of Table 1.2 records hourly compensation of production workers in manufacturing in 1992 across countries, also transformed into dollars by exchange rates. The position of American workers is different than it was in earlier decades. At 1992 exchange rates Americans received low pay compared with workers in other advanced countries. Hourly compensation was 60 percent higher in Germany than in the United States, 50 percent higher in Sweden, 44 percent higher in Switzerland, 36 percent higher in Belgium (which Gompers saw as a disaster case), and so on.[15] Given comparable levels of productivity, American workers are a low-wage bargain in the developed world.

However, pay comparisons based on exchange rates, while an appropriate guide to some business investment decisions, are misleading as an indicator of standards of living. Hourly compensation in PPP, given in column 2 of Table 1.2, tells a very different story. Measured in purchasing power, the United States is not *the* leader in

Table 1.2   **Hourly Compensation of Production Workers in Manufacturing in Advanced Countries, Relative to the United States**

Country	Hourly Compensation in Exchange Rates 1992[a]	Hourly Compensation in Purchasing Power 1992[b]	Hourly Compensation Projected to the Year 2000[c]
United States	100	100	100
Major Countries			
Japan	100	66	75
Germany	160	119	135
France	104	85	91
United Kingdom	91	82	98
Italy	120	100	105
Canada	105	97	96
Smaller Countries			
Australia	80	81	76
Austria	122	95	107
Belgium	136	113	114
Denmark	124	82	85
Netherlands	128	103	104
Norway	143	93	100
Spain	83	74	87
Sweden	150	90	92
Switzerland	144	89	95

[a] Column 1 data from U.S. Bureau of Labor Statistics, *International Comparisons of Hourly Compensation Costs for Production Workers in Manufacturing*, 1992 Report 844 (Washington D.C.: U.S. GPO, 1993), Table 1.
[b] Column 2 data adjusted by taking hourly compensation from Table 2 of the report and purchasing power parity figures for 1990 from OECD, 1992d (Table 1.3).
[c] Column 3 data based on projecting 1979–1990 growth of real hourly earnings in manufacturing from OECD, 1992b (Table 9.2) for each country except the United States, where I have made the more optimistic assumption of constant real earnings as opposed to the annual drop of 1 percent in the 1979–1990 period in the OECD figures.

pay it once was, but it trails only Germany, the Netherlands, and (Gompers would be stunned) Belgium. The difference in the U.S. position between columns 1 and 2 is that at 1992 exchange rates, consumer prices were much higher in Europe and Japan than in the United States. Adjusting for price differences via PPP rates greatly improves the relative American position.

But as with productivity, the growth rate of real wages (wages adjusted for inflation) in the United States portends a worsened relative position for American workers by the year 2000. The real earnings of manufacturing workers in the United States fell in the 1980s,[16] whereas the real earnings of manufacturing workers in Europe rose by 1.2 percent per year and the real earnings of those in Japan rose by 1.6 percent per year. If 1980s rates of growth of real earnings are maintained in other countries, and the United States manages to keep real earnings from falling (which would be an improvement over the 1980s), American workers will drop from near the top of the earnings table to the lower middle ranks (see column 3 of Table 1.2). If real earnings of American manufacturing workers fall in the 1990s at the same rate as in the 1980s, the United States will drop to the fourth lowest position. Some countries will undoubtedly do better in the 1990s than they did in the 1980s while others will undoubtedly do worse, but the general pattern is clear: a falling position for the United States.

Since most workers are not production workers in manufacturing, you may wonder whether the earnings of these workers provide a valid comparison of well-being across countries. As an indicator of the position of *average* workers, the pay figures in Table 1.2 are broadly representative.[17] Estimates of annual compensation for employees in the business sector, which covers the vast bulk of employees, confirm the story about the fall of the United States from its position as the high-wage country.[18]

Average earnings are, however, misleading in one important sense. The *distribution* of wages (and incomes) is more unequal in the United States than in other advanced countries. Lower paid workers do much worse compared with the average in the United States than in other advanced countries, while well-paid workers do much better. Figure 1.4 documents this with two statistics: the ratio of the hourly (weekly) earnings at the lowest decile of the earnings distribution (earnings that exceed those of just 10 percent of the male work force) to the median; and the ratio of the earnings of men in the top decile (those whose earnings exceed 90 percent of workers) also relative to the median. American men in the bottom decile earn just 38 percent of median earnings—barely half as much as Europeans in the bottom decile receive relative to the European median, and just 62 percent as much as Japanese in the bottom decile relative to the Japanese median. In contrast, men in the top decile do relatively better compared with the median in the United States than in other countries. The stories about U.S.

**Figure 1.4 Pay of Low-wage and High-wage Workers
Relative to Median: United States, Japan, and Europe.**

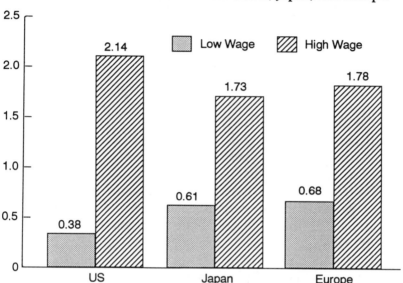

SOURCE: Calculated from OECD, 1993b (Table 5.2) with Europe estimated as a weighted average using 1988 employment for weights, from OECD, 1990b.

executives being well paid as compared with those in other countries are true, but it isn't only executives who do well: so do other American workers near the top of the earnings distribution.

Since average earnings in the United States are comparable in purchasing power to average earnings in countries like Germany or Norway or Belgium, the evidence that low-paid American workers are further below the average than low-paid workers in other countries implies that low-paid Americans have lower earnings and living standards than low-paid workers in those countries. Indeed I estimate that among men in the bottom decile, Americans earn roughly 45 percent of what Germans earn, 54 percent as much as Norwegians, half as much as Italians, and so on. Among bottom decile workers, if the United States is scaled at 100 as in the table, European earnings are 144 and Japanese earnings are 106.[19] Even worse, low-paid Americans have lower real earnings than workers in all advanced countries for which there are comparable data—which is due largely to the fall in their real earnings (see Chapter 2, this volume). The low and falling real pay of less skilled Americans contributes to the high and rising rates of child poverty, and to the extensive homelessness and large "underclass" that differentiate American society from that of other advanced countries.

TRADE-OFFS IN OUTCOMES?

The evidence that the United States has done better than Europe in employment growth but worse in growth of real wages and productivity suggests that perhaps these are two sides of the same coin. Maybe the United States "paid" for employment creation through low or declining wages, while Europe "paid" for high or rising wages with sluggish growth of employment. In fact, conditional on growth of real output (similar in Europe on a per capita basis to that in the United States, but more rapid in Japan than elsewhere), countries that had rapid growth of real wages, had smaller growth in employment in the 1970s and 1980s than countries with small growth of real wages and labor productivity (Freeman, 1988). From 1979 to 1990 in the United States employment per capita rose by 0.6 percent per year while GDP per worker grew by 1.0 percent, whereas in Europe employment per capita grew by just 0.3 percent per year while GDP per worker grew by 1.4 percent.[20]

One interpretation of this pattern of change in employment, wages, and productivity is that firms in different countries face two "givens": changes in demand for their product, which depends on rates of national GDP growth determined by long-term economic forces and national economic policy; and changes in wages that depend on pay-setting institutions in the country. Given what firms can sell, and the cost of labor, they necessarily hire fewer workers when wages rise rapidly. Whether this simple labor demand story captures the true difference in country performances, or whether (as I suspect) reality requires a more complex analysis, the observed inverse relation between wage growth and employment growth (conditional on GDP growth) highlights the fact that while the United States did well in job expansion, it did poorly in earnings growth.

DIFFERENCES IN RULES

In Economics I, the invisible hand of market forces sets wages, prices, and quantities, aided perhaps by a Wizard of Oz "auctioneer" who calibrates prices and wages until all markets clear. In real labor markets, however, matters are more complicated and interesting. Every country has its own labor market institutions—unions, management organizations, government agencies—and rules that help determine outcomes. Each has its own way of resolving labor-management disputes; setting wages and determining nonwage benefits; regulating hiring and firing decisions and personnel policies; and providing welfare "safety nets" for those lacking work. Some countries rely extensively on legal mandates to determine outcomes. Others use collective bargaining. Others give relatively free sway to management decisions and individual negotiations. All develop labor market policies intended to improve market outcomes. These differences in rules and institutions affect economic outcomes and are themselves an important element in working life.

Organization of Labor and Management

Consider first the ways labor and management are organized in advanced countries. Trade unions are probably the most idiosyncratic institution in modern capitalism. Each country's union movement has a distinct structure and mode of operating, in part due to its unique historical development. Employers have a greater similarity across countries—many of the same multinationals operate everywhere—but the organization of employers into employer associations and the role those associations play in economic life differ greatly among countries.

The United States has a business-oriented union movement (dating back to Gompers's leadership) based largely on relatively autonomous local unions who bargain for better conditions from individual employers. American labor relations is also characterized by exclusive representation: at any given workplace workers are either represented by one union, chosen by majority vote, or they have no union. On the employer side, American businesses rarely give the right to negotiate labor contracts to employer associations; organizations like the National Association of Manufacturers or the Chamber of Commerce are primarily lobbying and information groups. Since each employer and group of workers negotiates separately, whether a work site is union or not can greatly affect the wages of the workers relative to others and enterprise profitability, producing great conflict over the existence of unions at those sites.

European labor and management are organized differently. Unions play a smaller role in the local firm and a larger one at the industry or national level, as part of a social movement. They have historical links to political parties—in France and Italy, for instance, there are communist-led unions, Catholic-led unions, and socialist-led unions. In most countries, members of various unions are found at the same workplace, cooperating along some dimensions and competing along others. On the employer side, European employers' federations are powerful economic entities. Individual firms give employer federations the right to bargain with unions for wages and conditions in entire sectors or regions, or in some cases, for wages countrywide. The term "social partners," foreign to Americans, lies at the heart of the greater institutional organization of labor and management in Europe. The social partners are the main union federations and main employer groups. They conduct most collective negotiations, and European governments typically consult them on economic matters and often seek their consent on policies relating to wage inflation, job-creating initiatives, training programs, and the like.

In Japan, although the United States (in the form of General Douglas MacArthur) sought to establish U.S.-style labor relations during its post–World War II occupation, Japanese unions and employers are a different kettle of (raw?) fish. Unions are largely company-based, with memberships that include all workers in the firm up through middle management. Until the mid-1970s, Japanese firms encouraged company unions as part of their company personnel systems. The firms provided union facilities, advised workers to join, and regarded union leaders as candidates for advancement in management. The oil shocks of the 1970s, however, made the big Japanese firms less favorable to unions. On the employer side, Japanese employers are well organized; the Japan Federation of Employers' Associations (Nikkeiren) plays a more active role in wage setting than any such employer group in the United States.

The extent to which workers are organized into unions differs greatly among countries. In Sweden, virtually everyone is a union member. In the United States, at the peak of union strength in the mid-1950s, about 40 percent of private-sector workers were organized, while perhaps 5 percent of public-sector workers were in unions. In the 1970s and 1980s country differences in union representation widened greatly. In the United States unionism declined precipitously (see Figure 1.5); unionization in the private sector dropped to a bare 11 percent of workers. The expansion of public-sector unionism in the 1960s and 1970s was insufficient to offset the massive loss of representation in the private sector.

Although unions had difficulties in almost all countries in the 1980s and early 1990s, only in the United States did business seek to establish a "union-free" environment, and with considerable success. In Canada unions maintained their share of workers through the period, so that union density there went from roughly the same as U.S. density to twice the American level. In Japan, union density fell in the 1980s but remained above U.S. levels, and unions continued to play a role in national wage setting. In Europe the proportion

Figure 1.5   Trends in Unionization, 1970 to 1990: Europe, Japan, and the United States

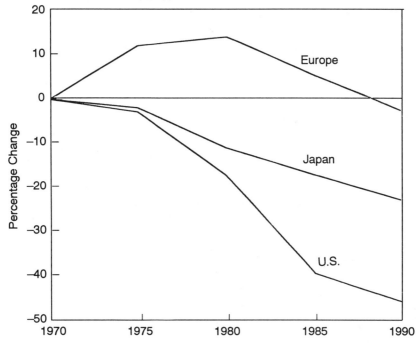

SOURCE: OECD, 1991; OECD, 1992c; U.S. Bureau of Labor Statistics, union membership data gathered from various sources, 1992; The Economist, *Book of Vital World Statistics* (N.Y.: Times Books (Random House), 1990).

NOTES: Europe includes Austria, Belgium, Denmark, Finland, France, Germany, Italy, Netherlands, Norway, Sweden, Switzerland, and the U.K. Union density figures for Europe were weighted using the 1988 labor force size for each country. For 1990, union density rates for Europe and Japan are 1988 figures.

of workers in unions declined in the 1980s, after a decade of growth. But even in countries where union membership fell massively (France and the Netherlands), institutional rules preserved a union presence and collective representation of labor within enterprises. In France, the only country with a lower union density in the early 1990s than in the United States, labor law required that most workplaces (regardless of union membership) have designated union representatives with legal responsibilities, and the number of company-level collective bargaining agreements increased despite falling union membership. In the Netherlands, unions continued to negotiate wages and to sit as social partners in diverse public agencies.

But perhaps the most important difference in the organization of labor between the United States and Europe is that European countries, save the United Kingdom and Ireland, mandate the election of works councils within enterprises—representative groups of workers with specified rights to information, consultation, and in some cases codetermination in selected decisions at the enterprise level (see Chapter 4, this volume). Councils cover all employees, including white-collar workers who are rarely union members in the United States. They provide representation inside firms regardless of how unions are doing, and they represent workers who oppose unions as well as those favoring unions. Through works councils, the typical European firm consults regularly with employee representatives in a cooperative venue that is not found in the United States and that could even be illegal under American labor law.[21] During the 1980s, when labor relations became more decentralized throughout the world and union strength weakened, works councils played an increasingly important role in European labor relations.

Barring a sudden reversal in the fortunes of American unions or a new American labor code, the United States will enter the twenty-first century with its work force having less collective representation than all other countries in the developed world. Gompers's 1909 statement that the union situation "in no foreign country can compare with the American Federation of Labor" will hold true, but not in the self-congratulatory way he intended it in the early 1900s.

Wage Setting

Modes of wage setting also differ substantially across countries. In every society, three groups are involved in determining wages—

employers or employer federations; workers, some organized into unions; and governments. In some countries, individual firms and workers determine wages largely in response to local market conditions, producing decentralized wage setting. In other countries, more encompassing groups of employer federations and unions bargain over wages, producing relatively centralized conditions. Still other countries have a mixed system, with collective bargaining in some sectors but market wage determination in others.

The United States represents the decentralized extreme in wage setting. Pay for the predominantly nonunion work force is determined by the interactions of tens of thousands of firms and millions of workers in the labor market. There is little formal coordination of wage settlements, though large firms use compensation surveys to see what other enterprises pay, job evaluation plans to determine the pay for jobs filled within the firm, and formal pay schedules to guide individual wage determination. But even the unionized sector of the United States is highly decentralized: local unions negotiate annually with individual firms. The head of the AFL-CIO does not negotiate collective bargaining contracts with employers, and nor do the presidents of many industrial or craft unions.

The virtue of decentralised pay setting is that pay settlements can be tailored to the particular situation facing individual workers and firms. The disadvantage is that, lacking any formal coordinating mechanism, differences in pay between seemingly similar workers tend to be high: the distribution of wages for workers of the same age, education, gender, and occupation is, for instance, much wider in the United States than it is in countries with more coordinated wage-setting systems.

At the centralized wage-setting extreme are the peak-level bargaining systems that characterize Austria and Norway, and that Sweden followed through the early 1980s and intermittently thereafter. In those countries, national employer associations, made up of associations of employers in different sectors, bargain with "peak level" union confederations to determine wages that cover the entire economy. But there is also, invariably, lower level industrial and firm bargaining and "wage drift"—wage changes that diverge from the bargained wages to reflect local market realities.

The virtue of a centralized wage-setting system is that central negotiators are forced to consider the effect of wage settlements on the entire economy. Unions and firms in centralized wage-setting systems often agree to "social pacts" to limit inflation. However, centralized wage-setting limits the ability of firms to respond flexibly to fast-moving market developments, and a centralized system is difficult to maintain in a world where different sectors and types of workers face different market conditions.

Many countries have other institutions for coordinating wage settlements across enterprises. Until the 1990s Italy had the Scala Mobile, a centrally negotiated moving scale that indexed wages to inflation and that greatly influenced wage settlements in the entire country. In France and Germany, ministers of labor extend the terms of collective bargaining contracts signed between unions and employer federations to all workers and firms in a given area, including those that were not party to the bargain. German law specifies that the national or state minister of labor can declare a settlement to be "generally binding" if companies employing at least half of the employees in the sector have signed the agreement and if the extension "serves the general interest." In addition, France relies heavily on the national minimum wage; changes in the minimum influence wages throughout the economy. Australia uses industrial tribunals in wage setting: unions and employers make presentations in court, and judges decide on the right wage settlement. Japan has its Shunto Offensive each spring, when all unions engage in a symbolic one-day strike to demand a given economywide wage change, to which the employers' federation responds with its recommendation for wage changes.

In the 1980s, wage-setting institutions became more decentralized in virtually all advanced countries. Some highly centralized systems, such as Sweden's, gave greater bargaining power to individual industries or firms; Italy abandoned its Scala Mobile; France relied more heavily on firm-level collective agreements; and Australian unions and firms engaged in plant-level negotiations. Even with these changes, however, the United States remains the exemplar decentralized wage-setting system.

Mandated Rights and Benefits

There are large country differences in the legal rights of workers at the workplace and in the nonwage benefits—pensions, unemployment benefits, health insurance, occupational disability insurance, and the like—that governments require employers to provide or fund. In Europe the Common Market's Social Charter commits EEC countries (except for the United Kingdom, which opted out of the charter) to provide "social rights of workers" in employment, remuneration, social protection, safety at the workplace, retirement benefits, and so on (EEC, 1992). As a general rule, European countries mandate greater rights and benefits for workers than does the United States. By legal statute European workers have, in addition to the works councils described earlier, the following workplace-related rights or benefits:

Extensive vacation and holiday time
Sickness leave, including pay during the leave
Maternity leave, including pay during the leave
Advance notice of dismissals
Severance pay on dismissal
Unemployment benefits that last longer than U.S. benefits
Social security pension benefits comparable to U.S. benefits

The United States does not regulate vacations, sickness leave, or severance pay, and it did not legislate maternity leave until the late 1980s and early 1990s (Table 1.3). In addition, the United States did not require firms to give workers early warning of mass dismissals until 1988. Provision of most benefits is the province of collective bargaining or the individual firms seeking to attract or retain employees, and the benefits and rights that American workers gain through collective bargaining or competitive market forces fall short of those that Europeans gain through legal mandates.

In some situations mandating may be the only way for the labor market to provide benefits or to attain the desired level of benefits. A single firm can face problems in providing benefits when workers differ in their potential use of the benefit. For instance, if firm A offers good sickness benefits, it risks attracting sickly workers, whose use of the benefit may make it too costly to maintain. If every firm offered the benefit, the sickly would be employed more or less randomly among firms, and no single firm would face excessive costs. Similarly, if an insurance company sold unemployment insurance on the open market it would face grave problems, as workers in cyclically sensitive industries or in firms in trouble would seek insurance in large numbers, while those whose jobs were secure would not buy any. Mandating provides a way around

Table 1.3   Statutory Regulations Governing Benefits and Rights to Workers in European Countries and United States, 1991

Benefits and Rights	Europe	United States
Public Holidays	12	8–10
Annual Vacation	4 weeks	no statute
Sickness Leave		
Maximum weeks of leave	54	no statute
Percentage of earnings paid during sickness	62 percent	
Maternity Leave		
Maximum weeks of leave	18	13
Percentage of earnings paid during leave	89 percent	0
Severance Pay		
Percentage of workers with severance pay	72 percent	no statute
Unemployment Insurance		
Months covered	16	6
Percentage of earnings paid during unemployment	47 percent	50 percent

NOTES: Tabulated from Ehrenberg, 1993 (Tables 2.3, 2.4, 2.5, and 5.1); and from OECD, 1991 (Table 7.2), where I used the replacement rate for persons without a spouse working, and gave Portugal thirteen months of unemployment coverage. I have formed EEC figures by weighting country figures by 1988 employment, as given in OECD, 1990b. Public holidays figures exclude Denmark and the U.K.; vacation data exclude Italy and the U.K. Belgium has an indefinite duration of unemployment insurance and is excluded. Most of the data are for Common Market countries; included are Belgium, Denmark, France, Germany, Greece, Ireland, Italy, Netherlands, Portugal, Spain, and the United Kingdom. The severance pay figures include Austria and the Scandinavian countries.

these difficulties, though at the cost of forcing uniform conditions onto workers who might do better with other arrangements. The woman who would trade the maternity leave benefit for a few extra cents in her paycheck cannot do so when the state mandates maternity leave.

The greater benefits and job security that European workers

have compared with Americans are costly. The compensation that employers pay a worker consists not only of wages paid for time worked but also payroll taxes for socially mandated benefits and wages paid for vacations and other time not worked. The nonwage components of compensation are markedly higher in some European countries, such as Italy, Belgium, and France than in the United States (U.S. Department of Labor, 1993). Employers often complain that employer-paid payroll taxes and mandated benefits add to their labor bill, but most economists believe that in the long run workers pay for these benefits in the form of lower wages (Ehrenberg, 1993). A European who costs her employer the same amount of money *per hour worked* as an American will receive a 20 to 25 percent lower hourly wage as a trade-off for a longer paid vacation and greater mandated social insurance benefits. In addition, many European workers pay a greater share of their wages in the form of payroll taxes and income tax. There is, in short, a price for the vacation and other benefits that Europeans obtain.

Welfare State

Finally, advanced countries differ in the state welfare support they provide persons outside the work force and the working poor. Some welfare benefits require that individuals have a history of work (social security pensions) or that the person be currently employed (the American Earned Income Tax Credit, which pays money to low-income workers as a form of negative income tax, or Swedish daycare subsidies, which require that the child's mother work at least part-time). When the state mandates benefits solely to workers or to those who have worked, the programs have a "workfare" flavor: they give people an extra incentive to find a job and to work for the amount of time that qualifies them for the benefits.

Other state welfare benefits are paid to people regardless of work status, such as family income allowances that provide money for every child in a family or national health insurance, which covers all citizens. Universal benefits also change the incentive to work. If the government provides health care for all citizens, regardless of work status, a worker may be more willing to change jobs, to go on strike, or otherwise to risk losing a job than if his health benefits were tied to his job. In general, the greater the *social wage*—defined as the resources provided people as citizens regardless of their work status—the smaller will be the need to work and the higher the wage that people will demand to work.

Other benefits are limited to people who may be incapable of working, such as the disabled; to the elderly who have retired; to able-bodied persons who cannot find work—the unemployed; or to children in single-parent families, when the single parent lacks work. By providing money for not working, these programs reduce the incentive to work and risk creating a "welfare trap," wherein the recipient's income would drop if he or she obtained a job. For example, the American Aid to Families with Dependent Children program provides health benefits that many small, low-wage employers cannot afford to provide, so that its potential disincentive effect is substantial, and goes beyond the loss of the income benefits. Single mothers in countries that have subsidized daycare for young children and national health insurance, such as France, face a very different set of incentives than those in the United States. (See Chapter 5, this volume.)

The welfare state affects the labor market in other ways as well. In a society in which many families are headed by a single parent, welfare benefits will affect the resources invested in children and presumably the qualifications of future generations of workers. In European countries with large state welfare programs, welfare is itself a major employer in the job market: a large share of women workers in Sweden, for example, are government employees. Last but not least, since welfare benefits are paid from taxes, the size of the welfare budget affects tax rates and take-home pay.

European countries generally have more extensive state welfare programs than the United States, for which citizens pay a larger percent of GDP per person in taxes. Some countries, notably Sweden, link most benefits to work, so that welfare becomes workfare. Almost all of the countries have generous unemployment benefit systems (Table 1.3) and provide housing and other subsidies that enable many persons to live for extended periods without a job. Lacking such an extensive state welfare system, the United States relies to a greater degree on the private sector to provide welfare-type benefits. Most retired Americans receive, in addition to their Social Security check, a pension from their employer. Americans donate time and money to charitable organizations that care for the needy to a far greater extent than citizens do in other countries. But even so the United States has a low ranking in the provision of welfare and the extent of the social wage or safety net that is guaranteed to citizens. This means that more than in other developed countries, the critical dimension in determining the economic well-being of Americans is how they fare in the labor market.

CONCLUSION

The superiority of the United States in the world of work that impressed Samuel Gompers in the early 1900s and that persisted for most of the twentieth century no longer holds true. Compared with most advanced countries, the United States does well in job creation but not in pay; it does well in flexibility and mobility but not in job security or worker representation. This country rates high in productivity and earnings but has alarmingly low rates of growth in productivity and real wages. And the United States pays less skilled workers lower wages than in many other advanced countries.

Some of the differences between the United States and other countries reflect implicit or explicit trade-offs of one outcome for another. But as the ensuing chapters will make clear, others reflect differences in the efficacy of alternative ways of organizing workplaces and structuring labor markets.

The mixed record of the United States compared with other advanced economies suggests that at the dawn of the twenty-first century the United States may have something to learn from others (just as they may have some things to learn from us). Perhaps finding out how other advanced economies determine wages, train workers, develop modes of representation, and protect workers through social safety nets will provide lessons for the design of American policy and labor market institutions. These considerations motivate the detailed comparisons in the rest of this volume.

NOTES

1. Gompers presented his findings in several speeches and in a book entitled *Labor in Europe and America* (Gompers, 1910). The first quote is the subtitle of the book; subsequent quotations are from pp. 59, ix, and 260, respectively. Gompers compares U.S. and European unions on pp. 249–260.

2. Throughout this chapter I will use "Europe" or "Europeans" to refer to those in the West, defined by OECD statistics as OECD-Europe. The

data are from OECD, 1990b, 26–27 (Table 4.0). The picture of greater job growth in the United States does not depend on the particular years chosen, though the precise numbers do.

3. Hours for France, Germany, the United States, and some additional European countries are given in *Employment Outlook July 1993* (OECD, 1993b) and in earlier editions.

4. These data are based on figures for 1985 from OECD, 1990b, and OECD, 1993b, (Table 1.2).

5. Because the unemployed have yet to find work, official statistics understate the length of joblessness. On average, an unemployed person will be halfway through a spell of joblessness when he or she is interviewed. Thus, many unemployed Europeans will be jobless for 2, 3, or even more years.

6. Some Americans who are unemployed one month leave unemployment without getting a job: i.e., they become discouraged and cease looking for work. This is less common among Europeans. Still, the difference in the figures is so great that differential movements out of the work force will not change the story in the text.

7. These data are taken from OECD, 1990a, (Table 1.2).

8. These statistics are from the Commission of the European Community (EEC, 1991, Table 4).

9. The OECD gives job turnover figures for various countries, where job turnover is defined as the sum of gross job gains and gross job losses among establishments, relative to employment. The United States, France, and Sweden had similar rates of job turnover, on the order of 23 percent to 25 percent. Germany had a lower rate, 17 percent, but the Japanese rate of job turnover was "off the map," at 8 percent. See OECD, 1987, chap. 4.

10. This has been recognized by the OECD; see OECD, 1993b, chap. 4.

11. Interest rates, trade surpluses, and anticipated economic changes may attract or deflect foreign exchange, altering the value of currency in a country relative to the dollar even in a short period.

12. World Bank, 1993, 239 (Table 1).

13. Measures of productivity in countries with differing levels of unemployment must be interpreted carefully. Since the unemployed consist disproportionately of less skilled workers, increases in employment in European countries would presumably decrease productivity relative to the American level.

14. From 1979 to 1990, real (that is, inflation corrected) output per worker increased by 1.0 percent in the United States compared with 1.4 percent in Europe and 2.9 percent in Japan; OECD, 1992b, 51 (Table 3.7). In manufacturing, American productivity growth was better: 3.1 percent per year in hourly productivity compared with 3.1 percent in Europe but 4.1 percent in Japan. The U.S. and Japanese figures are

from Neef and Kask, 1991 (Table 2). The figure for Europe is a weighted average of the output-per-hour figures reported in the same table, with 1988 employment in manufacturing in the countries from OECD, 1990b (Table 3 for each country).

15. The fact that at the exchange rates of the early 1990s the United States was "low wage" among developed economies is not something unique to the Bureau of Labor Statistics figures for production workers in manufacturing. The OECD publishes data on "compensation per employee in the business sector" for twenty-one member countries in dollar terms, based on exchange rates. In 1991 the United States ranked eleventh in compensation. The following countries had higher compensation than the United States ($30,200): Switzerland, $48,900; Sweden, $37,600; Finland, $37,000; Norway, $34,800; Japan, $36,600; France, $31,800; Italy, $30,300; Belgium, $34,600; Denmark, $31,200; Netherlands, $31,800. OECD, 1993a, 160 (Table 70).

16. OECD, 1992b, shows a change in real hourly earnings in manufacturing in the United States of -1.0 percent per year from 1979 to 1990 (Table 9.2, p. 94), according to the *Statistical Abstract of the United States*. The *Statistical Abstract of the United States 1992* shows a change in the real hourly earnings of these workers of -0.4 percent per year from 1980 to 1990 (Table 650, p. 410). But looking at the total compensation of all workers (including nonproduction workers) in manufacturing (*Statistical Abstract*, Table 649), one finds an increase in pay by 0.5 percent above the rate of inflation.

17. Wages are somewhat higher in manufacturing than in other sectors (more so in the United States than in Europe, which biases comparisons of earnings based on manufacturing workers in favor of the United States), but not markedly so.

18. This can be seen by adjusting the OECD estimated compensation per employee in the business sector given in exchange rate units in note 12 into PPP units. In these units the United States has higher earnings than all of the countries except for Belgium and Switzerland.

19. These estimates are obtained by multiplying the figures in column 2 of Table 1.2 by the ratios of lower decile to median earnings, from OECD, 1993b (Table 5.2). For example, German men in the lowest decile earn 71 percent of the median whereas American men earn 38 percent of the median. Thus, low-decile Germans earn 1.87 times what low decile Americans earn. Since Table 1.2 shows that Germans earn 119 percent of what Americans earn, Germans in the lowest decile would earn 222 percent of Americans in that decile. This implies that Americans earn 45 percent of what Germans earn. Calculations for other countries follow the same pattern.

20. OECD, 1992b (Tables 3.2 and 3.7).

21. The National Labor Relations Board made several decisions in the

early 1990s declaring that some company-sponsored committees of workers were illegal company-dominated unions, outlawed by the Wagner Act.

REFERENCES

Ehrenberg, Ronald. 1994. *Labor Markets and Economic Integration.* Washington, D.C.: Brookings Institution. Forthcoming.

European Economic Community (EEC). 1991. *European Economy* no. 47 (March).

―――. 1992. *Social Europe.* Luxembourg: EEC. First report on the application of the Community Charter of the Fundamental Social Rights of Workers.

Freeman, Richard. 1988. "Evaluating the European View that the United States Has No Unemployment Problem." *American Economic Review* (May): 294–299.

Gompers, Samuel. 1910. *Labor in Europe and America.* New York and London: Harper and Brothers Publishers.

Neef, Arthur, and Christopher Kask. 1991. "Manufacturing Productivity and Labor Costs in 14 Economies." U.S. Department of Labor, *Monthly Labor Review* (December).

Organization for Economic Cooperation and Development (OECD). 1982. *Historical Statistics 1960–1982.* Paris: OECD.

―――. 1987. *Employment Outlook July 1987.* Paris: OECD.

―――. 1990a. *Employment Outlook July 1990.* Paris: OECD.

―――. 1990b. *Labour Force Statistics, 1968–1988.* Paris: OECD.

―――. 1990c. *Labour Market Policies for the 1990s.* Paris: OECD.

―――. 1991. *Employment Outlook July 1991.* Paris: OECD.

―――. 1992a. *Employment Outlook July 1992.* Paris: OECD.

―――. 1992b. *Historical Statistics 1960-1990.* Paris: OECD.

―――. 1992c. *National Accounts.* Paris: OECD.

―――. 1992d. *Purchasing Power Parities and Real Expenditures.* Paris: OECD.

―――. 1993a. *Economic Outlook,* June 1993. Paris: OECD.

―――. 1993b. *Employment Outlook July 1993.* Paris: OECD.

U.S. Bureau of the Census. 1993. *Statistical Abstract of the United States 1992.* Washington, D.C.: U.S. GPO.

U.S. Department of Labor, Bureau of Labor Statistics. 1993. *International Comparisons of Hourly Compensation Costs for Production Workers in Manufacturing, 1992* Report 844 (April). Washington, D.C.

World Bank. 1993. *World Development Report 1993.* Washington D.C.: World Bank.

2

RISING WAGE INEQUALITY:
THE UNITED STATES
VS. OTHER ADVANCED COUNTRIES

Richard B. Freeman and Lawrence F. Katz

One of the "big stories" in American economic life in the 1980s was the large increase in income inequality. Inequality grew as the economic expansion of the latter half of the 1980s failed to benefit the majority of American families enough to offset the losses they had incurred during the recession of the early 1980s. In the early 1980s it was possible to make a plausible case for trickle-down economics, but by the end of the decade it was clear that policies to increase the income of the wealthy had not generated propserity for the majority of the population. Many American families saw a decline in their living standards in the 1980s. A large number were no better off at the outset of the 1990s than they had been ten years earlier; in 1989 the real money incomes for the bottom 40 percent of American families were similar to the incomes of the bottom 40 percent of families in 1979. In contrast, the incomes of the upper 20 percent of families in 1989 were almost 20 percent higher than those of analogous families in 1979 (U.S. Bureau of the Census, 1992, pp. B-11 and B-13).

Since most Americans make their living from work, the story behind this rising inequality and the deteriorating income of lower-paid workers is a story about changes in the labor market. Under-lying the rising disparity in the fortunes of American families was

The views expressed in this chapter are solely those of the authors and do not reflect the official position of the U.S. Department of Labor.

a rise in labor market inequality that shifted wage and employment opportunities in favor of the more educated and more skilled. Less educated men, particularly the young, suffered substantial losses in real earnings and were at greater risk of unemployment than in years past. For many of them, the American dream of economic progress was seriously threatened, as it had not been since the Great Depression.

Was the twist in the job market against less educated workers unique to the United States, or was it part of a general pattern of decline in the well-being of the less skilled in advanced countries? Does it mark a new era in modern economic development—a reversal of the broad trend of income inequality falling with economic growth?[1] Have other advanced countries avoided or ameliorated the rise in wage inequality that has characterized the United States?

To examine these questions we begin with a summary of the changes in the American wage structure during the 1980s, and then look at the extent to which similar changes occurred in other industrial nations. Our analysis of the overseas experience relies largely on studies by researchers at the National Bureau of Economic Research (NBER) that use computerized records of the earnings and employment of tens of thousands of workers in advanced Western countries—the United States and its major trading partners and competitors in the world economy.[2] Given the facts, we assess why inequality rose so rapidly in the United States, and draw lessons for the United States from the experience overseas.

Our analysis highlights four aspects of wage inequality across countries:

1. During the 1980s, the countries with the most decentralized labor markets and wage-setting systems—the United States and the United Kingdom—had exceptional increases in earnings inequality and in wage differentials by skill. Only in the United States, however, did low-wage workers (even those in full-time employment) have large declines in real earnings (earnings adjusted for inflation). Most other developed countries had only moderate or slight increases in wage inequality, and in Britain real wages rose even for low-paid workers.

2. The major cause of increasing inequality was a shift in relative labor demand that favored more educated workers and workers

with problem-solving skills combined with a reduced rate of growth in the supply of highly educated workers relative to less educated workers. The shift in demand was driven by skill-biased technological change associated with the "computer revolution" and, to a lesser extent, by changes in international trade. However, because shifts in demand were similar across countries, demand forces do not explain many of the differences among countries in the rise of inequality.

3. Slower growth in the supply of highly educated workers relative to less educated workers in the United States contributed to the especially great increase in wage differentials by education. The slackened growth was due largely to a slower expansion of the college-educated work force in the 1980s than in the 1970s, but was also affected by the influx of immigrants who had less than a high school education. Wage differentials by education increased much less in countries where the relative supply of more educated workers continued to grow rapidly in the 1980s.

4. Differences in wage setting institutions and training and education systems also contributed to international differences in the growth of inequality. Countries where unions, employer federations, and government agencies play a greater role in wage setting and where better training or education for non-college-educated workers is provided had smaller increases in inequality than in the United States. In addition, the decline of unionization in the United States and the United Kingdom contributed to the rapid rise in wage inequality in those countries, while the weakening of centralized wage-setting institutions in countries such as Sweden allowed for modest increases in historically compressed wage differentials.

CHANGES IN THE UNITED STATES

As a starting point for examining what happened in other countries, we summarize the facts about changes in the U.S. wage and employment structure in the 1980s. In this case, unlike in many areas of economic analysis, there is strong evidence and a broad consensus that lets us use the word *facts* rather than *claims* or *assertions*. Researchers using several data sources, including household survey data from the Current Population Survey (CPS), other household surveys, and establishment surveys, have documented that wage inequality and skill differentials in earnings and employment increased sharply in the United States (Bound and Johnson, 1992; Blackburn, Bloom, and Freeman, 1992; Davis and Haltiwanger,

1991; Katz and Murphy, 1992; Levy and Murnane, 1992; Murphy and Welch, 1992). The finding that inequality increased is not sensitive to the choice of data set, sample, or wage measure. The following is a summary of the changes in the American wage and employment structure that give us benchmarks for assessing the labor market performance of other countries.

FACT ONE: In the 1980s overall wage dispersion increased in the United States to levels greater than at any time since 1940. The hourly earnings of a full-time worker in the ninetieth percentile of the U.S. earnings distribution (someone whose earnings exceeded those of 90 percent of all workers) relative to a worker in the tenth percentile (someone whose earnings exceeded those of just 10 percent of all workers) grew by 20 percent for men and 25 percent for women from 1979 to 1989. This pattern was not offset by improved fringe benefits for less skilled workers[3] nor by increases in their chances of holding a job relative to more educated workers. It marks a worsening in the economic well-being of lower-paid workers.[4]

FACT TWO: Pay differentials by education and age increased. The college/high school wage premium doubled for young workers, as the weekly wages of young male college graduates increased by some 30 percent relative to those of young males with twelve or fewer years of schooling. In addition, among workers without college degrees the wages of older workers rose relative to those of younger workers. The only earnings differential that decreased was that between men and women, which dropped by 10 percent or so in all education and age groups in the 1980s.

FACT THREE: Wage dispersion increased within demographic and skill groups. The wages of individuals of the same age, education, and sex, working in the same industry and occupation, were more unequal at the end of the 1980s than they had been ten or twenty years earlier. Much of this increase took the form of greater wage differentials for "similar" workers across establishments in the same industry. A worker's formal educational qualifications and employer mattered more for his or her earnings in 1990 than in the past.

FACT FOUR: The real earnings of less educated and lower paid workers fell compared with the real earnings of analogous individuals a decade earlier. Most striking, the real hourly wages of young men with twelve or fewer years of schooling dropped by some 20 percent from 1979 to 1989.

This list of facts summarizes the evidence in terms of statistical measures of earnings distributions. But the same data can be organized in another way that some find more appealing: as changes in the share of jobs that provide "middle-class" earnings. For instance, rather than reporting the ratio of the wages of ninetieth percentile to tenth percentile workers, we could report the proportion of workers whose incomes fall within a fixed middle-class income band. Organized this way, the data show that the fraction of workers in the middle of the income distribution declined substantially. Published CPS Consumer Income Reports reveal, for instance, that in 1990, 35 percent of twenty-five- to thirty-four-year-old men had incomes that were in a 30 percent band around the mean for that age group, down 6 percentage points from 41 percent in 1980.[5] The middle of the income distribution was "squashed" relative to the top and bottom.

The "jobs" measure of changes in labor market inequality tells the same story as the income distribution measures, since both reflect the same changes in the pattern of individual earnings. Under reasonable circumstances, an increase in earnings inequality implies a decline in the proportion of jobs around the middle of the earnings distribution; conversely, a decline in the proportion of workers with middle-class earnings implies a rise in inequality.[6]

Did the 1980s' changes break with the past or do they continue earlier trends? In Figure 2.1 the graphs of relative hourly wages for full-time workers from the March Current Population Surveys show that most of these changes broke with the past. The college wage premium plotted in panel A did not trend upward for decades. It increased modestly from 1963 to 1971, then fell in the 1970s before jumping sharply in the 1980s, especially among younger workers.

Returns to experience increased greatly for less educated men in the 1980s, and they had not done so previously (panel B). The rise in the experience differential among less educated workers means that older or more experienced men without college education—fathers—did much better in 1989 relative to recent entrants in the job market—sons—than they had done before. The rise in the experience profile is, however, limited to the less educated; the

Figure 2.1   U.S. Relative Hourly Wage Changes, 1967 to 1989

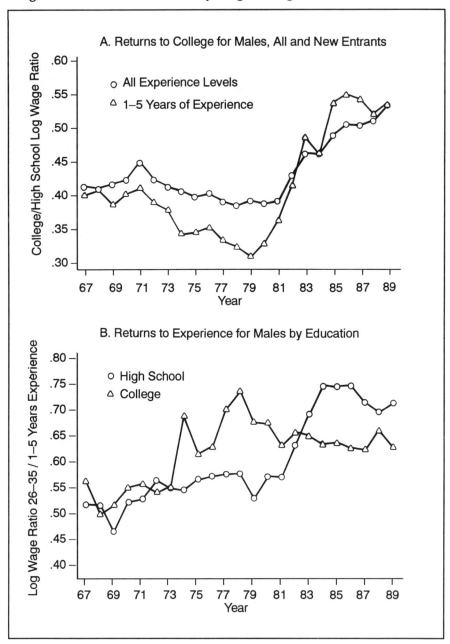

Figure 2.1   (*continued*)

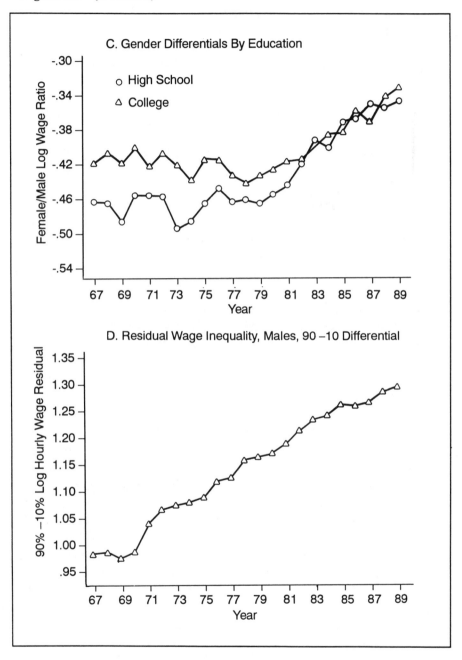

C. Gender Differentials By Education

D. Residual Wage Inequality, Males, 90 –10 Differential

earnings of male college graduates show no marked shift in favor of older or more experienced workers.

The reduction in the gender gap was also a 1980s development. Differentials in pay for women versus men changed little in the 1960s and 1970s, and then narrowed substantially from 1979 to 1989 (panel C).

The one change that began prior to the 1980s was the rise in within-group wage inequality for men. Panel D shows that even after controlling for education and experience the differential in earnings between men in the nineteenth percentile and those in the tenth percentile increased steadily from 1970 to 1989 period.

Will the increase in inequality continue into the twenty-first century? The increase in overall wage inequality was initially driven by rising within-group inequality but was counteracted, in part, by declines in the college wage premium in the 1970s. When within-group inequality and educational wage differentials expanded in the 1980s, inequality rose along all dimensions except gender. While there is no economic law preventing further increases in inequality, the rise in educational differentials has induced some offsetting forces—notably, increased enrollments in college in response to the increased payoff of college degress—that have arrested the upward trend in educational premiums in the early 1990s, and that will weigh against any sustained further rise in inequality.

CHANGES IN OTHER ADVANCED COUNTRIES

Did labor market differentials by skill and overall wage inequality rise in other advanced industrial nations as they did in the United States, or is rising inequality unique to the United States?

To answer this question, we used studies that gathered comparable earnings data and examined wage structures for many countries in the 1980s, including the United States, United Kingdom, Canada, Australia, Japan, Sweden, France, Italy, Germany, South Korea, and the Netherlands (Freeman and Katz, 1994). The data come from diverse sources, ranging from CPS-style household surveys to establishment surveys to surveys comparable to the United States' Survey of Consumer Finances.[7] Virtually all of the data sets measure earnings as before-tax earnings.

Table 2.1   Changes in Educational/Occupational Skill Differentials in Advanced Countries

Countries that Experienced:	1970s	1980s
Large Fall in Differentials	Australia Canada France Germany Italy Japan Netherlands Sweden United Kingdom United States	Korea[a]
Modest Changes in Differentials		
Modest fall in differentials		Netherlands
No noticeable change in differentials		France Germany Italy
Modest rise in differentials		Australia Canada Japan Sweden
A large rise in differentials		United Kingdom United States

SOURCES: For the 1970s, Richard B. Freeman "The Changing Economic Value of Higher Education in Developed Economies: A Report to the OECD," NBER Working Paper no. 820, December 1981; for the 1980s, Freeman and Katz, 1994.
[a] Developing country moving into advanced state.

the exception of the United States, all had a decline in overall wage dispersion for males in the 1970s—and all saw the trend toward lower educational wage differentials and a more compressed wage structure end by the early to mid-1980s.

In the 1980s, however, wage inequality changed differently in different countries.[8] Overall inequality and differentials by education grew in several countries, but much more modestly than in the United States. Canada, Australia, Japan, and Sweden had small increases in wage inequality and occupational differentials beginning in the early 1980s, and the Canadian rise seemingly began to reverse itself in the late 1980s (Bar-Or et al., 1992; MacPhail, 1993).

There are, of course, noncomparabilities between da
various countries. Definitions of educational and oc
groups differ depending on national education and tra
tems and data gathering procedures. Sample survey cov
measures of earnings differ. The meaning of earnings a
across countries. In the United States living standard
largely on personal earnings, whereas in countries with
welfare states the government provides elements of comp
to all citizens or workers, such as health insurance, th
Americans must buy with their take-home pay and giv
allowances and diverse forms of social insurance that ma
standards less dependent on earnings than in the United St
Chapter 5, this volume). If Europeans, for example, have
that Americans must buy with their pay, measures of in
based on wages will overstate inequality in Europe relativ
United States, since all European workers will obtain simi
efits that are not counted in their wages. Differences
progressivity of tax-transfer systems across countries also
how before-tax earnings translate into economic well-being
ings differentials based on before-tax earnings overstate ine
when the tax system is progressive. On the other hand
marginal tax rates induce firms to give in-kind payments to
ers (such as company cars, subsidies on transportation, lunc
so on), so that wage differentials may even understate true in
ity.

Differences in data sets by country and in modes of pay
cross-country comparisons difficult, but they do not make
comparisons impossible or meaningless. In many cases, we k
how reporting practices or definitions vary and can adjust re
for these differences or, if that is impossible, specify whethe
differences lead to an overstatement or understatement of ineq
ity compared with the United States. More important in term
the theme of this chapter, differences in definitions and repor
procedures that are constant over time are unlikely to distort tre
in inequality.

Table 2.1 categorizes countries by the way their wage p
terns changed in the 1970s and 1980s. From the late 1960s to t
late 1970s all of the countries shared a common pattern
narrowing educational and occupational wage differentials. Wi

Wage differentials narrowed in Italy and France through the mid-1980s with some hint of expanding differentials in the late 1980s. There is no evidence of rising wage inequality or educational differentials during the 1980s in the Netherlands nor in West Germany, and no evidence of rising educational differentials in Australia. The only country where wage differentials widened by an amount similar to the United States was Great Britain.

Table 2.2 measures changes in inequality in terms of the log of the ratio of the earnings of the top decile to the bottom decile of earnings from 1979 to 1990 (or the latest year available). The data show that only the United States and United Kingdom had double-digit increases in inequality. But there is a difference between the change in wages in the United Kingdom and in the United States (see Figure 2.2). In the United Kingdom, real earnings for all workers rose rapidly, so that despite greater inequality, the real pay of those at the bottom of the distribution grew (Katz, Loveman, and Blanchflower, 1994; Schmitt, 1994). By contrast, in the United States real earnings at the bottom of the earnings distribution fell sharply. From 1979 to 1989 the real earnings of lower-decile Americans dropped by 11 to 17 percent (depending on the survey used) compared to an *increase* in the real earnings of lower-decile British workers of 12 percent.

That low wage workers need not suffer losses in economic well-being even when inequality rises is also shown in the pattern of change in Japan. Inequality rose somewhat in Japan in the 1980s, but economic growth was so rapid that the living standards of the low-paid workers improved immensely. From 1979 to 1989, the real earnings of the tenth percentile Japanese male employee increased by more than 40 percent—an increase that exceeded that of the ninetieth percentile American male worker.

We conclude that less educated and lower-paid American workers suffered the largest erosion of economic well-being among workers in advanced countries.

Did the relative earnings of women improve in other countries as they did in the United States? Figure 2.3 shows that the gap in earnings between men and women declined in most countries during the period under investigation. Given the widening of the overall earnings distribution and the historical concentration of women in the bottom part of the distribution, the reduction in the male-female wage gap in the United States in particular was a

Table 2.2   Wage Inequality for Full-time Workers, Selected OECD Countries, 1970 to 1990[a]

Log of Ratio of Wage of 90th Percentile Earner to 10th Percentile Earner

Country	1979	1984	1987	1990	Change from 1979 to latest year
Men					
United Kingdom	0.88	1.04	1.10	1.16	0.28
United States	1.23	1.36	1.38	1.40	0.17
Japan	0.95	1.02	1.01	1.04	0.09
France	1.19	1.18	1.22	—	0.03
Italy[b]	0.74	0.69	0.73	—	-0.01
Netherlands	0.82	0.77	—	0.80	-0.02
Germany I[c]	0.78	0.80	—	—	}-0.03[d]
Germany II	—	0.96	0.91	—	
Canada[e]	1.23	—	1.44	—	0.21
Women					
United States	0.96	1.16	1.23	1.27	0.31
United Kingdom	0.84	0.98	1.02	1.11	0.27
Japan	0.78	0.79	0.84	0.83	0.05
France	0.96	0.93	1.00	—	0.04
Italy	0.87	0.69	0.69	—	-0.18
Men and Women					
Sweden, all	—	0.66	—	0.73	0.06
Sweden, blue-collar	0.30	0.30	0.31	0.35	0.05

SOURCES: The data for the United States, United Kingdom, France, and Japan are from Blanchflower, Katz, and Loveman, 1994; the data for Canada are from Davis, 1992; the data for Germany are from Abraham and Houseman, 1994; the data for Sweden are from Edin and Holmlund, 1994; the data for Italy are from Erickson and Ichino, 1994; and the data for the Netherlands are from Teulings, 1992.

[a] The samples consist of full-time workers, with the exception of Japan, which covers regular workers. Wages are measured by hourly earnings for the United States, United Kingdom, France, and Sweden; weekly earnings for workers covered by the social security system for Germany I; and gross average monthly earnings plus holiday allowances from the German socioeconomic panel for Germany II.
[b] The data in the second and third columns are for 1985 and 1989.
[c] The Germany I data are for years 1979 and 1983.
[d] This change is the sum of Germany I from 1979–84 and Germany II from 1984–87.
[e] Canada data are for years 1981 and 1985.

remarkable achievement. After all, when lower-paid workers are falling further behind higher-paid workers, one would expect a group that has traditionally been lower-paid, such as women, to lose ground relative to men who traditionally receive higher pay. That women gained ground against the tide of rising inequality implies that distinct forces were operating in favor of women in the job market (Blau and Kahn, 1994).

When looking at changes among countries in the ratio of employment to population or in unemployment rates by level of skill, two things stand out. In terms of levels, the ratio of employment to population in all countries was higher for the more educated workers. Similarly, the less educated were invariably more likely to be unemployed than the more-educated. In terms of changes, the trend was against the less educated. Their employment-population ratio fell relative to that of more educated workers in many countries during the 1980s (OECD, 1989, chap. 2); and the difference in unemployment associated with education tended to rise. While in the early 1990s white-collar unemployment became a larger problem in the United States, the fact that the more skilled and more

Figure 2.2   Change in Log of Hourly Real Earnings at the Tenth Percentile, Male Workers, 1979 to 1989

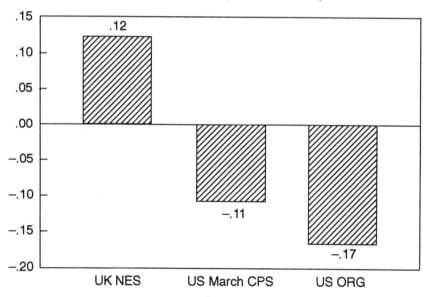

SOURCE: Blanchflower, Katz, and Loveman, 1994.

NOTES: UK NES - United Kingdom New Earnings Survey;
US March CPS - U.S. March Current Population Survey;
US ORG - U.S. Current Population Survey Outgoing Rotation Groups.
U.S. nominal wages are turned into constant dollars by using the implicit price deflator for personal consumption expenditures from the National Income and Products Account. British nominal wages are deflated by the Consumer Price Index.

Figure 2.3 Female-to-Male Hourly Earnings Ratios, Nonagricultural Workers, 1967 to 1990

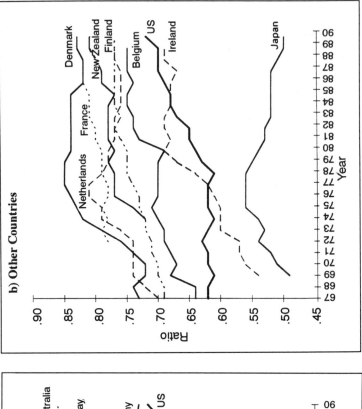

b) Other Countries

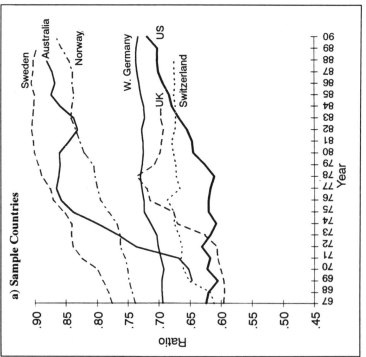

a) Sample Countries

SOURCE: Blau and Kahn, 1994.

42

highly paid workers can often do the work of the less skilled, while the latter lack the education needed for professional, technical, or many managerial jobs, implies that rates of unemployment are likely to remain higher among the less educated.[9]

EXPLAINING THE CHANGES

Why did wage inequality and educational wage differentials rise more in the United States than in other advanced countries? We attribute the exceptional experience of the United States to the way shifts in the supply of and demand for skills work themselves out in the decentralized U.S. labor market, compared with how they operate in other labor markets. Our explanation has three parts.

The first is that changes in the supply of and demand for labor skills substantially alter wages and employment of different groups of workers in the manner predicted by economists' supply-and-demand market-clearing model. This statement is more than the squawking of an economic parrot that knows nothing beyond supply and demand. For the supply-demand model to be relevant to the observed changes, wages must respond to market forces in situations with very different wage-setting institutions—collective bargaining, minimum wages, individual bargaining—and in situations where markets may not fully clear. Different demographic, education, and skill groups must be imperfect substitutes in production.[10] We further expect supply and demand to have their largest effect on young or less experienced workers on the active job market as opposed to experienced workers with substantial job tenure (Freeman, 1976).[11]

Supply and demand factors, however, cannot by themselves explain all of the differing changes in inequality among advanced countries. Why? Because supply and demand moved in roughly similar ways in these countries. Developed economies, after all, operate in the same world markets, using similar technology, and they have similar industry and occupation mixes. Changes in demand will not differ significantly among these countries. Supply changes will diverge more, because the countries expanded their higher education systems at different times, but even so a trend toward a greater proportion workers obtaining college degrees is found everywhere. To fully understand the differences in labor market outcomes across countries, something beyond supply and demand is needed.

The second part of our explanation identifies that "something" as differences in wage setting and other labor market institutions across countries (see Chapter 1, this volume). In a world in which the labor market is not a bourse (a stock exchange where prices continuously fluctuate), identical shifts in supply and demand will have different wage and employment consequences, depending on the wage-setting institutions or pay-setting norms in a country and on its education and training institutions. The stronger the role of institutions in wage determination, the smaller will be the effect of shifts in supply and demand on relative wages and, as a consequence, the greater will be their effect on relative employment. In addition, education and training institutions also mediate the effect of market forces on wages and employment (see Chapter 3, this volume). They determine the level of workplace skills for the less educated workers and the degree to which more and less skilled workers can be substituted for each other in production. A more egalitarian distribution of skills should dampen the effects of market shifts on wages and employment. Social insurance and income maintenance institutions also affect labor outcomes. For instance, generous income maintenance or unemployment benefits that allow workers to remain unemployed for a long period can reduce their willingness to take low wages to obtain work and thus reduce supply-side pressure for pay cuts.

For the third part of our explanation we turn to institutional changes, such as product market deregulation and changes in unionization that alter the wage-setting calculus. In part, forces outside the labor market, such as political developments, will change labor institutions, but these institutions also respond to shifts in supply and demand. The important institutional changes in the 1980s were the decline in trade union power, which was exceptional in the United States, and the decentralization of collective bargaining that characterized diverse European countries. Both of these developments are likely to produce greater earnings differentials.

Since our analysis links wage and employment changes both to the market forces of supply and demand and to labor market institutions, we call it the supply-demand-institutional (SDI) explanation of change.

DOES THE SDI EXPLANATION FIT THE UNITED STATES?

We ask first how well the SDI hypothesis fits the rise in inequality in the United States. An explanation of rising inequality in the United States clearly requires the operation of both supply and demand. By themselves, supply-side changes in the composition of the work force cannot account for recent U.S. wage structure changes. This is because the groups with relative wage increases in the 1980s, such as college graduates and women, also had increases in their relative numbers in the labor force. For example, a market or supply-demand explanation for rising education differentials would fit this pattern only if less educated workers had become less productive (as some critics of U.S. education allege), or if relative demand had shifted toward the more skilled.

We reject an explanation based on declining quality of less educated U.S. workers. The increase in wage differentials and inequality in the 1980s occurred for fixed-age cohorts of workers as they grew older. For instance, inequality grew among the cohort of workers who were twenty-five to thirty-four years old in 1979 as they aged ten years to become thirty-five- to forty-four-year-olds in 1989. Increases in inequality within the cohort of those educated twenty years earlier rule out explanations of rising inequality in terms of any decline in the quality of primary and secondary education in the United States.

This directs attention to shifts in relative demand for labor that favor more educated workers and workers with problem-solving skills as the key to understanding rising wage differentials. In fact, for many years the industrial and occupational distribution of U.S. employment shifted in favor of college graduates relative to non-college workers and in favor of women relative to men. Employment fell in goods-producing sectors that employed many blue-collar men and expanded in professional, medical, and business service sectors that employed many college graduates and in service industries that hired relatively more women. The loss of high-wage, blue-collar jobs in goods-producing sectors may account for as much as one-fourth to one-third of the increase in the college–high school wage differential for men during the 1980s (Blackburn, Bloom, and Freeman, 1990; Katz and Revenga, 1989; Bound and Johnson, 1992). One should not, however, exaggerate the shift in employment from goods to services. Most of the change in the job structure occurred within narrowly defined industries, where firms increased their usage of more educated workers relative to less educated workers and of professional, managerial, and technical workers relative to production workers. These changes could have arisen from moving production jobs to foreign countries, changes in technology, or changes in the organization of work.

The increased internationalization of the U.S. economy contributed to the changed supply-demand balance. In the 1980s, trade imbalances implicitly acted to augment the nation's supply of less educated workers, particularly those with less than a high school education (Borjas, Freeman, and Katz, 1992). Many production and routine clerical tasks could be more easily transferred abroad than in the past. The increased supply of less educated workers arising from trade deficits accounted for as much as 15 percent of the increase in the college–high school wage differential from the late 1970s to the mid-1980s. In contrast, a balanced expansion of international trade, in which growth in exports matches the growth of imports, appears to have fairly neutral effects on relative labor demand. Indeed, balanced growth of trade leads to an upgrading in the jobs for workers without college degrees, since export-sector jobs tend to pay higher wages for "comparable" workers than do import-competing jobs.

A critical factor raising demand for more skilled workers relative to less skilled workers is technological change that favors higher skills. In the 1980s, the increased use of microcomputers and computer-based technologies shifted demand toward more educated workers. In manufacturing, increases in the relative employment of more educated workers were positively correlated with investment in computer technologies and R & D intensity (Berman, Bound, and Griliches, 1992). A substantial wage premium for workers who use computers on their jobs explains a sizable part of increases in the college wage premium (Krueger, 1993). Whether because of computerization or other causes, the pace of relative demand shifts favoring more skilled workers accelerated within sectors (Berman, Bound, and Griliches, 1992; Katz and Murphy, 1992).

Separating the effects of technology and trade is, to be sure, somewhat problematic. Increased international competition could motivate firms to innovate, adapt new technologies, or change work organizations. And changes in technology affect trading patterns. The diffusion of technology overseas and the expansion of education in other countries has made foreign workers more substitutable for non-college-graduate Americans. Together, large trade deficits in manufactured goods and technological changes favoring computer-literate workers with problem-solving skills explain much of the increased wage inequality and wage differentials based on education.

But demand shifts are not the whole story. If changes in demand were all that drove wage differentials between more and less educated workers, those differentials would have risen in the 1970s. In that decade, as in the 1980s, relative demand shifted toward college graduates and away from less educated workers (though there was no trade deficit in the 1970s), but as was shown in Figure 2.1, education differentials fell in the 1970s.

The reason for the difference in the trends in wage differentials between the 1970s and the 1980s is found on the supply side of the market. In the 1970s the relative supply of college graduates grew rapidly, the result of the baby boomers who enrolled in college in the late 1960s and early 1970s in response to the high rewards for college degrees and the fear of being drafted for the Vietnam War. The growth in supply overwhelmed the increase in demand for more educated workers, and the returns to college diminished (Freeman, 1976). In the 1980s, in contrast, the growth of the relative supply of graduates declined with the "baby-bust" cohorts and the lower return to college education in the 1970s. Katz and Murphy (1992) estimate that the growth of the relative supply of "college-equivalent" to "high-school equivalent" workers declined from a 5 percent annual rate from 1971 to 1979 to a 2.5 percent annual rate from 1979 to 1987.

The lesson is clear. To understand changes in inequality, we must look at both blades of Alfred Marshall's famous market scissors: supply as well as demand.

Another important factor changing relative supplies in the 1980s was immigration, which contributed to rising inequality by bringing many less educated workers into the labor market. The skill distribution of new immigrants to the United States in the 1980s was bimodal. Many immigrant workers came with college degrees, but many from developing countries came with little formal schooling, which adversely affected the market for native-born Americans with limited schooling, those who failed to graduate from high school (Borjas, Freeman, and Katz, 1992).[12] Wage inequality increased most in the West, the region with the largest inflow of less educated immigrants (Topel, 1992). Immigration accounts for about 30 percent of the decrease in the earnings of male high school dropouts compared with other workers in the 1980s (Borjas, Freeman, and Katz, 1992). In addition, the influx of immigrants with college degrees may have slightly dampened the growth of college graduates' earnings.

In sum, sizable and accelerated shifts in demand favoring more educated workers, and reduced growth in their relative supply combined to increase wage inequality in the 1980s. But even in the United States, where market forces have great leeway to determine wages, institutional factors also played a role in increasing inequality.

THE ROLE OF INSTITUTIONS

The major institutional factor that affected the U.S. wage structure was the decline of unionism. By itself the precipitous drop in the union share of the work force in the 1980s explains one-fifth of the growth in wage differentials or overall wage dispersion among male workers (Blackburn, Bloom, and Freeman, 1992; Freeman, 1993; Card, 1992). It accounts for a similar share of the fall in employer- and union-provided pensions among men (Bloom and Freeman, 1992). The calculations behind these assessments are relatively simple. Consider, for example, what happened to young blue-collar men in the 1980s. The proportion who were in unions fell by some 15 percentage points, while the percentage of young white-collar men in unions was roughly constant (and low). Thus 15 percent of the less skilled workers lost the 20 to 25 percent wage advantage associated with union membership, the lower dispersion of wages found in union workplaces, and the greater provision of pensions and other fringe benefits under unionism. Multiplying the 15 percentage point decline in unionization by the effect of unionization on these outcomes provides a first-order estimate of the effect of the decline in unionization on the position of the less skilled. If, as many labor relations analysts believe, lower unionization rates reduce the pressure on nonunion employers to pay high wages and provide benefits, this calculation underestimates the full contribution of falling unionization to the rise in inequality.

Two other widely noted institutional changes during the 1980s appear, in contrast, to have only marginally affected the overall wage structure. First, the fall in the real value of the minimum wage did not greatly affect the distribution of wages, because the U.S. minimum has always been set so low that it determines the pay of only a small minority of workers. In other countries, such as France, where minimum wages cover large proportions of the work force, a fall in the minimum would be a logical explanation for changes in the wage structure. Second, while the reduced generosity of the welfare system in the 1980s induced some potential welfare beneficiaries to enter the job market, adding to supply pressures for lowering the wages of low-skill workers, this was at most a minor contributor to the rise in inequality (Moffitt, 1990).

A look back in U.S. economic history supports the notion that wage-setting institutions can greatly affect earnings inequality. The 1940s provide a striking contrast to the 1980s in terms of the direction of relative wage changes and institutional developments. In the 1940s education and establishment wage differentials and overall inequality decreased substantially (Goldin and Margo, 1992). Much of the narrowing of the wage structure was driven by the explicit policies of the national War Labor Board to reduce establishment wage differentials. At the same time, the increased strength of unions raised blue-collar wages. Market forces reinforced these patterns with a manufacturing boom that generated a strong growth in demand for blue-collar workers as well as a rapid growth in the supply of more educated workers. In the 1980s, institutional changes went in the opposite direction of those in the 1940s and reinforced market tendencies toward increasing wage inequality.

WHY OTHER COUNTRIES FARED DIFFERENTLY

Can international differences in changes in relative wages in the 1980s be explained by supply, demand, and institutions? Why did inequality increase more in the United States (and the United Kingdom) than in most other advanced countries?

Labor demand factors do not explain many of the international differences in the growth in wage inequality or education earnings differentials in the 1980s. All advanced countries experienced large, steady shifts in the industrial and occupational distribution of employment toward sectors and job categories that used a greater proportion of more educated workers. The share of employment in manufacturing declined everywhere but in Japan. In the United States, the manufacturing share of employment dropped by 4.2 percentage points from 1979 to 1989; in OECD Europe it fell by 4.1 percentage points. Only Japan's massive export success enabled it to maintain a near constant manufacturing share of employment. Still, even in Japan changes in technology and the internationalization of economic competition shifted labor demand in favor of more educated workers against non-college-educated workers.

Differential growth in the supply of workers by level of education, in contrast, contributed to the greater rise in education wage differentials in the United States than in other countries in the 1980s. In the 1970s the supply of highly educated workers increased rapidly in all OECD countries. The increase was more rapid than the shifts in demand favoring educated workers, so that skill differentials narrowed in every country (Table 2.1). In the 1980s, however, while the educational qualifications of workers continued to rise in all countries, the growth of the college-educated work force decelerated sharply only in the United States. Among young American men, the college graduate share of the work force actually fell, whereas other countries maintained supply-side pressure against rising inequality. Continued rapid expansion of the college-educated work force in Canada, for instance, explains the more modest rise in the relative earnings of college graduates in Canada than in the United States (Freeman and Needels, 1993). Countries whose education differentials did not increase during the 1980s—France, the Netherlands, and Germany—maintained their 1970s rate of growth in the supply of more educated workers into the 1980s (Katz, Loveman, and Blanchflower, 1994; Abraham and Houseman, 1994; Teulings, 1992; Hartog, Oosterbeek, and Teulings, 1992). The fact that this explanation is more than a "story" has been shown in diverse studies that have found a roughly comparable inverse relation between increases in the supply of educated workers relative to less educated workers and in the pay advantage of the educated workers, across countries. Holding fixed the growth of demand, a 10 percent increase in relative supply lowers relative pay by 3 percent to 7 percent in a variety of countries—as similar a magnitude as one might expect from studies that used various types of data, covering different time periods and with different wage-setting institutions.[13]

South Korea provides a striking example of the effect of relative supply changes on education differentials (Kim and Topel, 1994). In the 1980s South Korea saw a huge drop in the advantage that college graduates had over less educated workers, in contrast to stable or rising differentials in more advanced countries. Why? A major reason was that South Korea had exceptionally fast growth in the college-educated share of the work force. Unlike almost any other developing country (and many developed countries), South Korea has moved rapidly toward levels of college education for its young people characteristic of the United States and Japan.

In sum, the supply and demand forces that affected education differentials in the United States also operated in other countries, with differences in the growth of relative supply accounting for some of the cross-country difference in the increase in pay differentials. But just as for the United States, supply and demand do not fully explain international differences in changes in inequality. Differences in labor market institutions also influenced these outcomes.

WAGE-SETTING INSTITUTIONS AND
CHANGES IN INSTITUTIONS

There are many ways to categorize labor market institutions (see Chapter 1, this volume). Most analysts concentrate on the degree to which wage setting is centralized, differentiating between countries like the United States, with its highly decentralized labor markets in which hundreds of thousands of firms bargain with unions or individual workers over pay and working conditions with little governmental intervention, and the more centralized wage-setting systems of Western Europe. But European wage-setting institutions actually differ greatly among themselves. In Austria and Sweden, for example, peak-level union confederations and employer federations have historically bargained for national wage settlements that cover much of the work force but allow local employers and unions to increase wages above the national settlement through "wage drift". In Germany industry or regional collective bargaining determines basic wages for an area and the Ministry of Labor often extends those to all workers. In France the minimum wage is important in determining the overall level of wages, and the French Ministry of Labor also extends contracts. In

Italy the Scala Mobile, a form of negotiated wage increase designed to compensate for inflation and which applied effectively to all Italians, increased the pay of low-paid workers faster than that of high-paid workers throughout the 1980s.

Ranking these diverse institutions in terms of centralization of wage setting is not clear-cut. Some experts place Germany high on the centralization scale (Bruno and Sachs, 1985); others place it lower (Calmfors and Driffil, 1988). Although few view Italy as having highly centralized wage-setting institutions, the Scala Mobile resembles Sweden's peak-level bargaining system.[14] Some view Switzerland as decentralized, others as more centralized. Moreover, here as elsewhere Japan is a problem case. Is Japan highly centralized because of the importance of the Japanese employers' federation and the annual Shunto Offensive during which national unions and employer federations bargain over the "right" wage settlement for the country (Soskice, 1990)? Or is Japan decentralized because of its company unions, the importance of employee bonuses that are linked to company profits, and its low rate of unionization? Japan has sizable variation in wages across industries, which one normally associates with decentralized wage setting, but the percentage change in wages across sectors and firms in Japan is remarkably similar, which suggests a more centralized wage-setting mechanism. And in the 1970s Japan rapidly reduced its rate of wage inflation throughout the economy in a way that would do the most centralized wage-setting system proud.

Countries that change their wage-setting practices—as Australia did in 1983 when its unions made an agreement with the government to limit wage increases so that employment would grow; as Sweden did when it stepped back from national bargaining in the 1980s; as Germany did in 1993 when unions offered employer federations and the government a "social pact" to control the growth of real wages—create further classification problems. However, these difficulties notwithstanding, one thing about international differences in labor institutions is clear: the position of the United States. No matter which factors one stresses in categorizing countries, the United States ranks low in the role played by institutions in determining wage and employment outcomes and high in the role played by market forces. In contrast to European countries or even Canada, whose unions remain strong, the United States has developed few institutions to augment market wage setting.

Unionization is low. Employer federations are weak. The government rarely intervenes to set wages. Since institutional forces such as unions tend to dampen inequality, wage inequality ought to be higher in the United States than in most other countries, and it is. In addition, because it allowed the full brunt of shifts in supply and demand to fall on wages in the 1980s, the United States could have been expected to have especially large drops in the relative earnings of less educated workers, as it did. In Western European countries on the other hand, wage-setting institutions dampened the pressures for increased wage differentials.

Finally, there were important changes in wage-setting institutions in many advanced countries in the 1980s that affected wage differentials. After growing in the 1970s, unionization fell in many, though not all, countries (OECD, 1991). The union share of the work force dropped precipitously in the United Kingdom, the United States, the Netherlands, and France, but it held steady in Canada and Germany. However, because unionism means different things in different labor relations systems, even similar declines in unionism have different effects on the labor market. In the United States and the United Kingdom reduced union density meant a decreased role for collective bargaining and institutional forces in wage setting. But in France falling unionization did not diminish the importance of the national minimum wage in wage setting, and it was accompanied by an increasing number of plant-level collective contracts. Sweden and Austria offer another striking contrast. In Sweden the union share of the work force is exceptionally high, whereas union density is lower and fell sharply in Austria in the 1980s. Yet Swedish employers withdrew from peak-level bargaining in 1983 and moved to decentralize Sweden's traditionally centralized bargaining system, while Austria maintained centralized wage setting throughout the decade. In Europe "second channel" works councils gave employees a continued voice in many workplace decisions, even with declining unionism (see Chapter 4, this volume).

Weakened unionism and reduced centralization of wage setting contributed to the cross–country pattern of change in wage inequality in the 1980s. In the United Kingdom the fall in union density accounts for about one-fourth of the growth of inequality (Schmitt, 1994)—comparable to the estimated effect of declining unionism on U.S. inequality.[15] At the other end of the spectrum, the continued strength of unions in Canada partly explains the smaller increase in inequality there than in the United States. Approximately 40 percent of the difference in wage inequality between the United States and Canada appears to be due to the difference in the union shares of the work force (Lemieux, 1993). The decentralization of collective bargaining in Sweden contributed to the rise in inequality there in the 1980s, though Sweden's levels of inequality are modest by U.S. standards. Unification of East Germany with West Germany moved the former East German wage structure toward that of the West (Krueger and Pischke, 1994).

This discussion interprets institutional change as an outside force that affects labor market outcomes. But institutions are not immune to market forces. Shifts in supply and demand that raise relative wage differentials will reduce the strength of centralized collective bargaining and lower union influence on wage setting (Freeman and Gibbons, 1994). Institutions that go strongly against market forces face a difficult task. The fact that unionization fell in most countries in the 1980s, when market forces favored greater inequality, is no accident. Italy's dropping of the Scala Mobile, Sweden's move from peak-level bargaining to more industry- and company-based settlements, and the 1980s' trend toward more plant- or firm-level arrangements in France were responses to a changing economic environment, not random variations in modes of pay setting.

The evidence from overseas shows that there is space for institutions to affect outcomes, but only within limits. European countries that had small increases in inequality in the 1980s might see greater rises in wage differentials in the 1990s as their institutions adapt to market forces or are altered by those forces. However, few if any countries (except the United Kingdom) are likely to approach American levels of inequality, so long as they give greater sway to institutional forces in the labor market.

CONCLUSION: LEANING AGAINST THE WIND

Market forces are working to ameliorate the huge increase in inequality in the United States. The massive college-education-wage premium of the 1980s increased college enrollments despite sharply rising tuition costs (Blackburn, Bloom, and Freeman, 1992). In 1990, 60 percent of new American high school graduates enrolled in two- or four-year colleges in the October following their graduation, compared with 49 percent of the high school graduating class of 1980 (U. S. Department of Education, 1992)—a huge change that will accelerate the growth of the college-graduate work force in the 1990s. An increased supply of graduates will, in turn, offset demand increases favoring the more educated and act to lower education differentials. Having proportionately fewer workers with less than a college degree will decrease downward pressure on the pay of the less educated, and may possibly lead to real wage gains for them.

Will this be enough to restore an economic future to less educated workers? Given continued trade and technological changes favoring those who are more educated, we doubt that increasing the supply of college graduates and reducing that of less educated workers will by itself undo the rise in inequality seen in the 1980s. The experiences of other advanced nations suggest additional ways to lean against the forces toward greater inequality. Indeed, developments in Europe and Japan in the 1980s showed that international competition and the implementation of new technologies do *not* necessarily imply sharp increases in wage inequality and declines in the real earnings of less educated workers.

Two broad national strategies were associated with little increase in skill differentials and in overall wage inequality in the 1980s. The first was the European model of greater institutional influence in the wage-setting process through increases in minimum wages and extensions of the terms of collective bargaining agreements to firms not directly involved in such agreements. Strategies of this type succeeded in preventing the wage structures from widening in Italy and France in the early 1980s. But these policies do not deal directly with a changing demand for skills, and they can run into economic difficulties over the long run. Policies that limit market wage adjustments without directly addressing changed market conditions can prevent wage inequality from increasing, but they risk stagnant employment growth, persistent unemployment for young workers (as in France), and a shift of resources to an underground economy to avoid wage regulations (as in Italy).

The second type of national strategy combines some institutional wage interventions with education and training systems that invest heavily in non-college-educated workers. Of this approach,

Germany and Japan are exemplars in training (see Chapter 3, this volume). German and Japanese firms treat college-educated and non-college-educated workers as much closer substitutes in production than do U.S. or British firms, reducing the effect of technological change on relative skill demand and lowering pressure for wage structure changes in those countries as compared with the United States. German institutions affect wage setting, but they also offer apprenticeships to ensure that the nation's skill structure is consistent with its wage policies. Buffering the earnings of the less educated with institutional wage setting seems to work best when institutions augment workers' skills as well.

From this perspective, an economic strategy that involves policies to augment the skills of the less educated, that develops institutions to protect workers' interests in the labor market, and that encourages market responses in the form of greater investments in higher education could produce a more desirable long-term solution to the rise of inequality in the United States than could any of these approaches taken separately.

NOTES

1. The relation between development and inequality is known in the economic development literature as the Kuznets curve. Nobel laureate Simon Kuznets provided evidence indicating that income inequality first rose, then fell with economic development.

2. Even if one is interested solely in the United States, there are virtues to examining other countries. The experience of others can be used to "test" explanations that are explicitly tailored to fit the U.S. facts. If the same story fits the experiences of other countries, one can be more confident that the explanation holds for the United States. In addition, understanding how other countries have dealt with the same underlying market forces ought to provide some notions of what strategies might improve the economic position of less skilled Americans.

3. To the contrary, the same less skilled men who suffered losses in real earnings experienced losses in the likelihood that they would have an employer- or union-provided pension (Bloom and Freeman, 1992; Parsons, 1993; Even and Macpherson, 1993) and, as far as can be told from weak data, an employer-provided health insurance plan (Gittleman and Howell, 1993).

4. Despite the decline in the relative wages of less skilled men, the proportion employed fell relative to the proportion of more skilled men employed during the 1980s. This occurred by education and by deciles of the earnings distribution. But note that this pattern has somewhat reversed itself during the early 1990s. White-collar work-

ers have suffered more from unemployment in the last few years than in the past. The unemployment rate of executives in January 1993 was 3.9 percent, the highest it had been since 1983 (4.4 percent). By contrast, the unemployment rate of operators, fabricators, and laborers was 11.9 percent in January 1993 compared with 20.6 percent in 1983.

5. Specifically we computed the proportion of all men who had income between 1.3 times the mean and 0.7 times the mean income in the relevant tables reporting total money income by age, in CPS Consumer Income Reports Series P-60, *Money Income of Households, Families, and Persons in the United States.*

6. Because earnings distributions can be altered in various ways, there is no one-to-one correspondence between all measures of change in the earnings distribution and change in the share of jobs in specified income categories. The proportion of workers earning middle-class incomes could remain unchanged while the very poor got poorer and the very wealthy got wealthier, raising measured inequality. Summarizing changes in an income distribution with single statistics can always produce some problems.

7. While most of the analyses use individual-level data files, such data were unavailable in some cases. For example, Japan does not make public the micro-economic data from its Basic Survey on Wages. In these cases, the analyses are based on tabulations from published data.

8. This generalization is based on the following studies: Blanchflower, Katz, and Loveman, 1994; Edin and Holmlund, 1994; Freeman and Needels, 1993; Abraham and Houseman, 1994; Erickson and Ichino, 1994; Gregory and Vella, 1994; and Hartog, Oosterbeek, and Teulings, 1992.

9. In some countries, such as India, rates of unemployment are high for the more educated. A poor, uneducated Indian cannot spend time searching for the most desirable job, whereas a wealthier job seeker can. On the other hand, unemployment compensation, which replaces a larger share of the income of the low-paid worker than of the highly paid one makes it easier for the former to search for work.

10. In technical terms, the elasticities of complementarity (Hicks's term for the effect of changes in relative quantities on relative factor prices) must be noticeably greater than zero but less than infinite.

11. Going beyond the supply-demand story, economics offers general equilibrium analyses that stress the complex interactions of the entire economy. There are human capital investment stories that interpret declines in relative wages as indicating that workers are investing in future skills and will enjoy rapid increases in earnings in the future. There are quality of education stories that claim that the skills of workers in the bottom half of the education distribution have declined. And there are compensating differential stories in which

relative wage changes simply offset changes in taxes or employee benefits, so that the real economic well-being of workers does not change. For instance, the decline in marginal tax rates in the United States might have led firms to pay high-wage workers more in terms of salary and less in terms of in-kind or deferred benefits. If this were the case the increase in inequality would be illusory—reflecting a shift in the composition of compensation rather than in the real level of pay of highly paid workers versus low-paid workers.

12. Studies of local labor markets that compare changes in cities receiving many immigrants with those receiving few immigrants show little impact from immigrants on the wages of less skilled workers (Altonji and Card, 1991; LaLonde and Topel, 1991), in contrast to analyses that focus on the effects of immigration nationally on the relative supply of less educated workers. Several factors may account for this difference: compensating geographic mobility to gateway cities (Iowans who would have migrated to New York or Los Angeles, absent the immigrant flow, did not do so); immigrant-induced increases in demand; immigrants taking jobs that native-born Americans would not have taken in any plausible circumstance; and so on.

13. The countries covered are Canada (Freeman and Needels, 1993), the United States (Freeman, 1976; Blackburn, Bloom, and Freeman, 1990; Katz and Murphy, 1992), the United Kingdom (Schmitt, 1994), Sweden (Edin and Holmlund, 1994), the Netherlands (Teulings, 1992), and South Korea (Kim and Topel, 1994).

14. During its heyday, the Scala Mobile produced huge declines in the dispersion of wages that were accompanied by a shift of employment to the underground economy—just as during its heyday, Sweden's peak-level bargaining system produced huge declines in the dispersion of wages, accompanied by growing employment in the public sector. In both countries, moreover, wage drift allows particular sectors to deviate from the central settlement, and allows individual firms to deviateas well. A detailed comparison of the two systems of wage setting suggest that they are more alike than the wage-setting systems of many other European countries (Erickson and Ichino, 1994; Edin and Holmlund, 1994).

15. Gossling and Machin (1992) also find a big role for de-unionization in the rise in wage dispersion in the United Kingdom. In contrast to the United States wage dispersion in the United Kingdom rose much more in nonunion than in union establishments.

REFERENCES

Abraham, Katherine G., and Susan Houseman. 1994. "Earnings Inequality in Germany." In R. Freeman and L. Katz, eds., *Differences and Changes in Wage Structures*. Chicago: University of Chicago Press for NBER.

Altonji, Joseph G., and David Card. 1991. "The Effects of Immigration on the Labor Market Outcomes of Less-skilled Natives." In J. Abowd and R. Freeman, eds., *Immigration, Trade and the Labor Market*. Chicago: University of Chicago Press for NBER.

Bar-Or, Yuval, John Burbidge, Lonnie Magee, and A. Leslie Robb. 1992. "Canadian Experience-Earnings Profiles and the Return to Education in Canada: 1971–90." McMaster University, Department of Economics, Working Paper no. 93-04, December.

Berman, Eli, John Bound, and Zvi Griliches. 1992. "Changes in the Demand for Skilled Labor within U.S. Manufacturing Industries: Evidence from the Annual Survey of Manufacturing." Unpublished paper, NBER, July.

Blackburn, McKinley L., David E. Bloom, and Richard B. Freeman. 1990. "The Declining Position of Less-Skilled American Males." In G. Burtless, ed., *A Future of Lousy Jobs?* Washington D.C.: Brookings Institution. Pp. 31–67.

———. 1992. "Changes in Earnings Differentials in the 1980s: Concordance, Convergence, Causes and Consequences." NBER Working Paper no. 3901, November.

Blanchflower, David G., Lawrence F. Katz, and Gary W. Loveman. 1994. "A Comparison of Changes in the Structure of Wages in Four OECD Countries." In R. Freeman and L. Katz, eds., *Differences and Changes in Wage Structures*. Chicago: University of Chicago Press for NBER.

Blau, Francine, and Lawrence Kahn. 1994. "The Gender Earnings Gap: Some International Evidence." In R. Freeman and L. Katz, eds., *Differences and Changes in Wage Structures*. Chicago: University of Chicago Press for NBER.

Bloom, David E., and Richard B. Freeman. 1992. "The Fall in Private Pension Coverage in the United States." *American Economic Review* 82, no. 2 (May): 539–548.

Borjas, George, Richard Freeman, and Lawrence Katz. 1992. "On the Labor Market Effects of Immigration and Trade." In G. Borjas and R. Freeman, eds., *Immigration and the Work Force*. Chicago: University of Chicago for NBER. Pp. 213–244.

Bound, John, and George Johnson. 1992. "Changes in the Structure of

Wages in the 1980s: An Evaluation of Alternative Explanations." *American Economic Review* 82 (June): 371–392.

Bruno, Michael, and Jeffrey Sachs. 1985. *Economics and Worldwide Stagflation.* Cambridge, Mass.: Harvard University Press.

Calmfors, L., and J. Driffil. 1988. "Bargaining Structure, Corporatism and Macroeconomic Performance." *Economic Policy* 6 (April).

Card, David. 1992. "The Effect of Unions on the Distribution of Wages: Redistribution or Relabelling." NBER Working Paper no. 4195, October.

Davis, Steven J. 1992. "Cross-Country Patterns of Change in Relative Wages." In O. J. Blanchard and S. Fischer, eds., *NBER Macroeconomics Annual.* Cambridge, Mass.: The MIT Press.

Davis, Steven J., and John Haltiwanger. 1991. "Wage Dispersion within and between Manufacturing Plants." *Brookings Papers on Economic Activity: Microeconomics.* Washington, D.C.: Brookings Institution. Pp. 115–180.

Edin, Per-Anders, and Bertil Holmlund. 1994. "The Swedish Wage Structure: The Rise and Fall of Solidarity Wage Policy." In R. Freeman and L. Katz, eds., *Differences and Changes in Wage Structures.* Chicago: University of Chicago Press for NBER.

Erickson, Christopher, and Andrea Ichino. 1994. "Wage Differentials in Italy: Market Forces, Institutions, and Inflation." In R. Freeman and L. Katz, eds., *Differences and Changes in Wage Structures.* Chicago: University of Chicago Press for NBER.

Even, William E., and David A. Macpherson. 1993. "The Pension Coverage of Young and Mature Men." Paper presented at the U.S. Dept of Labor, Pension and Welfare Benefits Administration Conference on Pension Coverage, April 16.

Freeman, Richard B. 1976. *The Overeducated American.* San Diego: Academic Press.

———. 1992. "How Much Has De-Unionization Contributed to the Rise in Male Earnings Inequality?" In S. Danziger and P. Gottschalk, eds., *Uneven Tides: Rising Inequality in America.* New York: Russell Sage Foundation.

Freeman, Richard B., and Robert Gibbons. 1994. "Getting Together and Breaking Apart: The Decline of Centralized Collective Bargaining." In R. Freeman and L. Katz, eds., *Differences and Changes in Wage Structures.* Chicago: University of Chicago Press for NBER.

Freeman, Richard B., and Lawrence F. Katz. 1994. *Differences and Changes in Wage Structures.* Chicago: University of Chicago Press for NBER.

Freeman, Richard B., and Karen Needels. 1993. "Skill Differentials in Canada in an Era of Rising Labor Market Inequality." In D. Card and

R. Freeman, eds., *Small Differences That Matter.* Chicago: University of Chicago Press for NBER.

Gittleman, Maury B., and David R. Howell. 1993. "Job Quality and Labor Market Segmentation in the 1980s: A New Perspective on the Effects of Employment Restructuring by Race and Gender." Unpublished manuscript, March.

Goldin, Claudia, and Robert Margo. 1992. "The Great Compression: The Wage Structure in the United States at Mid-Century." *Quarterly Journal of Economics* 107 (February): 1–34.

Gossling, Amanda, and Steve Machin. 1992. "Trade Unions and Wage Dispersion in U.K. Establishments, 1980–90" Preliminary draft of paper, University College London, December.

Gregory, Robert, and Frank Vella. 1994. "Aspects of Real Wage and Employment Changes in the Australian Male Labour Market." In R. Freeman and L. Katz, eds., *Differences and Changes in Wage Structures.* Chicago: University of Chicago Press for NBER.

Hartog, Joop, Hessel Oosterbeek, and Coen Teulings. 1992. "Age, Wage and Education in the Netherlands." Unpublished paper, University of Amsterdam.

Katz, Lawrence F., Gary Loveman, and David Blanchflower. 1994. "A Comparison of Changes in the Structure of Wages in Four OECD Countries." In R. Freeman and L. Katz, eds., *Differences and Changes in Wage Structures.* Chicago: University of Chicago Press for NBER.

Katz, Lawrence F., and Kevin M. Murphy. 1992. "Changes in Relative Wages, 1963–1987: Supply and Demand Factors." *Quarterly Journal of Economics* 107 (February): 35–78.

Katz, Lawrence F., and Ana L. Revenga. 1989. "Changes in the Structure of Wages: The United States vs. Japan." *Journal of the Japanese and International Economies* 3 (December): 522–53.

Kim, Dae-Il, and Robert H. Topel. 1994. "Labor Markets and Economic Growth: Lessons from Korea's Industrialization, 1970–1990." In R. Freeman and L. Katz, eds., *Differences and Changes in Wage Structures.* Chicago: University of Chicago Press for NBER.

Krueger, Alan B. 1993. "How Computers Have Changed the Wage Structure? Evidence from Micro Data." *Quarterly Journal of Economics* (February): 33–60.

Krueger, Alan B., and Jörn-Steffen Pischke. 1994. "A Comparative Analysis of East and West German Labor Markets: Before and After Unification." In R. Freeman and L. Katz, eds., *Differences and Changes in Wage Structures.* Chicago: University of Chicago Press for NBER.

LaLonde, Robert J., and Robert H. Topel. 1991. "Labor Market Adjustments to Increased Immigration." In J. Abowd and R. Freeman, eds.,

Immigration, Trade and the Labor Market. Chicago: University of Chicago Press for NBER.

Lemieux, Thomas. 1993. "Unions and Wage Inequality in Canada and the United States." In D. Card and R. Freeman, eds., *Small Differences That Matter* Chicago: University of Chicago Press for NBER.

Levy, Frank, and Richard Murnane. 1992. "U.S. Earnings Levels and Earnings Inequality: A Review of Recent Trends and Proposed Explanations." *Journal of Economic Literature*, September.

MacPhail, Fiona. 1993. "Has the 'Great U-Turn' Gone Full Circle? Recent Trends in Earnings Inequality in Canada 1981–1989." Dalhouse University, Halifax, Department of Economics, Working Paper no. 93-01, January.

Moffitt, Robert. 1990. "The Distribution of Earnings and the Welfare State." In G. Burtless, ed., *A Future of Lousy Jobs? The Changing Structure of U.S. Wages*. Washington, D.C.: Brookings Institution.

Murphy, Kevin M., and Finis Welch. 1992. "The Structure of Wages." *Quarterly Journal of Economics* 107 (February): 285–326.

Organization for Economic Cooperation and Development (OECD). 1989. *Employment Outlook*. Paris: OECD.

————. 1991. *Employment Outlook*. Paris: OECD.

Parsons, Donald O. 1993. "The Contraction in Pension Coverage: Household Survey Evidence." Paper presented at the U.S. Dept. of Labor, Pension and Welfare Benefits Administration Conference on Pension Coverage, April 16.

Schmitt, John. 1994. "The Changing Structure of Male Earnings in Britain, 1974–88." In R. Freeman and L. Katz, eds., *Differences and Changes in Wage Structures*. Chicago: University of Chicago Press for NBER.

Soskice, D. 1990. "Wage Determination: The Changing Role of Institutions in the Advanced Industrialized Countries." *Oxford Review of Economic Policy* 6, no.4 (Winter).

Teulings, Coen N. 1992. "The Wage Distribution in a Model of Matching between Skills and Jobs." University of Amsterdam, October.

Topel, Robert. 1992. "Wage Inequality and Regional Labor Market Performance in the United States." Paper presented at NBER Labor Studies Meeting, Cambridge, Mass., November.

U.S. Bureau of the Census. 1992. *Money Income of Households, Families, and Persons in the United States: 1991*. Current Population Reports, Series P-60, No. 180. Washington D.C.: U.S. Department of Commerce, August.

U.S. Department of Education. 1992. National Center for Education Statistics, *The Condition of Education 1992* Washington D.C.: U.S. Government Printing Office, June.

3

PAYOFFS TO ALTERNATIVE
TRAINING STRATEGIES AT WORK

Lisa M. Lynch

In the 1970s labor market analysts and policymakers were concerned about absorbing into the labor market an "overeducated American"—the cohort of young, baby-boom college graduates who flooded the labor market and experienced reduced earnings and employment opportunities (Freeman, 1976). In the 1980s and 1990s discussion has focused on a very different issue: how to stimulate the skill development of an "undertrained America." In 1983, the National Commission on Excellence in Education, and later in 1989, the Secretary of Labor's Commission on Workforce Quality and Labor Market Efficiency, both concluded that for U.S. firms to compete internationally immediate reforms were needed in the education and training institutions in America.

What happened to cause such an apparently sharp reversal in the appraisal of U.S. workers' skills? In the past, many U.S. workers without a college degree could look forward to a good paying job with moderate skills requirements in manufacturing. The required skills could be obtained through a system of informal "learning by doing." However, as technologies changed and firms organized work in new ways to increase productivity, demand increased for workers with problem-solving skills and with knowledge to deal with the new, often computer-based, technology. Part of this increased demand for highly skilled workers has shown up in the increasing wage premium college graduates receive relative to those with a high school degree or less (see Chapter 2, this volume). Even nonmanagerial workers without a college degree are now expected to take on responsibilities for quality control and trouble-shooting that were not required under old, Fordist production systems. Leaner work organizations now require workers to have a broader range of skills. In addition, continuing technological change will mean that many workers, even if they remain with the same employer, may not be doing the same job ten years from now.

In a world of changing work force requirements workers must be retrainable and adaptable to new technologies and work organizations. The problem facing new entrants, especially those without a college degree, is obtaining the training needed for an entry-level high-skill, high-wage job as opposed to a low-skill, low-wage job. For older workers who have already completed their formal education, the problem lies in acquiring new skills. To understand the nature of this "training deficit," it is necessary to examine not only the skills development of new entrants to the labor force, but also the adaptability of workers already in the labor force to changing skills requirements.

While there seems to be an emerging consensus that U.S. workers' skills are not on a par with those of workers in Europe and Japan (see U.S. GAO, 1990; U.S. OTA, 1990; Lynch, 1991a and 1993b; Kochan and Osterman, 1991), this is based on limited evidence of how skills and skills preparation vary from country to country. There are relatively good studies of how education and government training programs affect labor market outcomes but much less evidence for how private-sector training affects wages or what impact alternative training strategies have on firm productivity and competitiveness.

This chapter summarizes new findings on the payoffs received from alternative training strategies in various advanced industrialized countries.[1] I will contrast the characteristics of national training systems and the institutional structures that support these systems, and seek to determine why different countries adopt different training systems. I will also present evidence on the "bottom line" question: how alternative types of training affect productivity and wages. Finally, I will draw lessons from different countries' experiences with training strategies for the development of alternative proposals to modify the system of post-school training in the United States.

CHARACTERISTICS OF TRAINING SYSTEMS ACROSS COUNTRIES

If there is an emerging consensus in the United States that training is necessary for competitiveness, why isn't everyone doing more training? Firms may not provide training, especially training which workers could use throughout the economy, for a variety of reasons. Smaller firms often have higher training costs per employee than larger firms, because they cannot spread fixed costs of training over a larger group of employees. In addition, the loss in production from having one worker in off-site training is probably much higher for a small firm than for a larger firm. As a result, the percentage of workers with company training in the United States is lower for small than for large firms: 26 percent of workers in large establishments report receiving formal company training compared with 11 percent in small establishments (Bowers and Swaim, 1992). Another reason that a firm may be reluctant to invest in training is high employee turnover. In fact, training may itself contribute to employee turnover: if the new skills will be valuable to other employers, the firm risks having the employee hired away (what is known as the poaching or "cherry-picking" problem). Therefore, investments in training that can only be used at the given firm (so-called firm-specific training) are more attractive to firms than training that can be used throughout the economy (so-called general training). This would not be a problem if workers could readily borrow money to finance more general training themselves, if the state would subsidize general training, or if employers could pay workers lower wages during general training periods. But workers cannot easily borrow money for training, the state might end up financing both general and firm-specific training with subsidies, and workers are reluctant to accept lower wages for training without a guarantee of employment security.

How do other countries address this problem?

Japan, which has an admirable record of providing firm-level training for workers, deals with the problem of capturing the returns on training by imposing high costs on employees who leave a firm. Wage gains associated with years of experience at a firm are four times greater in Japan than in the United States.[2] Firms are also more reluctant to hire workers away from other firms, because the social costs paid by poaching firms have historically been high. This is one reason why employees stay, on average, much longer with a single firm in Japan than in other developed economies.³ In addition, when demand falls Japanese firms are less likely to lay off workers than are their U.S. counterparts. Instead they often use periods of slack demand to do training. With their lower employee turnover, firms are able to capture the returns on investments in even relatively general training. However, the ability of this system to sustain itself may be challenged as employee turnover increases in sectors such as finance and banking.

Germany, which also has an admirable record in providing training, uses a different approach. Its tripartite structure of employers, unions, and government determines a national strategy for training; this arrangement also appears to have solved the problem of capturing returns from training. Local chambers of commerce use moral suasion in the business community to protect firms that train a large number of workers from excessive poaching by other firms. More generally, Germany's dual system of apprenticeship training is characterized by coinvestment in training by workers and firms; government provision of training-related schooling for apprentices; codetermination of training program content by unions, employers' associations, and the government; and nationally recognized certification of skills upon completion of training. German firms undertake a great deal of general skills training, and this generates a high-skill, high-productivity labor force.

Sweden and other Nordic countries have historically addressed the potential market failure in general training through their extensive support for government training. This support may take the form of government-sponsored programs in specially developed training institutions, or school-based vocational training for young workers, as is found in Norway. Regardless of the form of delivery of government training programs, the expenditures are much larger than what is spent on government-sponsored training in the United States. For example, in 1990 the Swedish government spent approximately .46 percent of its gross domestic product on training programs, in contrast to just .09 percent in the United States. Government-financed training in Nordic countries is targeted at both disadvantaged or unemployed workers and those in employment.

While this strategy of government sponsorship may help fund training it risks exploitation by firms that shift the cost of firm-specific training, which they would otherwise undertake themselves, to the public. Also, evidence of the effectiveness of government training programs on the employment experience of workers is mixed (see Bjorklund, 1990). For instance, recently unemployed young workers who are trained in government programs are more likely to experience future unemployment than those who just participate in job-search skills training. There is concern in Sweden that government-sponsored programs are not improving workers' skills appropriately to meet private-sector demand, and that some workers may even be stigmatized by participating in government training programs. This latter concern has also been raised in U.S. discussions of the effectiveness of government training programs. As a result of increasing pressure to reduce government expenditures and the lack of clear evidence for how much government programs actually improve workers' skills, Sweden may try to shift training expenditures from the public to the private sector.

The U.S. training system, in contrast to those in Western Europe and Japan, is highly decentralized and has little formal structure (see Carnevale et al., 1990; Carey, 1985; Lusterman, 1977; and U.S. OTA, 1990 for overviews of the U.S. training system). There are many possible sources of post-school training in the United States: formal and informal employer-provided training acquired on the job; off-the-job training from for-profit proprietary institutions and community colleges; government training programs, such as the Job Training Partnership Act (JTPA); and military training programs. One of the key features of training in the United States is that no national system exists for accrediting vocational skills acquired outside of formal schooling. Decisions to invest in training are made by workers themselves or by specific firms. Apart from limited programs to build basic skills, the training content of most programs is generally task specific and not geared to preparing workers for a lifetime of skills training as technology changes.

Why did the United States not develop a formal training system as did Europe or Japan? Part of the answer may lie in how U.S. firms fulfilled their training requirements in the past. It used to be that when U.S. employers faced a specific skill shortage they could increase immigration flow of workers with the necessary skills. One consequence of this practice was a failure to develop training and retraining institutions within the U.S. that could increase the skills of less educated and less skilled Americans. Another reason that post-school training is so decentralized in the United States may be that the American schooling system is itself decentralized. Compared with schools in Europe and Japan, U.S. schools have a high degree of local and state autonomy in setting standards. This structure is replicated in post-school training institutions. Generally the U.S. training system is one in which the decisions of individual workers or individual firms determines who gets trained and for what skills. This has resulted in a training system that is flexible at the individual level but that lacks a comprehensive national strategy to develop and coordinate individual investments to address potential market failures in the delivery of training.

In recent years several countries have attempted to reform their training institutions. Both France and Australia have adopted an employer's training tax to generate additional firm- financed training. The tax in France applies to all firms with more than ten employees; in 1971 the tax rate was 0.8 percent of the total payroll, but it rose to 1.2 percent in 1988 and to 1.4 percent in 1993. This tax is a "pay or play" tax, since what is required is the expenditure, not the training: if a firm cannot document training expenses greater than 1.4 percent of its wage bill, it must pay the difference between its actual training expenditures and the 1.4 percent. In Australia the payroll tax is called the Training Guarantee, and it has been in place since 1990. All enterprises that have a payroll greater than $200,000 (Australian) must spend 1.5 percent of their payroll on training. Plans for increasing the Australian tax to 2 percent in 1993 were abandoned because, according to the minister of employment, most firms were already well above that level of training expenditures.[4]

There has been only limited evaluation of the impact of the training tax in France and none in Australia at this writing, since that tax was instituted so recently. A survey of the training practices of French firms in 1988, after the increase in the rate from 0.8 to 1.2 percent, showed that while 29 percent of employees in firms with ten or more employees received training in 1988, very few unskilled employees and employees in small firms (those with ten to fifty employees) received company-provided training. Only 8 percent of workers in firms with ten to twenty employees received training, and only 12 percent of all unskilled workers received training. In contrast, 49 percent of workers in firms with 2,000 or more employees received training, and 47 percent of all managers and technical workers received training. Efforts to stimulate training through the tax seem to have had an uneven impact on the distribution of company provided training across workers and firms.

The various training strategies pursued by firms in the United States, Europe, and Japan are summarized in Table 3.1. The table divides national training systems into two broad categories: workplace-based systems and all other systems: school-based, individual-choice, and government-led systems. Examples of workplace-based training systems include apprenticeships (Germany), extensive company-provided training with low employee turnover (Japan), an employer training tax (Australia and France), and informal learning by doing in the United States. Examples of school based, individual choice, and government-led training systems include the school youth training programs in Norway and the system of formal schooling matched with training provided by for-profit vocational and technical institutions in the United States. The key difference between these two categories is that the workplace-based systems link structured formal training programs with employment while the school-based and government-led systems are not directly linked with jobs. The table highlights some of the characteristics of each system. Within the two broad groupings, it shows large variation across countries in their approaches to augmenting the skills of their work force. It also identifies issues associated with each of the training systems, such as the relevance of primarily school-based vocational training and the degree of certification of skills.

Figure 3.1 shows the impact of the different systems on the incidence of private-sector training across a range of countries. Most of the countries with workplace-based training systems have high rates of training. Germany, however, is a surprising exception: over the entire population of workers the incidence of training is low, but the incidence of training for workers twenty to twenty-four years of age in Germany is the highest in the world, with over 75 percent of these workers receiving workplace training. This suggests that the extensive training workers receive early in their worklife prepares them sufficiently well for adjusting to changes in their jobs in the future that they do not need much additional formal company training. Countries with extensive government involvement in training, such as Sweden and Norway, also have very high rates of company training.

The most striking finding in Figure 3.1 is the small percentage of

Table 3.1   Alternative Training Systems

System	Country	Basic Characteristics
	Workplace-based Systems	
Apprenticeship Training	Germany, U.K. (pre-1980s)	Codetermination (employers, unions, government) Coinvestment Certification of skills Incentives for all to do well in school
Low Turnover and Firm Training	Japan	Lifetime employment lowers turnover Firms provide general and specific training Training embedded in production process High degree of homogeneity in literacy and numeracy
Employer Training Tax	France, Australia	Distributes costs over wide range of employers Workers receive training from firms or centers funded by firms not providing in-house training
Learning by Doing	U.S.	Employer training is primarily firm specific, difficult to monitor and evaluate
	School-based, Individual-choice, and Government-led Systems	
Government-led, School-based	Sweden, Norway, U.K. (post-1980)	Government-funded general training Part of overall package of relocation grants and assistance to promote mobility into growth sectors and away from declining sectors
School-based, Proprietary Institutions	U.S., Canada	Individual autonomy on training investments Multiple sources of training Few nationally recognized qualifications outside formal schooling

SOURCE: Lynch, 1994.

Figure 3.1   Incidence of Firm-provided Training

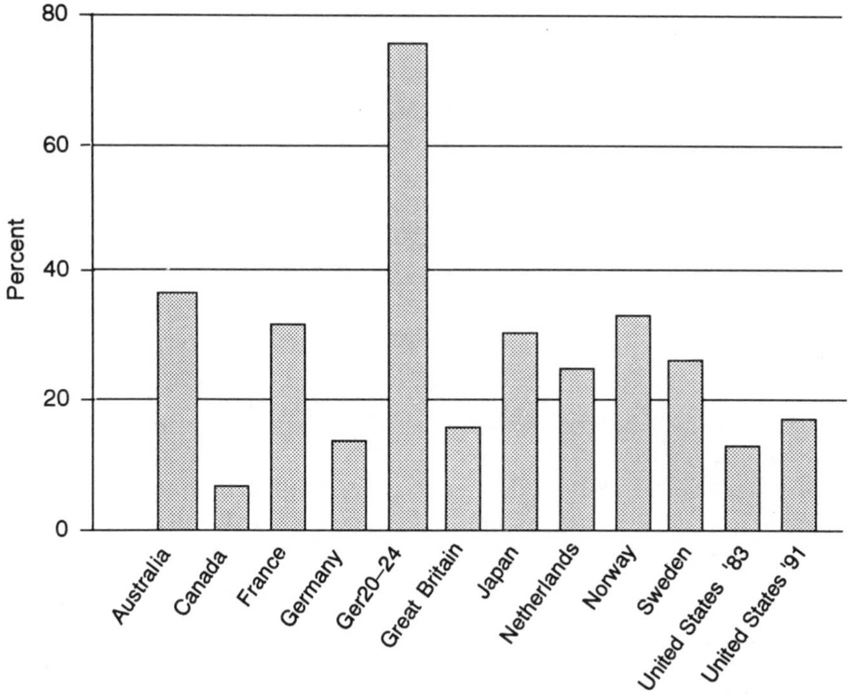

SOURCES: Current Population Survey 1983 and 1991 training supplements; OECD, 1991; CEREQ, 1991a,b; Ishikawa, 1992; and the 1985 Adult Training Survey, Statistics Canada, 1986. Data refer to the incidence of training in various years in the mid to late 1980s. "Ger20–24" indicates German workers age 20 to 24.

workers who receive company training in the United States compared with the other countries cited. This stands out even though the U.S. measure of training incidence is broader than that of other countries: the U.S. numbers reflect the percentage of workers who received any training at all at any time in their current job, instead of the percentage who were trained in the previous year, the measure used for the other countries. The only country with a lower incidence of training is Canada, whose training system is similar to the system in the United States. Most of the workers in the United States who receive employer-provided training are technical and managerial employees with university degrees.[5] Only 4 percent of young workers who are not university graduates get formal training at work.[6] Nonmanagerial and nontechnical workers receive very little skill-enhancing formal training in the United

States compared with workers in Europe and Japan. Most training for these workers is obtained informally, through learning by doing.

Since training is more informal in the United States than in Europe, one might conclude that U.S. firms do not spend as much on training as do firms in other countries. Measuring training expenditures from firm data, however, is not straightforward. Training costs for firms include direct costs that are fairly clearcut, such as materials, salaries of teachers, transportation, and other items associated with off-site training. But the treatment of trainee wages is more problematic. If, when receiving training, workers receive lower wages commensurate with their limited productivity, their wages should not be counted as training cost. If, as is more likely, workers' wages exceed the value of what they produce during the training period, so that firms recover a large part of their training expenditures well after workers complete their training, at least some of the firms' expenditures on wages should be included as costs of training. This suggests that national training expenditures should include some but not all trainee wages in firm training costs, yet it is common practice in the measurement of training costs across countries to include all trainee wages, which raises estimated expenditures.

Alternatively, a large share of training costs are indirect and not measured in company records: these costs result from lost output of trainees and co-workers or supervisors during the time spent training new hires. This suggests that firm training costs as measured across countries could understate the resources that go to training. Therefore, measuring actual training expenditures by firms is difficult, and existing statistics must be read gingerly.

When one examines firms' training expenditures across countries it is important to note that different countries use different accounting procedures to deal with wages and the indirect costs of training. Given this caveat, Table 3.2 presents the Organization for Economic Cooperation and Development's calculations on firms' training expenditures (OECD, 1991). On average, large firms in the United States (firms with 100 or more employees), and all firms in Germany, the United Kingdom, France, and Australia, spend roughly 1.5 percent or more of their total wage bill on training. The exception is Japan, where the official statistics show that only 0.4 percent is spent on training. Most of the discrepancy between the

Table 3.2   Average Percent of Total Wage Bill Spent on Training

Country	Expenditure (%)
United States	1.8 (1988)[a]
Canada	0.9 (1985)
West Germany	1.8 (1984)
United Kingdom	1.3 (1984)
France	1.6 (1984); 2.5 (1989)
Japan	0.4 (1989)[b]
Australia (private sector)	1.7 (1989)

SOURCES: OECD, 1991; for the U.S., *Training Magazine*, 1988; the Canadian data are from the Adult Training Survey, Statistics Canada, as reported by the Canadian Labour Market and Productivity Centre.

[a] Firms with 100 or more employees.
[b] Training expenditures as a percentage of monthly labor costs, excluding trainees' wages. All other countries include trainees' or apprentices' wages.

reported numbers for Japan and the other countries is due to the fact that the Japanese cost numbers are limited to direct costs associated with off-site training, and they exclude the major costs included in the other countries' estimates—trainee wages and the time that supervisors spend training workers. Given this difference, the apparently low numbers for Japan show how successful Japanese firms have been in incorporating training into the production process. The fact that Table 3.2 does not show the huge gap in spending that popular discussion on training deficiencies in the United States would suggest may reflect accounting practices in reporting training more than actuality. More important, the U.S. numbers reflect training investments by larger firms which one would expect to be able to invest more in training.

A more fruitful approach to comparing training across countries is to contrast how workers are trained in specific industries and occupations. This approach can reveal differences in training content, which may be even more important for competitiveness than crude, cross-country comparisons of expenditures. For example, in the auto industry the average worker in Japan or in a Japanese-owned U.S. plant spends two to three times as much time being trained as a worker in a U.S-owned plant (Krafcik, 1990). One might object to these numbers, because they do not control for age and experience; the smaller hours trained in U.S.-owned plants may result from the work force being older and more experienced here than in Japan or in the Japanese transplants. However, the gap in hours of training across the three types of plants is even greater for newly hired assembly workers. New hires in Japan or in Japanese transplants receive approximately 300 hours of training, while their U.S. counterparts receive only 48 hours of training.

To obtain a clearer understanding of how the German training system operates, comparisons have been made of the informal training system in the U.S. auto industry with the German auto industry's training system.[7] In automobile manufacturing there are three types of training for both skilled and unskilled workers: product and process awareness training, teamwork training, and technical training. In the first two forms of training, there is little difference between U.S. and German auto firms. Indeed, U.S. workers spend slightly more time in product awareness training than their German counterparts. But these two types of training constitute a very small proportion of overall training. Most employee development is in technical training and here there are large differences between the United States and Germany. German firms spend 1.5 to 10 times more in technical training than comparable U.S. firms. Moreover in Germany, as elsewhere, there are wide differences among firms. German firms that provide less technical training are characterized by less employee flexibility and look more like U.S. auto firms. Firms that provide considerable training are able to deploy their workers more flexibly in the workplace.

Cross-country differences in training in the nuclear power industry provides insight into a sector where the technology is identical in many countries.[8] It is also a highly regulated industry that spends large amounts on worker training to ensure safe operation of facilities. In the United States it is considered to be an industry with a highly developed training program. Workers in the U.S. nuclear industry, such as technicians, receive similar amounts of training compared to their European counterparts (excluding German technicians in plant operations). However, half of all formal technician training in the U.S. nuclear industry (560 hours over two years) is spent on teaching basic technical skills and in some cases remedial math and literacy skills, whereas European technicians use training hours for more advanced study of nuclear engineering and plant administration. This difference reflects the different level of preparedness that workers have coming into the industry. The more advanced training in Europe may improve workers' ability to respond to situations outside the parameters of the simulations they have been trained with; and it also allows firms to hire fewer supervisors. So, while the expenditures and hours may be similar across countries, the content and results vary dramatically. This factor helps resolve the paradox that has been noted: that while U.S. training expenditures are comparable to those of other developed countries, many analysts believe the United States suffers from a training deficit. In part because many American workers enter the job market with weak high school education and few technical work skills, U.S. firm-based training may be more basic than firm-based training in other countries.

In sum, aggregate estimates of training across countries show that U.S. workers receive much less formal training in the workplace than their European or Japanese counterparts. This is especially true for new entrants into the labor market who do not have a college degree. At the same time it appears that, at least for large firms, the U.S. does not spend less than other countries on training. But in some sectors, for the same level of expenditure, even large U.S. firms do not end up with employees that are as well qualified as their European or Japanese counterparts, apparently because their initial level of skills may be low, due to the education they receive before entering the work force.

I conclude from this that underinvestment in training in the United States may take two forms. In certain sectors, U.S. firms may spend less and provide their nontechnical or nonmanagerial employees with more limited training than competitors in other countries. In other sectors, the level of expenditure or the hours of training may be the same, but the investment may not achieve the skill proficiencies found in countries such as Japan and Germany. Moreover, since the purpose of training is to enhance the skills of workers, my analysis suggests that using a benchmark for training expenditures of some fixed percentage of payroll (say 1.5 per cent) to judge if firms train enough can be misleading for policy. Looking at outputs directly—in terms of the skill attainment of workers (say, through skill certification)—rather than in terms of often poorly measured dollar inputs, would be more accurate.

WHY DO TRAINING SYSTEMS VARY ACROSS COUNTRIES?

To understand why training systems vary around the world one must consider how and by whom the training is financed, its content, and its assessment and certification.[9] Conceptually, if trainees receive most of the benefits of training through higher wages, then trainees should pay for most of the training costs. Contrarily, if firms receive most of the benefits of training through higher productivity, then firms should pay for most of the training costs. Typically both workers and firms receive benefits from very specific training, so training costs should be divided between the two. Young workers may, however, need more general training than firms would like to provide, so that they will have the skills for greater flexibility in future career options. If the training is more general, the share of training costs borne by workers should increase. At the same time, however, workers will want some nationally recognized certification for the skills they have acquired and that they have paid for through lower wages. There is little incentive to invest in general training that is not recognized as such.

Traditional apprenticeship systems, such as those in Great Britain and the United States, provide much less general skill training than apprenticeships in Germany, in part because wages for the apprentices are much higher during training periods. German apprentices earn about one-third of the adult unskilled wage rate, while apprentices in the United States and Britain typically earn 60 percent or more of the adult rate. In detailed cross-country comparisons,[10] because wages were much higher in Britain, apprenticeship programs there focused on narrower occupational skills development than did apprenticeships in Germany. This resulted in a training system that did not prepare workers for the major technological and employment shifts of the 1980s.

The British government sought in the 1980s to reform its traditional apprenticeship system by replacing it with a new training system for all unemployed young workers. But this reform has not been particularly successful, and the problems with the British reforms are instructive for countries, like the United States, that are considering changing their post-school training system. In the new British system, the skill levels required for certificates associated with the new training programs are low, the certificates are too industry specific, and they fail to measure reliably an individual's actual skills in the workplace. As a result, trainees still have not been willing to accept the same reduction in wages that German apprentices accept. Since trainee wages have remained relatively high, British employers, in turn, have provided less training, and the training has been more firm specific than that provided by German employers. By lowering the skill-levels requirements from the higher standards of the traditional apprenticeship, the revised training system in Britain may have removed one key component of a successful training system.

In contrast, training standards are high in Germany and are widely viewed as valid, and apprenticeship training includes a general-education element. Consequently, young people find the payoff from investing in training more attractive in Germany than they do in the United Kingdom. Youths in Germany are willing to work hard in school to get better apprenticeships, and to accept lower wages during the apprenticeship. The lower wages allow firms to provide more general training, creating a virtuous circle. In the 1980s, while the United Kingdom moved away from apprenticeship training, Germany expanded its program and developed new apprenticeships in growing sectors of the economy, such as banking and finance. [11]

This process suggests why it is difficult for a single firm to change to a great degree the amount of training it provides. If a firm provides more general training, but there is no accepted national system to recognize and certify general skills, then workers will not be willing to accept lower wages during training. If firms pay for general training, there is a good chance that trained workers will later move to other firms in a highly mobile society. Thus, firms will choose to train workers in largely specific areas and in limited amounts. As a result the economy can become locked into a lower training equilibrium, even when individual firms are willing to invest in more general training and would do so if enough other firms did the same. This offers one explanation for the lack of training in the United States.

In a market that offers lifetime employment or limited mobility, as in Japan, firms can train workers in very general skills even without greatly lowering trainees' wages.[12] With low employee turnover, the firm that provides training can capture some of the returns from training that in a high-turnover labor market would go to workers, who could use those skills at a new firm. The Japanese training system also benefits from the focus in schools on producing students who have a relatively homogeneous and high-level set of literacy and numeracy skills, a willingness to learn and teach new skills, and an ability to function as team members. This lowers the cost of investment by firms in both technical training and employment relations. As in Germany, school performance is very important in determining post-school employment opportunities; many firms have close links with certain schools from which they recruit new employees. Because of the high level of basic knowledge that the work force shares, firms can rely to a large degree on more informal learning and individual study for technical training. This lowers initial training costs and allows training expenditures to be targeted at technical upgrading. More informal learning is not inconsistent with new work organizations per se, but it requires that workers have considerable basic skills when they enter the workplace.

INSTITUTIONAL SUPPORTS FOR ALTERNATIVE TRAINING SYSTEMS

Different countries provide various institutional structures to support their training system. The German apprenticeship system is bolstered by a range of institutional structures including the school system, banks, local chambers of commerce, unions, employers associations, and works councils.[13] One important factor affecting training in Germany is the percentage of the work force that is unionized and the role of unions in the organization of work. Union density in Germany in 1988 was over 30 percent while the rate in the United States was approximately 16 percent. In addition, the extension of collective-bargaining contracts by Germany's Ministry of Labor to all firms in a sector means that union-management agreements apply to much of the nonunion work force as well. Unions in Germany, through their representation on works councils in most firms and on supervisory boards of larger firms, are actively involved in codetermining with employers the content of apprenticeship training and retraining programs targeted at adult workers (see Chapter 4, this volume). Unions push for more general training, and employer associations argue for more specific training. This tension produces a balance between the two types of training needs.

The training system in Germany is supported by other structures as well. For example, there is a clear ranking in the quality and status of the various apprenticeships available. The better apprenticeships go to students who perform well in school, which gives those students not preparing for university an incentive to work hard.[14] Many trainers are older workers in the firm who have passed nationally recognized examinations certifying them as trainers. This maintains high training standards within the firms. Larger firms with well-developed internal labor markets carefully select and train young workers. They do this partly because bank lending policies allow firms to make longer-term investments, and because local chambers of commerce work to minimize other firms' poaching of trained workers. The local chambers of commerce also provide valuable training expertise to firms. While the training content for apprenticeship training is bargained over by unions and employers and then endorsed by law, the training programs are also then certified by the local chambers of commerce. The majority of apprentices remain in the firm after completion of their apprenticeship. Apprentices know that if they do well in their apprenticeship they will have a skilled, high-paying job.

What seems to be a key feature of the German training system is that it teaches people broadly how to learn, rather than training young workers to do a narrowly defined job. The emphasis on off-site, classroom training to develop general skills enables workers to adapt to future changes in their jobs. The classroom training is linked with employment so that youths see immediate workplace applications for the skills they learn in school. As a result of this training strategy initial training levels in Germany are quite high, as shown in Figure 3.1. But this high incidence is followed by relatively lower training rates after apprenticeships are completed.

Not all apprenticeships end in a job with the same firm in which a young worker was an apprentice. In small firms and in certain sectors such as bakeries and artisan establishments, there is much higher apprentice turnover at the completion of training. Even with this high turnover, however, firms are willing to hire apprentices because they can pay lower wages than they would pay for adult, unskilled labor. German trade unions' success in obtaining high wages in larger firms has had two consequences for apprentice training. Larger firms can pursue a high-quality, innovative, product market strategy that requires a highly skilled work force, and many smaller firms gain through hiring low-wage apprentices that allows them to remain competitive.

The institutions that support the training structure in Japan include, first and foremost, the long-standing links between employers and schools. For example, in recruiting for production jobs, employers will hire workers from specific high schools with which they have developed long-term relationships and where they pay close attention to the performance of the students. Students realize that how well they do in school will influence their ability to obtain certain types of jobs. High schools in Japan do not focus on teaching technical skills; rather they concentrate on developing math, science, reading, and "citizenship skills" that help workers communicate better when they are in teams in the workplace (Hashimoto, 1994). Another support for the Japanese training system is the government subsidy for in-house training, especially for smaller firms.[15] In addition, Japan has a national Trade Skill Test system. These tests are set to government standards and are limited mainly to manufacturing and construction skills. While passing these tests is not usually a condition of employment, many firms provide special bonuses to workers who do pass them. The well-documented links between large companies and their suppliers extends to the area of training as well. Many large firms will train smaller suppliers' workers. This maintains quality standards for the large firms and overcomes constraints smaller firms may face in training their own workers.

Outside the labor market, the system of training, as in Germany, is buttressed by the Japanese capital market. Banks, which provide much of the capital to Japanese firms, take a long-term view toward firms' investments in R & D and training (Aoki, 1988).

If a major component of the Japanese system is a high degree of shared basic knowledge, how easy would it be to transfer this training system to the United States?[16] Because there are no well-developed relationships between U.S. employers and schools, Japanese transplants in the automobile industry, for example, have had to adapt their training system for the United States. The transplants closely screen new hires—choosing workers much more carefully than American firms normally do. In addition, the transplants have had to provide more formal training than is required in Japan, both in technical skills and in employment relations skills.[17]

In sum, a range of institutions, including schools, banks, employers' groups, and unions support the diverse set of training systems that are found in advanced countries. The extent of workplace training is intertwined with the pattern of wages and the degree to which skills are certified. Both Japan and Germany create incentives for youths who do not obtain a university degree to perform well in secondary school by linking their ensuing progress in the job market to their school or apprenticeship record. These countries have developed training institutions that seem to overcome the potential market failure in the provision of general training. When Japanese transplants operate in the United States, they modify rather than replicate the Japanese system. Even with the modifications, the transplants in the auto industry devote more time to training workers than most of their U.S. counterparts.[18]

TRAINING OUTCOMES: RETURNS TO FIRMS

Most people assume that the rapid aggregate growth rates in German and Japanese manufacturing labor productivity in the 1970s and 1980s are partly due to their company training systems. The ideal way to examine this would be to compare productivity in firms that had extensive training programs with those that provided less training, either in the same country or across country lines. Such studies are rare, however. My assessment of the training-productivity link is based on limited evidence from new surveys of firms in the United States[19] and a new Dutch study. There is nothing comparable for Japan or Germany, so I must rely on the differences between the U.S. and Dutch findings to speculate on what the impact of alternative training systems might be for international comparisons of productivity.

Consider first the effect of informal, learning-by-doing skill development on productivity in the United States. Some argue that the apparent U.S. training deficit is overstated because it focuses on formal training, and underestimates the amount of informal training. This argument is at odds with evidence on the output of new hires in U.S. electronics assembly plants that have no formal training programs for new hires.[20] Workers in these plants do exhibit rapid productivity growth during the first month of employment, as they learn on the job. However, six months later there is little evidence of any further positive productivity changes associated with learning by doing. The effect of learning by doing thus seems to be a one-shot, short-term effect. The implication is that an overreliance on informal training may be one reason for lower productivity growth in the United States. Observing productivity growth due to informal training in initial periods on the job may overestimate its effect on longer term productivity growth.

Do existing studies indicate that formal training programs do a better job of raising the productivity of firms? Three recent studies show that formal training has a high payoff in the United States, but that the payoffs differ by type of training (see the firm productivity panel in Table 3.3). One study (Bartel, 1991) compared U.S. manufacturing firms in 1983 and 1986 and found that firms with formal training programs had gains in productivity (measured by net sales per worker) on the order of 17 percent. Using the personnel records of a large manufacturing firm, a second study found that training leads to an improvement in job performance as measured by supervisors' performance ratings of workers (Bartel, 1992). A third study, of new hires (Bishop, 1994), contrasted small- and medium-size firms in the United States across all sectors of the economy, with training divided into current on-the-job training, previous relevant employer training, previous "irrelevant" employer training, and current and previous training "off the job" in schools or institutes. This study measured productivity by asking employers to rate their most recent hire's productivity during the first two weeks of employment, during the next eleven weeks, and at the time of the interview, on a scale of 0 to 100. There appear to be sharp differences between the returns from formal on-the-job training and off-the-job training as workers switch employers. Formal on-the-job training received from a previous employer has little effect on a worker's current wage (as might be expected given the absence of certification), but it increases a worker's current productivity by an estimated 9.5 percent and lowers the amount of training that the new firm must give the worker for the worker to do the new job. However, if the worker receives no additional training from the current employer, the impact of training from a previous employer diminishes over time. Company-sponsored off-the-job training has a more lasting effect on wages, raises productivity by 16 percent and makes workers more innovative on the job.

Table 3.3 Payoffs from Alternative Training System

Type of Training	Increase in Firm Productivity (%)	Increase in Individual Wages (%)
Workplace-based Systems		
Formal, Employer-provided Training		
Current Employer		
1. U.S.	17	7
2. U.S.	16	11
3. U.S.	—	4.4
4. U.S.	—	4.7
5. U.K.	—	3–7
6. Netherlands	11–20	4–16
7. Australia	—	7–9
Previous Employer		
8. U.S.	9.5	0
9. U.S.		0
Apprenticeship		
10. U.S.	—	13
11. U.K.	—	9–12
12. Australia	—	8
Informal, Learning by Doing		
13. U.S.	Rapid increase, then flat or falling	Initial growth, then 0
Off-the-job Training		
14. U.K.	—	5–8
15. Australia	—	0
School-based Individual Choice, Government-led Systems		
School-based		
16. Norway	—	0
Individual-choice		
17. U.S. (community college)		3–5
18. U.S. (proprietary institutions)	—	5–10
Government-led		
19. U.K.	—	0 or negative
20. U.S. (JTPA women)	—	0
21. U.S. (JTPA men)	—	-7.9

SOURCES: (by line) 1) Bartel, 1991; Lynch, 1992a; 2) Bishop, 1994; Lillard & Tan, 1986; 3) Mincer, 1988; 4) Holzer, 1989; 5) Dolton, et al 1994; 6) Groot, 1993; Groot et al., 1994; 7) Tan et al., 1993; 8) Bishop, 1994; Lynch, 1992a; 9) Bishop, 1994; 10) Lynch, 1992a; Blanchflower & Lynch, 1994; 11) Blanchflower & Lynch, 1994; 12) Tan et al., 1993; 13) Weiss, 1994; 14) Dolton et al., 1994; 15) Tan et al., 1993; 16) Elias, et al., 1994; 17) Kane and Rouse, 1993; 18) Lynch, 1992a; 19) Dolton et al., 1994; 20) Bloom et al., 1993.

NOTE: JTPA = Job Training Partnership Act

These limited studies, the results of which are also summarized on Table 3.3, suggest that formal training increases productivity. Combined with the evidence that the United States does relatively little formal training, this is at least consistent with the claim that the slow productivity growth of U.S. firms is due to insufficient training.

TRAINING OUTCOMES: RETURNS TO INDIVIDUALS

The ideal way to study the effects of training on individuals would be to assign individuals randomly to training programs in firms and then observe the impact of the training on their productivity and wages. This assignment process has been used to evaluate government training programs but has rarely if ever been implemented in the private sector.[21] Most empirical studies of the returns from training follow a different approach, comparing wages and growth of wages of persons who report receiving training with wages of those who do not report that they received training.

These nonexperimental studies have a problem in that trainees are likely to be better workers even in the absence of training. On the one hand, employers are likely to pick their best (most trainable) workers for training. On the other hand, the workers who acquire training, particularly off the job, are likely to be the most motivated and those who see the largest benefits from such training. In this situation, differences in the wages or productivity of persons who have been trained and those who have not will overstate the effects of training on an average person. Analysts deal with this problem by identifying the characteristics most likely to affect the probability of receiving training and controlling for them in estimating the return on training for workers. For instance, the determinants of receiving company-provided training for non-college-graduate youths include such things as: having had some post-high school education, being white and male, and being covered by a union contract (Lynch, 1992a). Women and minorities are more likely to have participated in off-the-job training provided by for-profit proprietary institutions than to have received formal company training that lasted four weeks or more. Similarly, there is evidence that Americans who have received a general equivalency diploma (GED) are more likely to obtain additional post-school private-sector training than are noncertified high school dropouts (Cameron and Heckman, 1994).

There are many analyses of training and earnings based on nonexperimental data for the United States,[22] and a smaller number on how training affects wages in Great Britain, Australia, the Netherlands, and Norway, among other countries. These studies provide insights into how different types of training affect wages and wage growth and how training from a previous employer affects current wages. The effect of previous employer training is a critical issue in the United States, given the high rate of labor turnover. Most studies focus on young workers, since they typically make the largest investments in training, though some treat older, displaced workers.

The third column in Table 3.3 summarizes estimates of how training affects wages. The table highlights three major findings about the payoff from skills that seem to hold true for all the countries for which evidence exists:

1. Workers receive positive payoffs from company-provided training, apprenticeships, and off-the-job training.

2. Workers in the United States do not gain from previous company-provided on-the-job training when they move to a new employer.

3. Company-based training and apprenticeships have higher returns than government-led or school-based training.

In the United States the best estimates are that company-provided training increases wages from 4.4 to 11 percent. Returns in the Netherlands are similar, while those in Great Britain and Australia are somewhat smaller. Still, the uniformity of findings for different countries and data sets is impressive.

How should the U.S. studies be interpreted that show that formal on-the-job training from a previous employer does not raise wages in the current job? One interpretation is that the training was highly company-specific. Another is that when workers change jobs they accept lower pay to get skills at the new firm. However, the finding that workers with on-the-job training at a previous job raised productivity at their new firms suggests that the failure of such training to show up in pay may be due to the lack of certification of skills and the lack of information about those skills.

With respect to apprenticeships, there is also considerable cross-country similarity in the estimated effects on wages. Apprenticeships have a high payoff in the United States even after controlling for unionism. While it is difficult to obtain data on individual workers to estimate the returns on training for apprentices in Germany, the returns on training in the Netherlands, which has a training system similar to Germany's, are high. In the Netherlands there are numerous training funds jointly administered by unions and employers that are especially designed to assist small- and medium-size firms to train their workers. Youths in the Netherlands receive training that has a large component of workplace training in addition to school training and is linked to employment in a firm. Wage gains associated with firm-provided training are on the order of 4 to 16 percent (Groot et al., 1994). In addition, rates of return for firms from this type of training are on the order of 11 to 20 percent (Groot, 1993).

In Great Britain the small wage gains associated with completing a traditional apprenticeship were greatly increased if the apprentice also passed a nationally recognized qualification exam. Such exams do not exist in the United States. When the British government stopped financial support for the traditional apprenticeships program in the early 1980s in favor of the new government-led youth training program, the training became shorter in duration and its content was altered. As a consequence, young people were less likely to pass the national qualification exam, and wage gains associated with training were reduced.

The findings on the returns from training in the United Kingdom and the Netherlands shed some light on results presented in Chapter 2 of this volume, that wage differentials widened greatly in the United Kingdom (as in the United States) but not in the Netherlands in the 1980s. The higher incidence of training in the Netherlands and its high payoff to both workers and firms, as shown in the studies underlying Table 3.3, are likely reasons that the Dutch avoided a massive widening of the wage structure.

The bottom half of Table 3.3 shows that school-based and government-led training systems do not have as good a payoff as company-based systems. While Norway has a high incidence of employer-provided training, it has relied on school-based vocational training for new entrants into the labor market. There is a larger component of school training in Norway as opposed to workplace training in countries such as Germany and the Netherlands. One result of school-based training is that youths obtain vocational skills that are often poorly linked to the demand for labor, with a resulting negligible rate of return (Elias et al., 1994). The results from Norway are similar to findings in the United States that secondary school-based vocational education has low returns. As for government programs, those in Britain show no return. In the United States the substantial literature on government programs shows some modest effects for welfare recipients but little effect for most groups of young workers.

The general weakness of individual-choice and school-based training for workplace skills does not mean that a school-based system of post-secondary training is incapable of providing valuable training. In the United States, training acquired from such off-the-job sources as business, vocational, and technical institutes assists young people to move on to a new career path (Lynch, 1991b and 1992c). Their wages do not increase while they are being trained, but there are positive longer-term effects from this type of training as youths use the training to jump to better career paths. Despite instances of consumer fraud and the frequent failure of students to complete programs (which leads to defaults on loans), studies find that proprietary school training (conditional on not dropping out early in the program) has a positive effect on worker productivity and wages (Bishop, 1994; Lynch, 1992a). The return from proprietary schools is very similar to estimated returns from community and junior colleges in the United States (Kane and Rouse, 1993). Since more than half of all high school graduates go on to complete a year or more of post–high school education or to attend a course at a proprietary institution, this suggests that even for non-college-graduates there are positive returns on investments made in post–high school education.

LESSONS FOR ALTERNATIVE U.S. TRAINING POLICY INITIATIVES

The high returns from training shown in Table 3.3 bring us back to the question raised earlier: if the payoffs from company training are so high, why isn't firm-provided training as extensive in the United States as it is in some other countries? In broader terms, what determines the differences in firm-based training across countries?

My best answer is that the differences reflect the extent to which the various governments develop and support training institutions to overcome the potential market failure inherent in firm-based general training. Even when they would like to do more training, individual firms cannot move unilaterally from one training system to another: their best training strategy depends on what others are doing and thus on the institutional support, or lack thereof, for training.

How transferable might foreign training systems be to the United States? Table 3.4 summarizes some of the basic strengths and weakness of the alternative training systems from a United States labor market perspective. Apprenticeship training that includes nationally recognized certification of skills encourages investments in broad training even in a mobile society. The certification provides an incentive for workers to invest in the training and to accept lower wages during training periods. Employers are more willing to provide both specific and general skills because of the lower wages. Post-training wages increase sharply, and firm productivity increases as well. The German experience shows that it is possible to extend the apprenticeship model even into nonmanufacturing sectors such as banking, finance, and insurance.

The traditional Japanese system of training seems difficult to replicate in the United States. With high employee mobility, firms are reluctant to finance more training; even in Japan, the traditional system of training is being challenged as employee turnover increases in certain sectors of the economy. However, the Japanese companies transplanted here have shown that it is possible to upgrade skills in certain sectors.

While government-led training programs can target groups that are underrepresented in training and can be coordinated with other government policies, such as unemployment insurance and welfare assistance, government programs are often not relevant for current employer needs. An additional problem is that government-targeted training invariably applies to only a limited number of workers with training needs. Given the large returns on training obtained off the job, a better strategy might be to expand financial assistance to workers who wish to follow training courses. Establishing recognized standards for these programs should ensure quality is maintained.

Table 3.4 Lessons for U.S. Training Policies

System	Strengths	Weaknesses
Workplace-based Systems		
Apprenticeship Training	With recognized certification, provides alternative route to skills upgrading	Increased attachment to a specific occupation that may be obsolete in future Training model comes from manufacturing, while most new jobs are nonmanufacturing
Low Employee Turnover and Firm Training	Worker commitment to firm rather than to job increases flexibility	Cannot legislate reduced employee turnover. Cannot legislate moral suasion Increased worker mobility in Japan may challenge sustainability of system
Employer Training Tax	Immediately puts training on agenda of all firms	Does not guarantee training of unskilled and those in small firms
Learning by Doing	Inexpensive, individual, and firm specific	Skills associated with new technology and work organizations better obtained formally
School-based, Individual-choice, Government-led Systems		
Government-led and School-based	Can target groups traditionally under-trained Can coordinate with other labor market policies (e.g.,unemployment insurance)	Government may also fund firm-specific training Relevance of school-based programs questionable
School-based and Individual-choice	High degree of individual choice, especially to pursue formal higher education	Difficult to provide technical upgrading once out of school Technical skills provided in schools not relevant if no employer input Workers may lack information on which types of training they will need in the future

An employer training tax would put training on the agenda of every firm in the United States. It would reduce problems of poaching, since all firms would pay a portion of the training costs. However, even in centralized France the tax itself did not increase training of unskilled workers and workers in smaller firms. In the decentralized United States it would be extremely difficult to monitor whether reported training expenditures were in fact going to training. Outside the union sector, there are no workplace organizations (such as works councils) that would have an interest in making sure that firm training would be sufficiently general to be highly valuable in a mobile economy. The experiences of Norway and Great Britain in the 1980s show that training for training's sake does not necessarily result in higher productivity and wages.

I conclude from my examination of training in various advanced economies that the payoff to any effort to increase training in the United States would rise if there is:

1. Greater employer participation in training to increase the probability that skills will be related to demand. Firm-based systems seem to work better than school-, individual-, and government-based systems of training.

2. Employee representation in determining the content of training, to ensure that the training includes more general skills as well as firm-specific skills. Absent such employee participation, training would be too narrow.

3. Certification of skills through a nationally recognized process. This would increase general training and would increase workers' willingness to accept lower wages during training. Certification would also provide an alternative route to formal higher education for establishing technical skills, and would allow workers to obtain the benefits of their skills in other workplaces, in a society in which job-switching is frequent.

Finally, any effort to reform the U.S. post-school training system would be more effective if it is coordinated with reforms of the education system in general. Given the high participation of U.S. youths in post–high school education,[23] attempts to increase the workplace relevance of the courses they take should be encouraged.

NOTES

1. The findings are based on research given in Lynch (1994).

2. See Mincer and Higuchi (1988).

3. Hashimoto and Raisian (1985) find that for typical twenty- to twenty-four-year-old Japanese males with five years of work experience, 45.1 percent were with the same employer fifteen years later, while only 13 percent of their U.S. counterparts remained with their employer fifteen years later. A typical Japanese male worker will have five employers over his lifetime, while a U.S. male worker would have eleven employers.

4. See Lynch (1993) for further description and discussion of the training taxes in France and Australia.

5. Bartel (1989) gives details on the occupational distribution of training.

6. Lynch (1991b, 1992a) provides further details.

7. This discussion draws from Berg (1994).

8. These numbers are taken from Mason (1990).

9. See Becker (1964) for an overview of human capital theory and Oulton and Steedman(1994) for development of a theoretical model of international differences in training systems.

10. See Oulton and Steedman (1994), and Prais et al. (1989).

11. See Benton et al. (1991) for a discussion of training practices in the banking sector in Germany.

12. Much of this discussion is based on Hashimoto (1994).

13. See Soskice (1994) for more detail.

14. While historically most young people began their apprenticeship training around the age of sixteen or seventeen, more youths are now remaining in school longer. As a result, the age when youths began their apprenticeships rose in the 1980s to eighteen or nineteen.

15. See Sako (1990) for a more detailed discussion.

16. This section is derived from Hashimoto (1994).

17. As shown in Hashimoto (1994) and Higuchi (1987).

18. One important exception is the General Motor's Saturn plant, where there is extensive training of all workers.

19. See Weiss (1994) and Bishop (1994).

20. This section relies on Weiss (1994).

21. For a comprehensive review of large, randomized, experimental employment and training programs see Gueron and Pauly (1991).

22. Examples include Barron et al. (1987), Booth (1991), Brown (1989), Lillard and Tan (1986), Lynch (1991b, 1992a, and 1992c), and Mincer (1983 and 1988).

23. See Lynch (1992b).

REFERENCES

Aoki, M. 1988. *Information, Incentives and Bargaining in the Japanese Economy.* Cambridge: Cambridge University Press.

Barron, J., D. Black, and M. Loewenstein. 1987. "Employer Size: The Implications for Search, Training, Capital Investment, Starting Wages, and Wage Growth.", *Journal of Labor Economics* (January): 76–89.

Bartel, Ann. 1989. "Formal Employee Training Programs and Their Impact on Labor Productivity: Evidence from a Human Resource Survey." NBER Working Paper no. 3026.

———. 1991. "Productivity Gains from the Implementation of Employee Training Programs."NBER Working Paper no. 3893, November.

———. 1992. "Training, Wage Growth and Job Performance: Evidence from a Company Database." NBER Working Paper no. 4027, March.

Becker, Gary. 1964. *Human Capital: A Theoretical and Empirical Analysis with Special Reference to Education.* New York: NBER.

Benton, Lauren, Thomas Bailey, Thierry Noyelle, and Thomas Stanback. 1991. *Employee Training and U.S. Competitiveness: Lessons for the 1990s.* Boulder, Colo.: Westview Press.

Berg, Peter. 1994. "Strategic Adjustments in Training: A Comparative Analysis of the U.S. and German Automobile Industries." In L. Lynch, ed., *Training and the Private Sector: International Comparisons.* Chicago: University of Chicago Press for NBER.

Bishop, John. 1994. "Formal Training and its Impact on Productivity, Wages, and Innovation." In L. Lynch, ed., *Training and the Private Sector: International Comparisons.* Chicago: University of Chicago Press for NBER.

Bjorklund, Anders. 1990. "Evaluations of Swedish Labor Market Policy." *Finnish Economic Papers* 3, no. 1 (Spring): 3–13.

Blanchflower, David, and Lisa M. Lynch. 1994. "Training at Work: A Comparison of U.S. and British Youths." In L. Lynch, ed., *Training and the Private Sector: International Comparisons.* Chicago: University of Chicago Press for NBER.

Bloom, Howard, Larry Orr, George Cave, Stephen Bell, and Fred Doolittle. 1993. *The National JTPA Study: Title IIA Impacts on Earnings and Employment at 18 Months.* Bethesda, Md.: Abt Associates.

Booth, Alison. 1989. "Earning and Learning: What Price Specific Training?" Mimeo, Birkbeck College, London, England.

Bowers, Norman, and Paul Swaim. 1992. "Recent Trends in Employment-Related Training and Wages." Mimeo, U.S. Joint Economic Committee.

Brown, James. 1989. "Why Do Wages Increase with Tenure?" *American Economic Review* (December): 971–999.

Cameron, Stephen V., and James J. Heckman 1994. "Determinants of Young Male Schooling and Training Choices." in L. Lynch, ed., *Training and the Private Sector: International Comparisons.* Chicago: University of Chicago Press for NBER.

Carey, M. L. 1985. *How Workers Get Their Training.* U.S. Bureau of Labor Statistics, Bulletin no. 2226. Washington, D.C.: U.S. Government Printing Office.

Carnevale, Anthony, et al. 1990. *Training in America.* San Francisco: Jossey-Bass.

CEREQ. 1991a. *Training and Employment Newsletter,* Winter.

———. 1991b. *Training and Employment Newsletter,* Spring.

Dolton, Peter, Gerald Makepeace, and John Treble. 1994. "Public and Private Sector Training of Youths in Britain." In L. Lynch, ed., *Training and the Private Sector: International Comparisons.* Chicago: University of Chicago Press for NBER.

Elias, Peter, Erik Hernaes, and Meredith Baker. 1994. "Vocational Education and Training in Britain and Norway." In L. Lynch, ed., *Training and the Private Sector: International Comparisons.* Chicago: University of Chicago Press for NBER.

Freeman, Richard B. 1976. *The Overeducated American.* New York: Academic Press.

Formation Emploi. 1991. "La Formation Professionnelle Continue (1971–1991)." Special Issue, April–June.

Groot, Wim. 1993. "Company Schooling and Productivity." Mimeo, Leiden University.

Groot, W., J. Hartog, and H. Oosterbeek. 1993. "Returns to Within Company Schooling of Employees: The Case of the Netherlands." In L. Lynch, ed., *Training and the Private Sector: International Comparisons.* Chicago: University of Chicago Press for NBER.

Gueron, Judith, and Edward Pauly. 1991. *From Welfare to Work.* New York: Russell Sage Foundation.

Hashimoto, Masanori, (1993) "Employment Based Training in Japanese Firms in Japan and the U.S.: The Experience of Automobile Industries," in L. Lynch ed. *Training and the Private Sector: International Comparisons,* Chicago: University of Chicago Press for NBER.

Hashimoto, Masanori, and John Raisian. 1985. "Employment Tenure and Earnings Profiles in Japan and the United States." *American Economic Review* 75: 721–735.

Higuchi, Y. 1987. "A Comparative Study of Japanese Plants Operating in the U.S. and American Plants: Recruitment, Job Training, Wage Structure and Job Separation."

Center on Japanese Economy and Business, Graduate School of Business, Columbia University. Working Paper no. 13, May.

Holzer, Harry 1989. "The Determinants of Employee Productivity and Earnings." NBER Working Paper no. 2782.

Ishikawa, Toshio. 1992. "Vocational Training," Japan Institute of Labour, Japanese Industrial Relations Series. Tokyo.

Kane, Thomas, and Cecilia Rouse. 1993. "Labor Market Returns to Two- and Four-Year College: Is a Credit a Credit and Do Degrees Matter?" Mimeo, Harvard University.

Kochan, Thomas, and Paul Osterman. 1991. "Human Resource Development and Training: Is There Too Little in the U.S.?" Paper prepared for the American Council on Competitiveness, Cambridge, MA.

Krafcik, John. 1990. "Training and the Automobile Industry: International Comparisons." Report to Office of Technology Assessment, February.

Lillard, Lee, and Hong Tan. 1986. "Private Sector Training: Who Gets It and What Are Its Effects?" Rand monograph R-3331-DOL/RC.

Lusterman, S. 1977. *Education in Industry.* New York: Conference Board.

Lynch, Lisa M. 1991a. "Private Sector Training and Skill Formation in the United States." In G. Libecap, ed., *Advances in the Study of Entrepreneurship, Innovation, and Economic Growth*, vol. 5. JAI Press. PP. 117–145.

———. 1991b. "The Role of Off-the-Job vs. On-the-Job Training for the Mobility of Women Workers". *American Economic Review* (May): 151–156.

———. 1992a. "Private-Sector Training and the Earnings of Young Workers." *American Economic Review* (March): 299–312.

———. 1992b. "Young People's Pathways into Work: Utilization of Postsecondary Education and Training." Report prepared for the National Academy of Science, March.

———. 1992c. "Differential Effects of Post-School Training on Early Career Mobility." NBER Working Paper no. 4034.

———. 1993. *Training Strategies: Lessons from Abroad.* Washington, D.C.: Economic Policy Institute.

———, ed., 1994. *Training and the Private Sector: International Comparisons.* Chicago: University of Chicago Press for NBER.

Mason, John H. 1990. *International Comparative Analysis of Training Requirements for Technical Professionals: A Case Study of the Nuclear Power Industry.* Master's thesis, MIT Sloan School of Management.

Mincer, Jacob. 1962. "On-the-job Training: Costs, Returns, and Some Implications." *Journal of Political Economy* 70 (part 2): 50–79.

———. 1974. *Schooling, Experience, and Training.* New York: Columbia University Press.

———. 1983. "Union Effects: Wages, Turnover, and Job Training." *Research in Labor Economics*: 217–252.

———. 1988. "Job Training, Wage Growth and Labor Turnover." NBER Working Paper no. 2690, August.

Mincer, Jacob, and Yoshio Higuchi. 1988. "Wage Structures and Labor Turnover in the United States and Japan." *Journal of the Japanese and International Economies* 2: 97–133.

OECD. 1991. *Employment Outlook.* Paris: Organization for Economic Cooperation and Development.

Oulton, Nicholas, and Hilary Steedman. 1994. "A Comparison of the British, German and French Systems of Youth Training." In Lynch, ed., *Training and the Private Sector: International Comparisons.* Chicago: University of Chicago Press for NBER.

Prais, Sig, Valerie Jarvis, and Karin Wagner. 1989. "Productivity and Vocational Skills in Services in Britain and Germany: Hotels." *National Institute Economic Review* 130: 52–74.

Sako, Mari. 1990. "Enterprise Training in a Comparative Perspective: West Germany, Japan, and Britain." Report to the World Bank (Mimeo) London School of Economics, September.

Soskice, David. 1994. "Reconciling Markets and Institutions: The German Apprenticeship System." In Lynch, ed., *Training and the Private Sector: International Comparisons.* Chicago: University of Chicago Press for NBER.

Tan, Hong, Bruce Chapman, Chris Peterson, and Alison Booth. 1993. "Youth Training in the U.S., Great Britain, and Australia." *Research in Labor Economics.*

U.S. General Accounting Office (GAO). 1990. *Training Strategies: Preparing Noncollege Youth for Employment in the U.S. and Foreign Countries.* Washington, D.C.: U.S. GPO, May.

U.S. Office of Technology Assessment (OTA). 1990. *Worker Training: Competing in the New International Economy.* Washington, D.C.: U.S. GPO, September.

Weiss, Andrew. 1994. "Productivity Changes Associated with Learning by Doing." In L. Lynch, ed., *Training and the Private Sector: International Comparisons.* Chicago: University of Chicago Press for NBER.

4

WORKPLACE REPRESENTATION OVERSEAS: THE WORKS COUNCILS STORY

Joel Rogers and Wolfgang Streeck

In the labor relations systems of most advanced countries, unions or other mechanisms of wage regulation and collective bargaining are supplemented by a "second channel" of industrial relations. This second channel consists of workplace-based institutions for worker representation and labor-management communication that have status and functions distinct from, though not necessarily in competition with, those of unions. Typically, second channel institutions benefit from statutory supports that define their rights and obligations and, not incidentally, extend their reach beyond the unionized sector.

The purpose of second channel institutions is to give workers a voice in the governance of the shop floor and the firm, and to facilitate communication and cooperation between management and labor on production-related matters, more or less free of direct distributive conflicts over wages. Where there are workplace-based unions, as in Japan, employees articulate their interests through the union, and second channel arrangements take the form of labor-management consultation committees. Where unions and collective bargaining are centralized at the national or sectoral level, outside the firm—as in the Netherlands and Germany—or where unions are weak and not widely present at the workplace—as in France and Spain—second channel functions are usually performed by what are known as *works councils*.[1]

Works councils are representative bodies elected by all workers at a particular workplace, regardless of union membership and inclusive of white-collar and many supervisory employees. They are typically statutorily "mandated" for a given class of firms, and they enjoy presumptions against their discontinuance once established.[2] The councils institutionalize rights of *collective* worker *participation*, including rights to information and consultation on the organization of production and, in some cases, formal *codetermination* in decision making.[3] Commonly, in addition to thus institutionalizing worker power-sharing in firm governance, works councils monitor and help enforce state regulation of the workplace in such areas as occupational safety and health.

The United States and United Kingdom are exceptions to this pattern of dual channels for worker representation. Apart from direct state regulation of the workplace, the formal labor relations systems in the United States and United Kingdom consist entirely of unions and collective bargaining. But while the United Kingdom still has a sizable union movement, unionism in the United States is in an advanced and possibly irreversible state of decline. Approaching the twenty-first century, the United States effectively stands alone among the developed nations, on the verge of having *no* effective system of worker representation and consultation.

There are reasons to be concerned about this. First, basic democratic ideals are compromised by the absence of collective representation for those workers who want it. Survey data indicate that some 30 to 40 million American workers without union representation desire such representation, and some 80 million workers, many of whom do not approve of unions, desire some independent collective voice in their workplace.[4] These numbers dwarf the 16 million or so members of organized labor and point to a large "representation gap" in the American workplace (Weiler, 1990; Freeman and Rogers, 1993). Second, there is good evidence that this gap harms the economy. Many studies show the critical role of effective labor relations in economic performance and the dependence of effective labor relations on worker representation.[5] Third, in many areas of public regulatory concern in the workplace—occupational safety and health, wages and hours, and work force training among them—an effective system of workplace representation appears vital to the achievement of social goals.

In this context, this chapter presents the findings of a nine-country comparative research project on works councils, the dominant second channel organization in the developed world. The discussion has two main parts. First, we provide an overview of councils, indicating their incidence and general powers, organizational character, and contributions to democracy, efficiency, and state regulation. Second, we review the experience of councils in a number of European countries and in North America. A brief conclusion follows, summarizing the cross-national findings and pointing to a striking convergence among developed nations (the United States and United Kingdom excepted) in the importance they attach to their council systems.

WORKS COUNCILS: WHERE THEY ARE, HOW THEY WORK, WHAT THEY DO

Incidence and Powers

All Western European countries, except Ireland and the United Kingdom, have legislatively mandated works councils.[6] Some countries supplement these with mandatory health and safety councils; in others these functions are performed by the works councils themselves. Typically, national law requires elected works councils in establishments above a certain size; the law specifies the size and structure of the councils, rules for council elections, and other elements of procedure, and it provides enforcement mechanisms for agreements, conditions for works councilors to obtain paid time off for council activity, and sanctions against violations of specified rights.

The formal scope of issues addressed by councils varies inversely with the degree of extra firm wage setting. In Northern Europe, where unions are strong, negotiations are centralized, and legal extension of collective contracts is easy, the scope for council activity is often explicitly defined to exclude subjects dealt with by unions and employers' associations outside the individual firm. For example, the German Works Constitution Act forbids councils to bargain over basic wages and holds them legally responsible to uphold and supervise the implementation of any collective agreement applicable to their firm. Also, to emphasize the difference between unions and councils, the latter are typically placed under a legal obligation to seek cooperation with the employer. Thus Belgian law declares that works councils "exist to promote collaboration between employer and employee," and in France, where the Ministry of Labor extends collective contracts and where minimum wages are important, councils administer a firm's social funds but have little power in other areas. In contrast, where the external institutional structure is less elaborated, as in Spain, Greece, and Italy, council powers more closely resemble those of a local union. Spanish law, in fact, permits councils to bargain over wages and allows them to call strikes. In Italy, council functions are performed by union workplace organizations and their elected delegates, which for historical reasons often include workers not belonging to unions.

More important than the formal scope of permitted council activities is the *depth* of their power. The critical distinction is between councils that enjoy information and consultation rights only and those that also enjoy rights to codetermination in certain management decisions.

Information and consultation rights are universal and effectively define what is meant by a "mandated" council. Works councils laws invariably obligate employers to disclose to the council information about major new investment plans, acquisition and product market strategies, planned reorganization of production, use of technology, and so on. And council laws typically require employers to consult with the council on workplace and personnel issues, such as work reorganization, new technology acquisition, reductions or accretions to the work force, transfers of work, overtime, and health and safety. Typical of the information and consultation requirements are the provisions of the 1971 Dutch Works Council Act (Sections 31, 25):

Information: The employer must provide the council with all information which it may reasonably demand for accomplishing its tasks, more in particular, and at least once every year, with respect to the legal status of the firm, its financial and economic position, its long-term plans, and its social and personnel policies. . . .

Consultation: The employer must seek the council's advice with respect to decisions concerning a transfer of ownership of (parts of) the firm, merger, takeovers, plant or shop closure, major reduction, change or extension of activities, major changes in work organization, change in the location of production, the employment or lease of temporary staff, major investment, major capital loans, and assignments given to outside consultants or experts on any of the above issues. The council's advice is also needed on proposals concerning the dismissal and appointment of members of the executive board. The right of advice in matters of merger, takeovers and consultants does not apply when one of the firms involved is located outside the Netherlands.

Deeper rights to codetermination—requiring the employer to get works council approval for a decision to be "valid" or to withstand legal challenge—complement the information and consultation rights in stronger union systems. The German case is exemplary. German works councils enjoy information rights on financial matters, and information and consultation rights on personnel planning and work reorganization. In addition, however, they have codetermination rights on such matters as principles of remuneration, introduction of new payment methods, fixing of job and bonus rates and performance-related pay, allocation of working hours, regulation of overtime and short-time working, leave arrangements, vacation plans, suggestion schemes, and the introduction and use of technical devices to monitor employees' performance (Section 87 of the Works Constitution Act). They also enjoy prescribed codetermination rights on individual staff movements, including hiring, evaluation, redeployment, and dismissal,[7] and the right to a "reconciliation of interests" between the council and the employer on a wide range of other matters bearing on the operation of the firm. The latter include those matters bearing on:

> reduction of operations in or closure of the whole or important departments of the establishment; transfer of the whole or important parts of the establishment; important changes in the organization, purpose or plant of the establishment; introduction of entirely new work methods and production processes (Section 111).

In countries where councils have codetermination rights, the law provides mechanisms for resolving disputes without the use of economic force. Depending on the dispute and the country in question, such mechanisms include assignment of the dispute to a special joint grievance committee, to an outside arbitrator with binding powers, or to a labor court.

Organizational Character

If these are the formal attributes of councils, two aspects of their more substantive organizational character bear special note. The first is that councils are designed to guarantee some measure of *collective participation*. As *collective* institutions, they perform functions different from regimes in which workers express themselves as individuals. As *participatory* institutions, with obligatory status and real rights to information, consultation, and sometimes codetermination, councils are distinguished from new forms of work organization that are designed to increase, more or less contingently, the "involvement" of workers through decentralization and expansion of competence and responsibility in production tasks. While works councils may help managements implement work reorganization—or may demand such reorganization themselves—they are outside the managerial line of authority and not part of the functional organization of production. Their distinctive contribution to production decisions is based on a right to represent their constituents, not on job assignments or occupational competence. And while they make it easier for individual workers to speak up, as collective representatives they aggregate the views of workers, transforming individual views into some expression of what they take to be the interest of the work force as a whole.

As institutions of collective participation in the enterprise, works councils perform functions that unions and collective bargaining cannot easily perform, especially in the joint solution of problems and the resolution of conflicts in production. Where they are well developed, councils support collective bargaining by relieving it of tasks to which it is not well suited. By providing management and workers with a reliable channel for problem-oriented communication, they also help integrate workers into the firm. Councils are generally aided (except in Spain) in performing this intermediate role not only by statutory supports but also by their insulation from wage setting. With this crucial union function and source of conflict with management removed, they serve as instruments of negotiated exchange over such "qualitative," nonwage matters as work organization, technological change, personnel policy, and training—issues often best resolved at the level of the individual firm. They also serve as a mechanism, within the firm, for the enforcement of more encompassing social agreements. In centralized bargaining systems, works councils are commonly obliged not only to respect such general agreements but also to supervise their implementation at the workplace in ways appropriate to local conditions. More generally, they do the same for public labor regulation.

What is important to see, however—and this is the second key feature of councils' organizational character—is that performance of this distinctive role requires that councils be "compromised." To be effective, they must be neither fish nor fowl—not merely disguised unions nor, surely, disguised management. They are mixed institutions, varying along a line of compromise between worker interests in institutionalized representation and collective voice, and employer interests in work force cooperation and communication to enhance economic performance. Depending on the distribution of power between capital and labor and national labor relations policies, the substance of that compromise differs across countries and over time. While French councils are presided over by the employer, German councils are worker-only bodies. For most of the postwar period, Dutch councils were employer-led, but legal changes in the 1970s reorganized them on the German model. German councils have the legal right to veto certain managerial decisions, while Italian councils do not. In the immediate postwar period, European councils were generally more consultative and employer-dominated, often to the extent of being rejected by unions as overly paternalistic, but in the 1960s and 1970s they become more representative, to the point that in Germany today, for example, they are often perceived as the "extended arm of the unions" at the workplace. In all cases, however, councils typically accommodate concerns and interests of both management and labor and serve to reconcile them, at least in part, in their daily operation.

Because of their mixed and compromised status, works councils have been alternately supported and rejected by both unions and managements in different countries and at different times. Employers have favored works councils to the extent that councils give them access to "reasonable" worker representatives who were not "outsiders"—that is, not full-time union officials—and in the hope that councils would foster worker loyalty to the firm by stressing their shared interest with the employer in the firm's success in the marketplace. But employers also worry that councils might interfere with the free exercise of managerial prerogative.

Unions have their own reasons for ambivalence. Certainly many unions have come to regard works councils as a chance for expanding collective worker representation beyond the limits of collective bargaining, through an institutionalized voice in managerial decisions. In Germany, unions accepted codetermination as an alternative to socialist demands for the nationalization of industry, as a way of sharing economic power between capital and labor. At the same time, however, unions are often suspicious that council participation will draw workers into responsibility for business decisions that workers have no capacity to affect; that employers will influence the selection of worker representatives; and that councils may turn into company unions that crowd out "real" unions, cutting the work force off from broader solidarities beyond company boundaries and identifying worker interests with those of the firm.[8]

Such concerns are ubiquitous and ongoing, even in mature council systems enjoying very broad union and managerial support. In substantial measure they are intrinsic to any functioning council system.

Contributions to Democracy, Efficiency, and Regulation

Workers and employers, then, seek different benefits from works councils. Workers are interested in representation and expanded democracy, while firms look for gains in efficiency and performance. Councils exist and function well to the extent that work forces are persuaded to contribute to efficiency in exchange for representation and managements are persuaded to accept worker voice as a condition of cooperation. Councils generate economic benefits by mobilizing for economic purposes what one may call the "productivity of democracy." Through its existence in the firm, a council legitimates a plurality of interests within the firm and gives workers a secure status as industrial citizens, with quasi-constitutional rights to participate in decision making at their place of employment that parallel the rights of citizens in political communities. Indeed in Germany the legislation that institutes works councils is called the Works *Constitution* Act.[9] Industrial citizenship of this kind can benefit democracy in society at large as well as within firms, and can improve national economic performance. It can also enlist industrial citizenship in the service of general public goals in workplace regulation.

Contributions to Democracy

Political democracy and citizenship secure social integration by enabling people to hold authority accountable, to question and influence decisions, and to redress outcomes regarded as illegitimate by the community at large. Democracy is based on the belief that social integration through citizenship is normatively and practically superior to monolithic unity imposed from above; that an accepted plurality of interests is more conducive to social cohesion and productive cooperation than an authoritatively enforced unity of purpose; and that, at least in the long run, constitutional recognition of different interests is the most effective way of reconciling such interests. The rationale for industrial democracy put forward by its defenders in the countries we have studied consists to a large part in the extension of this view from the polity at large to the firm.[10] The central claim is that not only is it normatively desirable for employees to have a say at their workplace but that a guaranteed voice for workers is also more effective than even enlightened managerial unilateralism in productively integrating capital and labor.

That councils are a substantive form of democratic participation is evident from workers' involvement in them. Regular works council elections give workers a chance to express their views on the representation provided to them by their unions. German works councils, for example, are elected every four years on a nationwide election day, with opposing slates of candidates in each workplace that has a council and turnout averaging 90 percent. During the election campaign, unions contend with opposition from competing unions and from nonunion groups, which often try to win votes by distancing themselves from unionism and emphasizing their closeness to the employer. For the largest German union confederation, the DGB (Deutscher Gewerkschaftsbund), the fact that the candidates of its affiliates regularly win about 80 percent of works council seats nationwide (more in most large firms) has been a source of strength, legitimacy, and pride. In countries with multiunionism, works council elections force unions to match their policies to the preferences of large numbers of workers, unionized or not, and to measure regularly and publicly their support against that of their competitors. In these ways, a council system promotes a certain accountability among unions themselves to those they purport to serve.[11]

Further benefits for democracy result from the difference a works council makes for the relationship between workers and their superiors. Works councils provide employees with a safe institution in which to raise concerns and complaints without fear of sanctions. Because they are in continuous discussions and negotiations with the employer, works council members can easily take up minor worker complaints with management and settle them without undue bureaucracy (Williams, 1988). By comparison, where people can express discontent with the exercise of authority only to those wielding that authority, they will usually remain silent—unless they can make themselves believe in the benevolence of those who they believe have violated their rights. Thus grievances will rarely be redressed, especially if they are more than trivial. The consequence can be a sense of powerlessness and inferiority on the part of workers that may disable their performance as workers and as citizens. Reciprocally, much benefit redounds, in public arenas as well as private ones, from permitting people to express discontent without fear.

Contributions to Efficiency

The economic contribution of works councils can be summarized in different ways. Concentrating on council functions themselves, we note their demonstrated ability to generate trust between employers and workers, to increase the flow of information within the firm, to aid in the diffusion and implementation of advanced production practices, and to force economic upgrading.

Trust. Trust between management and workers is central for good economic performance under modern technological and market conditions. For firms to decentralize production decisions, managers must trust workers not to misuse their increased discretion. For workers to contribute to efficiency, they must trust management not to exclude them from the benefits of their effort. Generally trust is required to support cooperative exchange over longer periods, where outcomes and contingencies are not entirely predictable. Where deferral of rewards or long-term investments are important for competitiveness, lack of trust will make self-interested actors "cash in" too early, for fear of being victimized by opportunistic, short-termism on the part of others.

The availability of trust as a social resource depends on the extent to which actors can expect their counterparts not to defect from shared norms of reciprocity and "fairness," even when defection might be attractive. The firmer such expectations are, the more trust is available to underwrite extended operating under some uncertainty. Most immediately, and particularly where (as between employers and employees) economic power is not equally shared, credible information that the other side has noneconomic as well as economic reasons not to defect—moral commitments or legal obligations that preclude opportunistic behavior—is an effective condition for the growth and consolidation of trusting relations.

Works councils provide such credible assurance and thereby assure a foundation for trusting relations. With strong works councils, employers cannot abolish worker participation unilaterally. Since they know this, they will consider it a waste of effort to try, and will direct their efforts to building constructive relations with the councils. Thus the operations of the councils themselves will not be shadowed by a history of employer resistance (as union relations typically are in the United States). On the side of workers, knowing that the employer cannot abolish the council and therefore will not try permits workers to be less defensive than they would be under less safe conditions. Finally, the permanence of the council structure permits both sides to extend their time horizons in mutual dealings through it. A council can extend "credit" to the employer over long periods. And because it does not have to ensure against aggressive short-termism from worker representatives uncertain of their long-term status, management is more inclined to assume the costs of building cooperative structures that precede payoffs to them.

In short, the formal institutionalization of worker participation rights—moving such rights outside the discretion of the parties involved, and especially that of the employer—can contribute to the growth of trust. While trust is an intangible resource that cannot itself be legislated, legislation can ensure against the self-interested short-term actions that destroy trust and can foreclose options whose mere exploration may undermine trust for a long time. This is what strong council legislation does.[12]

Information Flow. Modern analyses of the firm recognize that in devising competitive strategies, managements face information problems that go beyond simple "black box" neoclassical models of the firm. These analyses stress the crucial role of different information held by different employees, as well as employees' strategic behavior in using that information. Recognizing that information exists at many levels of an organization leads to the understanding that, in many situations, it is inefficient for management to make key decisions without mobilizing information held by others and investigating the validity of divergent information in collective deliberation. Just as the center cannot efficiently run a centrally planned economy, neither can the center efficiently run a large modern enterprise.

The routes by which employee representation can improve enterprise efficiency through the flow of information have been modeled by Freeman and Lazear (1993). The authors stress the virtue of increasing information flows from management to labor, which can lead to worker concessions in difficult economic times, saving troubled enterprises; increasing information flows from workers to management outside the hierarchical chain; and providing a forum in which both sides can devise new solutions to problems. In this analysis, collective voice in the workplace has benefits for the enterprise beyond discouraging strikes due to unmet grievances (a major goal of the Wagner Act), saving the costs of turnover by reducing the number of workers who quit, or giving workers the compensation package they desire. It alters the way management and labor operate, creating a more cooperative and informed decision process. Because they are able to draw on formal entitlements to truthful information and are supported by obligations on the part of management to provide such information, irrespective of present inclinations and market constraints, works councils neutralize temptations for management to underinform or to inform only as suggested by short-term market pressures. They thereby increase employee confidence in the information they receive.

Employer obligations to consult with councils create in many situations an incentive for works councils to provide truthful information to management, in the hope of affecting managerial decisions. The more input work force representatives feel they can have in decisions, the more they will invest in mobilizing valid information, for example by researching the views of the work force at large. Workers, in turn, are more likely to give information and reveal their preferences to their elected representatives than to management. They may also speak to management more easily when they know that their rights and interests to be protected by a strong works council.

Furthermore, consultation and codetermination rights vested in representative bodies create space for joint deliberation of decisions between management and worker representatives. Typically the exercise of consultation and codetermination rights delays decisions while at the same time improving their quality; this is the tenor of research findings on the impact of codetermination on German management. Works councils that provide managers with skillful interlocutors able to analyze proposals and projects in depth cause management to consider intended decisions more carefully and to mobilize extensive information for their justification. Codetermination, which gives works councils temporary veto power over decisions, may protect managements from narrow, short-term responses to market signals, helping them avoid costly mistakes arising from lack of reflection.

Diffusion of "Best Practice." In successful works councils systems, councils serve liaison functions with the environment outside the firm, often helping the firm perceive and import good practice. In this way councils help diffuse innovations across firm boundaries. In dealing with technical change and its consequences for work organization, for example, councils in several countries may call in experts in ergonomics to advise them and the employer on state-of-the-art solutions.[13] Expert advice helps standardize conditions across firms and draws the attention of firms to advanced solutions that they might have found on their own only with delay and at high cost. In Germany, council members have rights to attend training courses, often organized by unions or employers' associations, on company time and at the employer's expense. These courses deal with questions of new technology, work organization, working time regimes, health and safety regulations, changes in labor law, and the like. Such courses spread information on high standard solutions to a large number of workplaces.

Industrial Upgrading. Councils can pressure managers to consider productivity enhancement as opposed to other competitive strategies. Through their influence on firm decisions, they force managers to consider decisions in light of the interests of employees, to explore alternatives before presenting them for approval, and to learn about their interlocutors (the workers themselves) and the conditions under which they work. This creates a management style that looks closely for solutions compatible with employees' interests. Moreover, the sheer imposition of employees' demands, for example for further training, submits managers to certain productivity-enhancing constraints. Councils cannot bargain over wages, but they can effectively pressure management in ways that can push it toward high-wage strategies. These pressures, diffused throughout the economy, exert a cumulative force for restructuring along the path of upgrading labor.

Contributions to Regulatory Performance

Finally, works councils can make a major contribution as supplements to state inspectorates in government regulation. Every society regulates some market outcomes and some aspects of the exercise of hierarchical authority in organizations. However, regulation through general rules, created by legislation or otherwise, is typically beset with a twofold enforcement problem: a limited bureaucratic capacity to supervise the innumerable sites where regulated activity occurs, leading to a potential enforcement gap; and the inevitable rigidity of rules applying uniformly to a large number of diverse local conditions.

Works councils are often enlisted as on-site enforcement agents to supplement government inspectorates, and sometimes they make government inspection altogether dispensable. Together with the employer, councils may be given discretion to modify general rules in line with local conditions, increasing the "bite" of rules by making them more flexible. In this way works councils may reduce enforcement costs for the government and contribute to the effectiveness and sophistication of regulation. Rule-making agencies, in turn, can leave the details of regulatory enforcement to local interlocutors (providing, of course, that their interlocution is structured to "keep each other honest"). This option relieves pressure on the state either to write elaborate rules or to abandon regulatory projects simply because local conditions are too varied for uniform rules to apply. Rule makers may (and almost always do) still want to review the results, but on net they benefit from this debureaucratization of regulatory strategies.

The nearly universal European practice of using worker committees as deputy "inspectors" for health and safety regulation is one example of this phenomenon. The most developed example of councils taking on broader regulatory functions, however, may again be found in Germany. German works councils are charged by law to monitor the employers' observance of pertinent labor regulations. In addition to health and safety regulations, these include legislation on employment protection and equal employment opportunities. Works councils that fail to comply with the law, or that allow a employer to circumvent it, may be taken to the Labor Court by individual employees or by the union, and councilors may be removed from office.

German works councils are also bound by any industrial agreement that unions and employers' associations may negotiate at the sectoral or the national level—which, given extension agreements, takes on at least the color of more general public regulation. They have the duty to ensure that employers do not pay wages below those set in the industrial agreement. Works councils also supervise employer compliance with statutory or collectively bargained worktime regulations, and they are typically charged with negotiating the details of their local implementation. Finally, works councils have the right and obligation to monitor employer compliance with Germany's public-private system of apprenticeship vocational training. They monitor implementation of the nationally standardized curricula for apprentice training at the workplace, and they are obligated to ensure that apprentices are not used unduly for production and that the skills they are taught are portable and not primarily workplace specific (see Chapter 3, this volume).

In all these areas the availability of competent enforcement agents—who have the interest and the powers to make regulation "work" in ways respectful of local variation—facilitates the achievement of public goals by facilitating cooperation both between labor and capital and between the private sector and the state. Employers would not have been willing to accept the German industrial agreements on work-time reduction in the 1980s, for example, had they not known that enforcement of those agreements through councils would allow flexible adjustment for local preferences and circumstances, and unions would not have been content with such enforcement had they not known that "flexibility" would not amount to subversion. Neither unions nor employers would support Germany's fabled apprenticeship-based vocational training system as strongly as they do without the same confidence in council flexibility and powers. Nor could the state plausibly contemplate governing such a system—with two-thirds of each age cohort undergoing three-and-a-half years of apprenticeship in any one of about four hundred certified occupations—without the contribution of local enforcement agents who enjoy the confidence of private parties. And German industrial policy would not be nearly so extensive and sophisticated if the state could not look to councils as it regularly does, to provide information on emerging needs, worker perspectives, and the effectiveness of past use of government monies and other supports—information of a sort not necessarily provided by employers.[14]

COUNTRY STUDIES

How do councils and council-like structures function in the context of different industrial relations systems? In the following section, we review the history and present state of councils in several countries. We examine Germany and the Netherlands, where works councils operate on a strong legal base; France and Spain, which have weaker councils functioning in an environment of declining, politicized multiunionism; Sweden and Italy, where councils are not prescribed in law but have developed through a more or less formally bargained consensus between employers and strong unions; and conclude with the U.S. and the Canadian experience with councils or council-like structures.[15]

Germany

The idea of worker representation through works councils first surfaced in the revolutionary Constitutional Assembly at Frankfurt in 1848 and was included in its draft constitution for a democratic German republic. Legislation, however, came only during World War I, when the Imperial Military Command instituted limited participation rights for councils of workers in factories, to mobilize support for the war effort and shield collaborating mainstream unions against pacifist and radical-socialist opposition. By the end of the war, that opposition had turned into a powerful, clandestine workers councils movement that had successfully organized a number of illegal strikes in the armaments industry. Like the Russian soviets, the movement saw itself as the political and institutional cornerstone of a postwar socialist order.

After their defeat at the hands of the Social-Democratic Party and the Socialist unions, which were supported by the remnants of the Imperial Army, the councils were incorporated in the liberal-democratic constitution of the Weimar Republic. Stripped of their political functions and purged of their militancy, they were given legal powers to represent workers and consult with employers. Collective bargaining was reserved for unions at sectoral and national levels, with councils legally bound to observe and implement collective agreements. This division of labor, which was designed to protect the primacy of industrial unions and sectoral collective bargaining, would in its basic contours be recreated after World War II.

Both unions and works councils were abolished by the Nazis in 1933. Later, in the period immediately following World War II, works councils reemerged earlier than unions, organizing production in the absence of owners and managers who had been associated with the Hitler regime and defending plants and equipment against Allied dismantling.[16] While unions and the Left had at first hoped for large-scale nationalization, and later for economic power sharing under broad-based codetermination, in 1951 the first government of the Federal Republic, formed by conservative parties, legally reinstituted works councils as bodies of cooperation and consultation between workers and employers. Unions perceived the legislation to be directed against them and opposed it. It was only after the consolidation of the collective bargaining system in the early 1960s that unions began to regard works councils as an acceptable legal-institutional device for worker representation at the workplace. This development culminated in the revision of the Works Constitution Act in 1972, in response to union demands, under the first federal government led by the Social-Democratic party.

German works councils are elected by the entire work force in establishments with five or more employees. While councils are not mandatory, only three employees, or a union with just one member in the establishment, are required to call an election; if necessary, elections are overseen by a labor court to prevent employer interference. Elections are at large, with blue- and white-collar workers represented in proportion to their numerical strength. Both unions and nonunion groups may run slates of candidates. If there is only one slate, voting is for individuals, and candidates are seated according to votes received. The term of office for councilors was recently extended from three to four years. Companies with more than one establishment form central works councils composed of delegates of local works councils.

The number of council members varies with establishment size and is determined by law. For example, establishments with 50 employees have five works councilors; with 300, nine; and with between 2,000 and 3,000, nineteen. According to union statistics, in the 1990 elections some 180,000 works council members were elected in 33,000 establishments. It is estimated that these account for between 70 and 80 percent of all establishments eligible to have a works council. Since all large firms have councils, the proportion of the work force covered is much higher.[17]

Council members are entitled to release from work for council duties; in establishments with more than 300 employees, some members must be released full-time. For example, of the nineteen council members in an establishment with between 2,000 and 3,000 employees, four are full-time. Council members have employment protection and must not suffer disadvantages with respect to promotions. All council expenses, including the costs of elections, are paid by the employer. As a minimum, councils are entitled to office space and staff, and councilors may attend union training courses; in larger firms they may, in addition, employ a small professional staff of lawyers, accountants, or economists, also at employer expense.

Apart from works councils, there are two other mechanisms of collective representation in large workplaces in Germany. In plants with a strong union presence, there is a caucus of union delegates elected by union members. In addition, codetermination under company law (as distinguished from the Works Constitution Act) entitles work forces in large corporations to elect one-half of the members of the company's supervisory board. In practice, both systems are closely linked to the works council and controlled by it. While union caucuses were originally introduced to counterbalance council collaboration with employers, today they typically serve as grassroots organizations for the works council and as a recruiting ground for its future leaders. Also, the leading works councilors are normally elected, in addition, to the supervisory board, a position they use for better access to information on economic matters and to increase their bargaining power in relation to company management.

Works councils have legal rights to information, consultation, and codetermination, the last being limited to work-related matters and those aspects of management decisions that may have negative effects on workers. They are furthermore charged with overseeing the implementation of any law or industrial agreement applicable to the workplace. Councils often find ways to expand their rights beyond the limits of the law. For example, works councils may threaten to exercise their legal rights and obligations formalistically, thereby delaying urgent decisions, unless management agrees to give them more information than is legally required, or to seek consensus for decisions that are formally outside the council's domain. Table 4.1 shows how members of works councils perceive their most important functions.

Works councils may negotiate binding agreements with the employer that differ in legal status from industrial agreements. They cannot call strikes, however, and their principal power resources are their legal rights. If no agreement is reached, an arbitration committee is formed that has authority to make binding

Table 4.1   Main Tasks of German Works Councils, as Perceived by Councilors

Tasks	Percent Identifying Task as one of "Three Most important Council Functions"
Personnel matters	68
Technical change	47
Health and safety	44
Wage group classification assignments	42
Working hours	33
Overtime	26
Further training	15
Initial vocational training	9
Social benefits	7

SOURCE: Hans-Bückler-Stiftung 1992 survey of 315 works councilors in the German printing, publishing, electrical engineering, and ceramics industries (Müller-Jentsch, 1994).

awards. Arbitration committees are rarely used, since employers and works councils equally dislike having outsiders take issues out of their hands.

Wage bargaining in Germany takes place at the sectoral and national levels, and is conducted by a small number of broad-based industrial unions and employers' associations. While union density has long been stable at about 40 percent, collective agreements cover almost all workers in the German economy, due to the high membership in employers' associations and the possibility of making agreements generally binding by legal decree. Works councils have no role in wage setting, except with respect to piece rates and job evaluation; there, too, however, they must respect and apply existing industrial agreements. Recently an increasing number of industrial agreements have included so-called "opening clauses," charging works councils and employers with local regulation of "qualitaive" subjects that are difficult to regulate centrally or uniformly, like work organization under new technology, training, and working time. Frequently industrial agreements define limits for local works agreements or offer a range of options between which local negotiators may choose.

In the immediate postwar period German unions rejected works councils as undermining working class solidarity. With time, however, they began to rely on them as their extended arm at the workplace, especially when union candidates began to win the vast majority of council seats, and surveys showed that workers made no distinction between unions and councils. Accommodation with the councils gave German unions access to the workplace earlier than their European counterparts had it, and to worker interests not easily covered by multiemployer bargaining. After the spontaneous strikes of 1969, unions relied even more on the councils, resulting in the gradual subordination of the union delegates under council control. This trend was reinforced by the Works Constitution Act of 1972, which expanded the rights of works councils and formally recognized the links between them and the unions. Today, full-time union officials are entitled to attend works council meetings, and they often serve as members of works council negotiating teams bargaining with management. Not only are the vast majority of works councilors union members, but many of the elected nonmembers also join soon after their election, to have access to union resources and support.

German industrial unions provide works council members with extensive training and advice. Most works councilors have attended a number of union training courses, and in large firms it is hard to be nominated as a union candidate for the council without having gone through training at union schools in economics and labor law. Many council members also hold union office at the regional, state, or national level, or sit on union committees that bargain with the employers' association. In this capacity, they are free to take part in strikes. In practice, German works councils are union workplace organizations that operate within the legal form and that have the means of codetermination.

Unions, in turn, benefit from works councils in that the councils make it possible for them to represent workers on vital nonwage interests, without jeopardizing industrial unionism and centralized wage bargaining. In fact, in a period when they were moving joint regulation closer to the workplace through "opening clauses," German unions were better able than unions in most other countries to defend centralized wage setting, and with it low interfirm and interindustry wage differentials. Works councils also provide for easy *de facto* union recognition and are used by unions as a convenient device for recruiting members. In the past decade, works councils have in addition served as a ready receptacle for a broad range of new subjects of joint regulation that might otherwise not have been covered, or that could not have been effectively taken up at the industry-wide level. Support for the council system has become unambiguous among German unions, which are well aware that their relatively strong position after years of deep economic restructuring is very largely owed to councils' firmly enshrined statutory powers at the workplace. German employers, while still hostile to codetermination on the supervisory board, have never seriously tried to make the conservative government undo the 1972 legislation, in part because of the economic benefits of improved cooperation and more reasoned decision making, and in part because no German government can touch the Works Constitution Act without damaging its electoral fortunes.

The Netherlands

Dutch works councils date from 1950, when they were made mandatory in law as a channel of communication between workers and employers, designed explicitly to improve the firm's economic performance. In 1971 representation of worker interests was added to council tasks, although the employer still presided over council meetings. Eight years later this was changed, and Dutch councils have since been worker-only bodies. Dutch law specifies procedures for the interaction between employers and councils that discourage the overt expression of conflict and promote a problem-solving approach through improved communication and mutual accommodation of interests. Council and employer must meet at least six times a year and deal with each other cooperatively and in good faith.[18]

Like their German counterparts, Dutch works councils enjoy extensive rights to information and consultation, obligations to uphold public regulation, and rights of codetermination on selected matters. (Management is obligated to provide all information necessary for the exercise of these rights and duties.) Under the Works Council Act of 1979 employers must give works councils "the opportunity to tender advice on any proposed decision" regarding, among other things, transfer of control over (parts of) the enterprise; merger with or takeover of other enterprises; termination of operations or plant closure; any major reduction, expansion, or change of activities; major organizational changes within the firm; changes in location; use of temporary staff; major investment projects; major capital loans; and assignments given to outside consultants on any of the above matters. Consultation may also be initiated by the council on any subject or proposal on which it considers consultation desirable. Councils oversee employer compliance with legal and other regulations concerning the terms of employment and the health, safety, and welfare of the work force. They are also charged with promoting public policy objectives, such as job referrals, worker participation and involvement, prevention of discrimination, equal treatment of men and women, and the integration of handicapped persons at the workplace. Codetermination rights are enjoyed for any rules on employee conduct, and for any stipulation of general terms of employment not covered by an industrial agreement between the relevant unions and employers' associations; for company pension, profit-sharing, or savings plans; working hours and vacations; job evaluation; health and safety at work; rules regarding hiring, dismissals, and promotion; training; assessment of worker performance; and the handling of grievances. If agreement cannot be reached, the law provides for a waiting period of one month; thereafter the employers can implement their decisions. Both parties can appeal to the courts, which may void an employer's decision or a council's veto on the grounds of being "unreasonable." Codetermination rights do not apply where the matter in question has been settled in an industrial agreement applicable to the enterprise.

Works councils are mandatory for firms with more than 100 employees; about 55 percent of Dutch workers work in firms of this size. Firms may ask to be exempted for a certain period from having a council, but about 83 percent of firms in the 100-plus size group have works councils.[19] There are councils with limited rights in firms with between 35 and 100 employees; these employ another 18 percent of the work force. Firms with between 10 and 34 employees are required to hold a number of consultative meetings each year with their full work force.

Works councils in the Netherlands cannot call strikes, and as a rule they are not involved in wage bargaining. Wages and other employment conditions are negotiated at the sectoral and national levels between unions and employers' associations. Large international firms, however, negotiate special company agreements with the unions, and a growing number of firms, especially in the service sector, do not belong to an employers' association and therefore are not covered by sectoral agreements. There are pressures for more decentralized bargaining, or at least for greater space for the negotiated application of industrywide agreements to the specific conditions of individual firms. While unions strongly object to the involvement of works councils in wage setting and employers also fear a "second bargaining round," although they would like to see more flexibility, there is no legal reason why works councils in firms that are not subject to an industrial agreement cannot negotiate over wages and other matters, and there are cases in which this occurs.

Dutch works councils are elected every three years, but not all at the same time. Voter turnout is around 75 percent, and it is higher in larger firms. The number of members on a council depends on the size of the workplace; a plant with 1,000 employees, for example, has a council of thirteen, while on average councils have nine or ten members. Representative unions may submit lists of candidates directly; smaller unions and nonunion groups may also run, but they have to collect a number of signatures to be admitted. Councilors in firms with more than 100 employees are entitled to paid leave for meetings, training, and preparation, as well as to office space and secretarial assistance. They may also hire experts or even sue their employer at the employer's expense. Council members use, on average, about 20 hours of paid leave per week; large firms have full-time council presidents. The average council meets ten to eleven times a year and consults seven times with the employer; again the numbers would be higher for larger firms. Three out of four council members receive about five days per year of training, organized and paid for by the Joint Training Board for Works Councils, which is run by unions and employers together and funded by the employers.

The Netherlands offer an example of strong multiunionism, with no legal provisions for privileged recognition of a "most representative" union. The largest union federation, the FNV (Federatie Nederlandse Vakbeweging)—an amalgamation of the former Catholic and Socialist unions—represents about 60 percent of all union members. Another 20 percent are organized in a Protestant federation, the CNV (Christelijk Nationaal Vakverbond). There also is a white-collar federation, MHP (Vakcentrale vor Middelbaar en Hoger Personeel). The FNV and CNV are organized on an industrial basis. Unionization declined in the Netherlands in the 1980s, from 37 percent of the work force in 1979 to 25 percent in 1989, and to 18 percent in the private sector. Part of this decline has been attributed to councils substituting for unions, but in spite of their shrinking membership, Dutch unions regularly take two-thirds of the works council seats (in 1985, 41 percent were held by the FNV, 11 percent by the CNV, and 12 percent by other unions), and the proportion of councils with a nonunion majority fell during the 1980s from 34 to 25 percent.

Dutch unions were divided over the 1979 works council legislation, with the more radical FNV opposing what it regarded as collaborationist elements in works councils.

But the FNV also recognized that council reform offered unions a more realistic chance for in-plant influence than further extension of union rights. Demands for legal rights for union plant committees, in addition to and alongside works councils, were accordingly dropped, and as in Germany the works council has become the main organizational base for unions at the workplace, in spite of multiunionism.

As to councils' economic consequences, studies indicate that councils both prolong decision time and improve the quality of decisions, as perceived by the unions as well as many employers. Among the latter the view is frequent that the rigorous economic restructuring of the 1980s would have been more difficult without councils. Employer fears in 1979 that the introduction of councils would result in higher workplace militancy have not materialized, and the 1979 council system has become an established part of Dutch industrial relations. Recourse to external adjudication of conflict is extremely rare. In addition to services provided by union headquarters and districts, councils draw on a growing number of private consulting firms that have sprung up alongside the council system and contributed to the professionalization of council policy.

France

Works councils are legally prescribed in France for all private-sector establishments with fifty or more employees.[20] They have rights to information and consultation. French works councils are presided over by employers; a secretary is appointed from among the worker members. Councils are elected every two years. They meet monthly, and the employer has to provide them with their own budget, equal to 0.2 percent of total payroll, though many firms may provide more funding. In addition council members receive paid time off from work for their official duties. Councils may set up commissions for special tasks. They are entitled to training in economic matters and to the assistance of a certified accountant, and they may obtain the help of an outside expert on matters relating to technological change, at the employer's expense.

Each establishment or plant has its own works council; companies with more than one plant form a central works council in addition. In 1990, 79 percent of establishments with fifty or more employees, including all large firms, elected works councils; 65 percent also elected health and safety committees. Under the law, all employees are eligible to vote, regardless of union membership. There are two rounds of voting. In the first, only recognized unions that are considered "representative" can present lists of candidates. The second round, in which nonunion candidates may run, is held only in workplaces where union lists have received less than 50 percent of the vote.

French works councils have three kinds of legal rights. First, they administer the social welfare funds a company maintains for its work force. Second, they may negotiate with the employer on profit-sharing and other financial participation plans; this is their only role in collective bargaining. More than 10,000 such plans were in effect in France in 1990, many introducing bonus pay in a remuneration system in which this had been largely unknown. Third, works councils have rights to information and consultation on the organization, management, and general operation of the firm. Recent national agreements and legislation obligate firms to provide explicit training plans for their work force, and to involve their works councils in setting them up. French councils have no rights to codetermination, however; their role is strictly advisory. Moreover, sanctions against employers that fail to inform and consult them in a timely manner—generally understood to be one month before a major decision is taken—are weak. Works councils may delegate two representatives to the company's board of directors where, however, they also have only an advisory role.

Councils operate alongside other institutions, in particular employee delegates, union branches, and health and safety committees. Employee delegates are elected, also by the entire work force, in establishments with more than ten employees, including those that have works councils. Their role is to monitor the employer's compliance with legislation and collective agreements and to present the employer with any grievances and demands raised by workers in this respect. Employee delegates do not, however, negotiate; this role is reserved for the union branches. There may be up to four union branches within a firm, given the division of French unions into four competing federations, all of which are deemed "representative" under French labor law. External unions have a legal right to designate a number of official union delegates in the workplace to represent them in relation to management and to negotiate collective agreements. Union delegates are entitled to limited time off for performance of their union functions, and like elected council representatives and employee delegates they are protected from dismissal. Health and safety committees were legally established in

1982 for workplaces with more than 49 employees; they have absorbed some of the functions of the employee delegates. The complex relations among the various bodies representing work force interests in a French workplace can be understood only in historical context; they also vary greatly between firms.

The situation of works councils in France is shaped by their position in a labor relations system that includes traditionally assertive employers bent on defending managerial prerogatives; politically divided and numerically declining unions; and weak collective bargaining that has moved from the national to the enterprise level. French industrial relations is characterized by a tacit consensus between employers and unions that the workplace is not an appropriate site for joint regulation. French employers are more insistent on managerial prerogative than their counterparts in other countries, while French unions have always sought to avoid responsibility for co-management of a capitalist economy. As a consequence, with collective bargaining centralized, French workplaces remained almost entirely unregulated for a long time. Workplace industrial relations were not institutionalized until 1936 when, under pressure from a militant union movement, employers demanded legislation mandating the election of employee representatives by all workers, unionized or not, as a lesser evil compared with union branches. Limited to raising worker demands and barred from both consultation and collective bargaining, employee delegates were acceptable to employers and unions.

In 1945, France passed a law setting up works councils as bodies for mutual information and consultation, designed to improve economic performance through cooperation and "social dialogue." However, lack of interest among unions and employers rendered the councils insignificant. In response to the unofficial strikes of 1968 that were attributed to excessive centralization of industrial relations and a lack of representative institutions at the workplace, the French government enacted legislation allowing unions to set up workplace branches and designate union delegates. In 1971 it established the legal possibility for collective bargaining and collective agreements at the enterprise level, but unions failed to respond to this. With works councils weak and often captured by competing, politicized unions, employers embarked on a concerted policy of employer-controlled, nonrepresentative communication with work forces and individualized participation ("direct expression") by workers, circumventing unions and collective bargaining and undermining the position of the unions.

In 1982, the newly elected Socialist government responded to a perceived need for a fundamental recasting of French industrial relations by passing the "Auroux laws," named for the minister of labor at the time. Blaming the lack of cooperation and the institutional deadlock in French workplaces equally on employer unilateralism and union intransigence, and in an effort to save the unions from the consequences of their inability to react constructively to the employers' direct participation offensive, the legislation strengthened the information and consultation rights of works councils, especially on economic matters; obliged employers to negotiate with unions at the enterprise level on a wide range of subjects; created special health and safety committees to supervise the implementation of applicable regulations; and enabled unions to regulate direct work force participation by collective agreement, in an effort to eliminate employer unilateralism in this area.

Works councils are defined by the Auroux reforms as institutions of social dialogue between the employer and the work force. Councils are given consultation rights, accommodating political pressures for protection of managerial prerogative and the preservation of a space for independent action of competing trade unions. Being almost entirely cut off from joint regulation,[21] French works councils are relatively weak institutions unless they find a way of coordinating their activities with union branches willing to use their new right to collective bargaining. But French unions declined rapidly in the 1980s, with density in the private sector dropping to about 10 percent in 1990. As Table 4.2 indicates, from 1985 to 1989 the proportion of establishments with designated union delegates fell in all sizes of establishments. And in spite of the union monopoly in the first round of voting for council elections, the share of votes for nonunion candidates has risen in all sizes of firms. In 1990–91 nonunion candidates drew 29 percent of the works council vote (62 percent in firms with between 50 and 100 employees), as compared with 19 percent (and 48 percent) in 1979.[22] This decline, coming at a time of enhanced institutional opportunities and responsibilities for unions at the workplace, undermined the reconstruction of enterprise-level industrial relations that had been intended by the Auroux legislation.

Table 4.2   The Weakness of French Union Influence in Small Firms

Size of Establishment	Presence of Union Representatives (%)		Votes for Nonunion Candidates in Work Committee Elections (%)		
	1985	1989	1979	1985	1989
50–99	41.7	35.9	48.2	56.0	61.7
100–199	63.4	57.1	35.9	40.1	45.3
200–499	83.6	77.7	18.5	20.7	25.5
500–999	93.6	89.4	7.3	9.4	13.5
1,000 or more	96.6	92.3	2.0	2.1	2.8

SOURCE: "Dossiers statistiques du travail et de l'emploi," Ministry of Labor, Employment, and Professional Training (Tchobanian, 1994).

By mandating that employers accede to union demands for enterprise-level bargaining on wages, hours, and direct participation of employees, the Auroux reforms tried to draw unions into joint regulation, with the hope that this would produce more cooperative and constructive attitudes. This is in contrast to the traditional, centralized collective bargaining in France, in which employer associations and unions reached sectoral agreements that did not significantly affect the operation of firms, doing no more than laying down minimum conditions that employers were free to modify. Unions often refused to sign agreements, to avoid becoming involved in the management of a capitalist economy. At the workplace, unions preferred to raise unilateral demands through unionized employee delegates, leaving it to the employer to respond or not, at the risk of industrial conflict. While only partly successful, the Auroux legislation did contribute to the decentralization of the collective bargaining system. Although the law does not require that negotiations result in agreement, 6,750 enterprise agreements covering 2.5 million employees were signed in 1991, as compared with 2,067 agreements in 1982.

The economic effects of French works councils are difficult to determine, in part because they are weak institutions. Some studies argue that their improved information and consultation rights have enabled some works councils to make employers invest more in training and improve workers' career opportunities in the internal labor market. As French companies experience the limits of

"Taylorist"[23] work regimes, works councils are described as supportive of major organizational changes, and a small but growing number of large firms are finding advantages in a cooperative relationship with a well-informed council. In many firms of between 50 and 200 employees, works councils have *de facto* come to be the only mechanism of worker representation.

Overall, "social dialogue" in French firms is often formalistic and superficial, without much effect on management decisions. Moreover, direct employee participation, organized through collective bargaining and outside the jurisdiction of the works councils, is generally considered to have failed, in spite of the more than 4,000 collective agreements signed on the subject between 1983 and 1986. Meetings of "expression groups" are rare and are often used only to present grievances. In many firms participation procedures have fallen in disuse, with employers favoring alternative mechanisms, like quality circles, that they can control, and the politically divided unions have failed to develop a consistent policy on participation. For larger firms, national and sectoral collective agreements on the "modernization" of French industry signed in 1988 and 1989 sought to redefine the relations between the various representative bodies at the workplace with respect to matters like technical change, working conditions, working hours, training, and equal opportunity. The objective was to facilitate what a government report calls "negotiated modernization," to be pursued jointly and consensually through coordinated information, consultation, collective bargaining, and direct participation, on the basis of nationally defined, inclusive procedures. However, only one major union federation signed the agreements, and only a few very large companies have applied them.[24]

Spain

Works councils were instituted in Spain under the Franco regime. Although unions were outlawed, the government recognized the need for some form of workplace representation, especially for local implementation of central legislation and wage guidelines. In the 1960s, councils gradually became *de facto* agents of collective bargaining and in the process were partly taken over by a semiclandestine, Communist-led union movement whose activists were often elected works councilors. After Franco's death in 1975 unions were legalized, but councils were not abandoned; on the contrary, their position was strengthened in that they were legally institutionalized as the unitary representative of workers in all firms with more than ten employees. While under Franco councils had included the employer, new legislation made them exclusive to worker representatives.

Council formation is not automatic but must be triggered, either by one-half of the work force or by a "representative union" in the area or industry in which the firm or plant is located. Spanish unions use their triggering privilege extensively, especially where they expect to win the election. Unions and nonunion groups run lists of candidates in the elections, which are held every four years on a nationwide basis. Seat allocation favors lists that draw a high number of votes. Voting is by different "colleges," for blue-collar and white-collar workers. Electoral turnout is quite high: 79.8 percent in 1986 and 74.0 percent in 1990. Councils in firms with more than 250 employees include by law a small number of non-voting, direct union representatives, whose seats are assigned on the basis of the election result.

Works councils elections decide which unions are designated as "representative" and "most representative" under Spanish law. Unions with more than 10 percent of the council seats in a given jurisdiction (a firm, a region, or the country as a whole) are considered "representative" and as a result have various organizational privileges. Unions, or combinations of unions, with more than one-half of the council seats have sole collective bargaining rights. The system contributes to the stability of Spains's two-union "representative duopoly"—the Socialist UGT (Unión General de Trabajadores) and the Communist CCOO (Comisiones Obreras)—by curtailing the growth of splinter organizations.

The size of councils varies with that of the firm. A firm with 1,000 employees will have 21 works councilors and 2 direct union delegates. In 1990 works councils were elected in 109,133 work-places, with 5.4 million employees electing 237,261 council members. It is estimated that about 70 percent of all workplaces in Spain elected councils, and among them are almost all large firms with more than 500 employees. Table 4.3 shows the distribution of representatives of different unions and groups in Spanish works councils elections from 1978 to 1990. In 1990 the UGT and the CCOO won about 80 percent of the seats; the rest went to regional

Table 4.3   Respective Union Shares in Spanish Works Council Elections, Shown as Percents

Elections	UGT	CCOO	USO	ELA	CIG	CSIF	Other Unions	Non-Union
1978	21.7	34.4	3.9	1.0	—	—	20.85	18.12
1980	29.3	30.9	8.7	2.4	1.0	—	11.94	15.77
1982	36.7	33.4	4.6	3.3	1.2	—	8.69	12.09
1986	40.9	34.5	3.83	3.3	0.7	—	9.95	7.6
1987[a]	23.1	24.2	—	—	—	24.9	27.8	—
1990	42.0	36.9	2.9	3.2	1.5	2.6	7.1	3.8
1990[a]	26.9	28.4	0.9	2.0	1.8	19.4	18.2	2.4
1990[b]	43.1	37.6	3.0	3.2	1.5	1.4	6.4	3.9

SOURCE: Ministry of Labor and Social Security (Escobar, 1994).

NOTES:
UGT   - General Union of Workers
CCOO - Workers' Commissions
USO   - Union of Syndicated Workers
ELA   - Solidarity of Basque Workers
CIG   - Galician Interunion Coalition
CSIF - Independent Union Confederation of Civil Servants

[a] Public administration only.
[b] Exclusive of public administration.

unions and nonunion groups. Since the works councils system was rebuilt in the transition to democracy, the more moderate socialist CGT has doubled its vote while the Communist CCOO has stagnated. The biggest losers have been the nonunion groups that had occupied 18.1 percent of seats in 1978.

Spanish works councils have the legal rights to information on a range of subjects regarding the economic situation of the firm. In addition they must be consulted on matters such as working time, redundancies, work organization and reorganization, redeployment of workers, training, incentive systems, job evaluation, and methods of supervision. In cases of redundancies (layoffs) and major changes in work organization, management has to get authorization from public authorities unless an agreement is reached with the works council. Works councils also monitor employers' compliance with applicable laws and industrial agreements, including health and safety, and may take legal action for this purpose, and they coadminister any social welfare funds provided by the firm.

Spanish works councils are entitled to office space and time off at the expense of the employer; council members are protected from dismissal. In return, they are obliged to cooperate with the employer in increasing productivity, to keep the work force informed of their activities, and to maintain secrecy with sensitive business information to which they may become privy in the exercise of their functions. Unlike councils in other countries, Spanish works councils also negotiate wages, and they may call strikes. Historically this is because councils had those functions under Franco, and for some time during the transition union branches at the workplace did not exist, which left the bargaining role of councils untouched.[25] Later attempts to centralize bargaining were tied to the idea of a nationally negotiated income policy. That policy failed, however, and the question of the level at which to bargain over wages has remained unresolved. Decentralization of wage bargaining has increased the independence of local unions from their national organizations.

Unions are weak in Spain. Membership density peaked at about 40 percent in 1978 and has since fallen to between 10 and 15 percent (25 percent in manufacturing). The unions are also poorly funded, though they receive some government money on the basis of works councils elections. As a consequence, works councils have widely come to serve as substitute unions, and some argue that they may have crowded unions out by providing representation without membership.

While originally divided over their attitudes toward the government, both the Socialist and Communist unions have moved closer together, especially at the local level. In December 1988, the UGT and the CCOO called a general strike against the government's economic policy that was widely supported. Still, Spanish unions have not played an important role in the restructuring of the workplace. Works councils sometimes cooperate with management to increase productivity and reduce absenteeism, but more frequently they are under pressure from workers to defend employment. Further complicating their position is the unsettled question of the level of wage bargaining, which stands in the way of a stable division of labor between unions and works councils. Employers, fearing that consultation at the workplace will produce redistributive wage bargaining, have sought to keep the role of works councils as limited as possible.

Sweden

Sweden is a case of workplace codetermination without works councils, where only joint health and safety committees are legally required. Swedish codetermination arrangements at the plant level are exclusively union-based. The 1976 Act on Codetermination at Work gives internal union bodies—the so-called union "clubs" at plants and enterprises—the possibility to negotiate a wide range of participation rights, creating a unique amalgamation of collective bargaining and second channel "industrial democracy." The result is a variety of consultative and participatory mechanisms in Swedish firms that have been jointly created by unions and employers and that include "codetermination councils," health and safety committees, and employee board representation, in addition to the bargaining role of union workplace organizations.

The main reasons for the absence of a conventional works council system in Sweden are the strong Swedish blue-collar union federation, LO (Landsorganisationen i Sverige), which has historically rejected legal regulation of industrial relations in general and works councils in particular, and the radicalization of the Swedish union movement in the 1970s, when workplace participation assumed high priority on the political agenda. In the 1920s "joint councils" were suggested to reduce Sweden's notoriously high level of industrial conflict, but they were never established. In 1946 the central employers association, SAF (Sveriges Arbetares Centralorganisation), and LO signed a national agreement on a system of "joint councils" of employers and work force representatives at the plant level, for "problem solving" in support of "rationalization." While union demands for similar councils at company and industry levels failed, union members' refusal to cooperate with nonmembers of unions on the plant councils ensured that these remained entirely union-based, and only union members were eligible to vote for or be elected as representatives. White-collar unions later joined the national agreement, turning the councils into multiunion arrangements.

The joint councils established in 1946 had information and consultation rights only. As a consequence, the LO unions did not perceive them as adding to their capacity but instead as potentially undermining their members' solidarity across company or plant boundaries and detracting from the role of collective bargaining. Joint councils therefore never became important in the Swedish workplace, being more often than not boycotted or sidestepped by the unions. Beginning in the late 1960s, LO, under the pressure of a wave of unofficial strikes, began to press for increased participation and codetermination rights for workers at the workplace. Rejecting initial proposals to reorganize and expand the joint council system, LO opted for a general right for local unions to bargain collectively on any decision employers may make. Where vital interests of workers were concerned, LO demanded veto rights, based either in law or in collective agreement.

Insisting on the principle of managerial prerogative, Swedish employers refused to grant these demands through a national collective agreement. In response, LO turned to the Socialist government for legislation. During the discussion of the Codetermination Act, one proposal was to vest new participation rights in works councils set up at the initiative of either the employer or the union. Even the latter alternative, however, was rejected by the unions, who argued that legally based councils were unnecessary for unions as strong as the Swedish unions, and instead demanded codetermination without legal guidance, based on collective bargaining. In some parts of the union movement, this was seen as a radical alternative to German codetermination. When the Codetermination Act was passed in 1976, superseding the 1946 joint councils agreement, it did no more than create a broad obligation for employers to negotiate with local unions on a wide range of subjects that had in the past been decided by management unilaterally. Still, the fact that the unions chose to procure their new rights through legislation instead of a central agreement was seen by the employers as an irreversible departure from the traditional pattern of Swedish industrial relations.

Participation in Swedish workplaces rests on several pillars:

Joint health and safety committees: Workplaces with fifty or more employees are legally obliged to have joint employer-worker committees on health and safety to oversee implementation of the Work Environment Act. Work force representatives are appointed by unions, in keeping with the union-based structure of Swedish industrial relations. Committees work with a national and regional labor inspectorate, which is jointly governed by unions and employers' associations and empowered to resolve disputes. A central agreement between employers and unions provides for majority representation of workers on joint committees, but decisions with financial implications for the company require unanimity.

Board representation: Under the Act on Board Representation for Employees in Joint Stock Companies and Cooperative Associations, passed in 1972 and amended in 1977 and 1988, employees in companies with a work force of more than 25 can have two or three "worker directors" on the company board. Worker directors have the same standing as other board members. They are appointed by the unions, except in the few nonunionized companies, where they are elected by the work force. Worker directors are always in the minority and do not participate in matters under collective bargaining. Board representation is today regarded primarily as a means of keeping unions and work force representatives informed, rather than as an instrument for them to influence managerial decisions.

The Shop Stewards Act: Passed in 1974, this act entitles elected trade union officials at the workplace to leave work for union duty. Shop stewards are the pillars of the workplace union organization, and they often are involved in health and safety councils, are appointed as board representatives, or serve as members of other bodies and councils.

The Codetermination system: Under the 1976 legislation, almost all matters concerning employer-employee relations are in principle subject to codetermination procedures. Negotiations are supposed to be cooperative, and the employer always makes the final decision. Noncompliance with procedures is referred to labor market organizations at the industry level; there also is recourse to the labor courts or to special arbitration boards. However, sanctions are weak and diffuse. In practice, the Act on Codetermination at Work has led to a vast expansion of information and consultation at the workplace, but not to codetermination in which worker representatives can veto specific management decisions.

The intention of the legislation was that the Codetermination Act would be followed by a central agreement between unions and employers' associations, that would fill in the details of how to carry out codetermination at the workplace, but private employers strongly opposed the act and moved slowly. Not until 1982 did the parties reach their "agreement on efficiency and participation." The agreement obliges employers and local unions to negotiate how codetermination is to be exercised. Three models are offered: bipartite negotiations between company and unions; "line negotiations" between managers and union representatives at all levels of the company; and "bipartite participation and information bodies." Very few local agreements have been concluded, however. Instead local parties have set up consultative bodies, joint project groups, or autonomous work groups for specific subjects; while they are regarded as codetermination bodies, their legal status is unclear. Bipartite negotiations and, where they exist, codetermination bodies proper are often bypassed. In this way, codetermination oriented toward collective bargaining and agreements is being replaced with information and consultation in joint bodies and along the managerial line of authority. If cooperation in the new bodies is not satisfactory for local unions, they may demand negotiations under codetermination procedures; in this sense, the Codetermination Act is still in force. However, recourse to its formal provisions is rarely taken.

In effect, the Codetermination Act facilitated the growth of a diverse, workplace-specific, informal infrastructure of communication between employers and work forces. This in turn has introduced traits of enterprise unionism into previously highly centralized Swedish labor relations. It has also recreated elements of the old joint councils that were pushed aside in the 1970s. Management antipathy towards the act has declined as management has seen its capacity to generate worker identification with the economic fate of the enterprise and to replace formal representation and negotiation with informal "involvement." While unions admit that the act has not given them what they might have expected, they recognize that it provides a voice on a range of subjects that had been beyond the reach of their highly centralized structures.

The development of Swedish codetermination in the 1980s coincides with the transformation of the "Swedish model" of industrial relations toward more decentralized collective bargaining.[26] While in Germany legally based codetermination at the workplace arguably supported centralized wage setting and protected the role of industrial unions and employers' associations, this was not the case with the union-based Swedish system. Union density is very high in Sweden, reaching as many as 90 percent and more of workers in core sectors of manufacturing. But Swedish unions are becoming increasingly fragmented, due to the changing composition of the work force and the growth of white-collar unions. Although Swedish unions have negotiated an interunion agreement on the use of their codetermination rights at the workplace, enabling them to have more unified representation of work forces, they remain exposed to employer demands for enterprise-level, unitary "co-worker agreements" that would abolish the traditional distinction between blue- and white-collar workers and end the separate negotiations for the two categories.

The impact of codetermination on Swedish economic performance is seen in its contribution to the emergence of informal cooperation and worker involvement in the enterprise. While by itself the Codetermination Act has not had major economic consequences, the workplace-level participation agreements negotiated on the basis of the act seem to have provided firms with the institutional foundation on which to build a structure of joint councils and committees that are involving the work force in a radical reorganization of production away from Taylorism. Swedish industry has benefited from the willingness of unions, conditional on their ability to have recourse to codetermination procedures and collective bargaining, to support modernization through participation in project groups and joint committees. Although employers had originally opposed the Codetermination Act, the vagueness of its content has helped their efforts in recent years to move Swedish labor relations from its former corporatist structure of central agreements and joint labor-management boards to individual enterprise negotiations and informal, production-centered, competence-based, and individualized worker involvement, and the growth of a "cooperative culture" at the workplace.

Italy

While works councils are of growing importance in Italy, they are only indirectly based in law; strictly speaking, their status is that of legally supported union workplace organizations. In line with the fluid structure of Italian industrial relations, Italian works councils are informally organized, and their structures and functions differ widely among workplaces. They also coexist with a politically divided union movement that nevertheless periodically attains high degrees of unity, especially at the local level. The functions of Italian works councils are defined in a way that leaves space for independent action of union branches at the workplace, provides for representation of workers that are not unionized while preserving the status of councils as union bodies, and allows for cooperative relations with external unions and full-time union officials. In recent years employers have become interested in works councils as unitary representatives of the work force and for their potential contribution to building consensus for and within a more flexible, less Taylorist organization of production.

As early as the beginning of the twentieth century there were examples in large Italian firms of elected worker committees providing unified workplace representation under conditions of craft-based multiunionism. While some committees were elected by all workers, others were elected only by union members; tension between the two organizational principles has continued until the present. During World War I, "internal commissions" were created in large firms that were exclusively union-based, to ensure industrial peace and the commitment of workers and unions to production goals in the war economy. Shortly thereafter, the commissions were confronted by a union-independent, revolutionary council movement opposing the war. The revolutionary councils were defeated in 1920, partly at the hands of the official union movement. Five years later, the fascist government abolished unions and internal commissions.

After the Second World War, internal commissions were reintroduced under a national agreement between unions and employers. After several revisions of their functions by national industrial agreement, internal commissions came to be defined in the late 1940s as works councils in the strict sense—that is, as plant-based bodies representing the entire work force, separate from unions, not taking part in collective bargaining, without the right to call strikes, and with the functions of consulting with the employer to facilitate cooperation and supervising the implementation of legal regulations and collective agreements. Unlike their counterparts in most other countries, however, the internal commissions were never regulated by legislation.

In subsequent years, the internal commissions were affected by the breakup of the trade union confederation into three politically divided organizations. While the Communist union defended the commissions as the sole, unified representative of workers at the workplace, the minority unions demanded in addition a space for workplace union branches and insisted on equal representation of all federations on the councils. Over time, the internal commissions fell into disuse, due to both lack of union interest and employer resistance to a union presence at the workplace. When the spontaneous strike wave of the late 1960s challenged managerial control, nobody regarded the internal commissions, with their emphasis on labor-management cooperation, as a possible basis for a reinstitutionalization of Italian labor relations.

The strikes of the late 1960s resulted in the first major piece of labor legislation in Italy, the Workers' Statute of 1970. Rather than trying to revive the works council system, the law institutionalized the presence of unions at the workplace by allowing "representative" unions—basically the three national federations—to set up workplace union branches. In part this was to enable the unions to structure, and perhaps control, what had in many places developed into a union-independent, radical council movement. With the new law unions were able to penetrate a sizable number of workplaces and increase their membership density, in the process effectively undoing the remaining internal commissions (though the national agreements on internal commissions were never formally rescinded). Along with increased organizational opportunities, the new situation presented the unions with a number of puzzles, such as how to relate to each other and to nonmembers at the workplace and how to coordinate workplace collective bargaining, which had become possible, with traditional, centralized bargaining at the national level.

The Workers' Statute gives unions legal rights in the workplace without prescribing the structure of union representation. The most common form of workplace union organization is a committee of work force representatives elected by all workers regardless of union membership; this is sometimes referred to as a factory council or a council of delegates and in many important respects corresponds to works councils in other countries. To give a council the legal status of a union branch under the Workers' Statute, the three federations designate an equal number of elected council members as their representatives or, alternatively, appoint a small number of their activists as additional members of the council.[27]

In the absence of legal regulation, election procedures are informal, based in part on agreements between the national union federations and in part on local traditions. Works council elections must be triggered by a certain small number of employees, or by the three union federations acting in unison. Elections are usually held every two or three years, and informal provisions are made to have all groups of employees represented. Large councils tend to appoint an executive committee. In multiplant companies, local councils sometimes form enterprise-level coordinating committees. The law entitles councils, *qua* workplace union branches, to a certain amount of paid time off from work; most other allowances and facilities are negotiated locally between the council and the employer. Councils are worker-only bodies with no employer presence. Employers must not interfere with the formation of councils, to the extent that they are protected union branches under the Workers' Statute. According to union data, in the early 1980s there were some 32,000 works councils in Italy, with more than 200,000 members, representing about 5 million workers or about 50 percent of the work force in manufacturing and private services. The number of councils grew after 1984 in spite of renewed conflict between the three federations at the national level, so that by 1990 almost all firms with more than 100 employees (and about 80 percent of firms with between 20 and 99 employees) had council-like representation.

In their relation to employers, Italian works councils originally emphasized their role as local agents of (conflictual) collective bargaining. However, with the growing importance of "qualitative" issues such as working time regimes and adjustment to technological change, and with increasing interest among employers in building consensus with their work force amid rapid restructuring, works councils moved into the center of an extensive web of largely informal information, consultation, and negotiation practices that are neither required nor encouraged by law. In part this shift is expressed in a proliferation of joint employer–works council committees on specific matters, and in a growing willingness of employers to involve councils in decisions, especially on working time, internal mobility, technical change, and training. The result is a peculiar mix of formal and informal modes of joint consultation and regulation at the workplace, premised simultaneously on employer self-interest and union organizational strength, and differing widely among firms. Remarkably, this has developed even though there is no legal or contractual obligation for Italian employers to inform, consult, or share decision making powers with their work force or the workplace union branch. Moreover, local cooperative practices are often in conflict with the official positions of both unions and employers' associations.[28]

As already stated, Italian works councils represent both unions and the general work force. Unions are represented through elected council members (of which union representatives are the vast majority), and through directly appointed union delegates, the latter being the main organizational device to accommodate multiunionism. Full-time union officers may attend council sessions and take part in important meetings with management, and council leaders often hold union office in addition. External union organizations provide a range of training and advisory services to councils, and sometimes support councils financially. As unified union branches, works councils have the right to collective bargaining, which, however, they normally exercise together with the external unions. Individual company agreements have become increasingly common, resulting in broad decentralization of the Italian collective bargaining system. This has been sought by the unions, who have been keen to reestablish their presence on the shop floor after the centralized, "neocorporatist" bargaining of the

1970s, as well as by employers looking for ways to establish more flexible work rules and working time regimes and to involve union representatives in day-to-day operational decisions.

Overall, the Italian works council system—indirectly legally supported but not legally regulated—has proven surprisingly stable and adaptable to the twists and turns of multiunionism as well as to changing economic contingencies. It also seems to have helped Italian unions in the 1980s protect themselves against a dramatic decline in their membership. Still, national union federations seek to consolidate their workplace branches by defining their functions and structures more clearly. The three federations have agreed to standardize election procedures and clarify the status of their joint representative bodies at the workplace in relation to the unions. Some observers argue, however, that any rationalization of the existing council structure is unlikely to have a lasting impact without some legal support.

North America

The United States and Canada provide no statutory guarantees of worker rights to information, consultation, and codetermination. Their labor relations systems are governed by the "Wagner Act model" of single channel worker representation, under which the presumptive state of workers is nonunion, and unionization is the only recognized form of plenary collective worker representation regarding the terms and conditions of employment. Union-management relations, moreover, are viewed largely as adversarial. To protect worker autonomy, employer support for organs of worker representation is explicitly prohibited.[29] In both Canada and the United States, moreover, collective bargaining is highly decentralized, extension laws are exiguous, and social benefits are tied closely to employment status. As a result cooperative labor relations within the firm are routinely frustrated by conflict over essential material terms of worker welfare.

These conditions granted, there is still a long history of nonunion workplace committees in both Canada and the United States and some experience with statutorily mandated committees with limited regulatory purposes. We will use the U.S. experience to illustrate the function of nonunion voluntary committees and the Canadian experience to illustrate regulatory functions.

U.S. Experience with Representation Committees

Although U.S. shop committees date back to the nineteenth century, the first great wave of employer representation plans in the United States came during World War I. Introduced to curb wartime strikes (they typically involved explicit renunciation of the strike weapon) and with an eye to inoculating the public against communist agitation, "works councils" or "shop committees" were promoted by various wartime authorities. From virtually zero in 1917, their number grew spectacularly. By 1919 the National Industrial Conference Board (NICB) reported 225 plans covering half a million employees, and by 1922 there were 725 plans operating throughout the country. Employers reported decreased threats of unionization, lower union turnout, and reduced grievances as benefits of the plans. However, with the exception of a small number of plans that provided more or less extensive participation rights, including representation in plant committees or on boards of directors and participation in profits and stock ownership or collective bargaining, most of these plans gave workers no real power in decision making.

While some large firms continued their company unions and welfare programs, these generally faded in the immediate postwar period. In the mid-1920s, however, the "American plan" open-shop drive to prevent unionization led many smaller firms to introduce representation plans. Between 1919 and 1928, total worker membership in employer-initiated representation schemes grew from 0.4 million to 1.5 million. Along with declining union membership during the 1920s, this shifted the relative strength of the two forms of representation. In 1919, plan membership had equalled only 10 percent of union membership; by 1928 the ratio was 45 percent (Millis and Montgomery, 1945, 837).

With the coming of the Depression, representation plans ebbed again: membership fell to 1.3 million over the years 1928 to 1932. But the National Industrial Recovery Act (NIRA) of 1933, which brought about a marked growth in trade union organization, also led to a resurgence in company unions. The NIRA forbade employers to force employees to join company unions but not to encourage the formation of such bodies (and such encouragement was often tantamount to force). Under increased threats of union organizing, the company union movement grew quickly. Data from NICB and the Bureau of Labor Statistics (BLS) indicate that by 1935 more than 3,100 companies, with 2.6 million employees, had some significant percentage of their employees covered by representation plans, two-thirds of which had been established after 1933 (Wilcock, 1957). The ratio of representation plan membership to trade union membership surged to 60 percent (Millis and Montgomery, 1945, 841). In some sectors coverage was even more widespread: for example, after passage of the National Recovery Act (NRA), most basic steel companies established employee representation plans, which then spread to 90 to 95 percent of the industry work force (Bernstein, 1970). This, however, was the highpoint for representation plans. In the late 1930s the massive organizing drives of the Congress of Industrial Organizations (CIO), aided by the prohibition of employer "encouragement" of worker representation in Section 8(2) of the National Labor Relations Act, killed most of them.

During World War II the government again promoted cooperative workplace relations, this time in the form of joint labor-management committees chiefly in union shops. These grew to cover some 7 million workers in the war years, but they faded thereafter (de Schweinitz, 1949). In the early postwar period, again chiefly in the organized portion of the work force, scattered efforts were made to formalize labor-management cooperation, including a variety of schemes aimed at increasing employee productivity through profit sharing and bonuses. Outside a few specific sites, however, these efforts never caught in on the union sector; economy wide their appeal was also limited (Derber, 1970, 478–482).[30] One survey found that no company with more than 1,000 employees and no establishment with more than 5,000 employees enjoyed an actively cooperative relationship with its union. With very rare exceptions, the "cooperative" strategy was limited to medium-size, closely held firms or to marginal companies; even there it essentially disappeared in the late 1950s (Harris, 1982, 195).

As the prime case of employer-initiated works councils operating in a largely nonunion, decentralized labor market, the U.S. experience in the 1920s through the 1950s provides insight into the potential for councils in such a setting. It shows, first, that employer-initiated councils were neither a long-lived stable institution nor were extended to the majority of the work force. Even at its peak the council movement covered only a minority of workers, mostly in big firms, and the peak came under threat of outside unionization. Still, this minority exceeded at times the modest private-sector U.S. unionization rates of the early 1990s. Second, NICB reports and historical investigations of the operation of councils show considerable diversity (NICB, 1919 and 1922; Jacoby, 1989; Jacoby and Verma, 1992; Nelson, 1993). In many cases, company unions were the sham that unionists usually claimed them to be, but in some cases they offered significant and meaningful means of worker representation. According to the NICB, "successful" worker representation depended on management commitment—as evidenced in regular meetings, worker education, and, ideally, concrete payoffs to workers through, for example, the profit-sharing (collective dividend) system (NICB, 1922, Report 50). Not contemplating an extension of enforceable worker rights within the firm, the NICB concluded that "where management is not thoroughly sold to the idea . . . a Works Council should not be formed" (NICB, 1922, Report 50, 10).

Renewed interest in employee participation began in the early 1970s. Focused on "quality of work life" (QWL) programs, it was initially motivated by concerns about worker alienation (the "blue-collar blues"), which many viewed as being responsible for an increased militancy of assembly-line workers. The National Commission on Productivity and Quality of Working Life and the Ford Foundation sponsored a number of QWL experiments in the early 1970s in both union and nonunion plants. The most widely known included those conducted at the Rushton Mining Company, and the General Motors (GM) Tarrytown plant, which prior to the QWL program had had one of the poorest labor relations and production records of all GM plants but which, within a few years of QWL adoption, became one of the company's best performing assembly plants. Implementation of QWL programs was never widespread, however, and most experiments faded by the late 1970s when government funding stopped (Kochan, Katz, and Mower, 1984, 6–7). In the 1980s, worker involvement programs enjoyed a resurgence, so that in 1990 some 30,000 U.S. firms, including 80 percent of the top 1,000 firms, reported having some such program—an increase of 50 percent in the incidence of programs over 1987 (Katz, 1992). These programs had various names—QWL committees, quality circles, autonomous work teams, gain-sharing and employee stock ownership plans (ESOPs)—and varied considerably in structure, representativeness, scope of issues, substantive decision making power, and links to other changes in work organization. Cutcher-Gershenfeld (1987) estimates that 10 to 15 percent of all American organizations had worker participation programs in the 1980s, covering about 20 percent of the work force. Cooke (1990) estimates that 40 to 50 percent of the unionized sector is involved with quality circles, QWL programs, or some form of employee involvement; of these, between one-third and two-thirds are jointly administered. About one-third of the unionized sector has committee-based participation, with health and safety being the most common focus.

Studies of these programs confirm the experience of the 1920s. The economic effects of worker involvement are most likely to be positive when workers have real power in decision making and receive concrete payoffs for cooperation (Blinder, 1990). The greatest gains from cooperation are seen in unionized settings, where worker power exists independent of management (Eaton and Voos, 1992; Kelley and Harrison, 1992). In nonunionized settings, where workers have no reserved rights, the performance and stability of the programs depends on management attitudes, which vary widely across firms and over time and which are subject to an important core ambivalence: even where managers recognize worker autonomy in their decision making as necessary to productivity gains, they are reluctant to relinquish control. Outside organized settings, much of the talk of worker "empowerment" is only that, involving a relatively trivial routinization of management access to employee opinion, rather than a substantive change.

Canadian Experience with Regulatory Committees

Within the United States or Canada, labor market regulations are typically enforced directly through state inspectorates or indirectly through "private attorneys general" pursuing statutory rights through civil actions. For reasons that have been suggested, however, in many areas of public concern neither of these means of regulatory enforcement is adequate. Sites of regulated activity are too numerous (in the United States, there are 6 million work sites) for any plausibly sized state inspectorate to monitor, and activity within them is too heterogeneous for a distant state agency to decide the best means of achieving desired outcomes. Private litigation, on the other hand, is a very costly and brittle way to settle disputes about standards of behavior, and its cost means it is least amply supplied to the less skilled, who typically are most in need of enforced standards. Indeed, the prominence of regulatory agents and lawyers in the compliance process is widely perceived as a barrier to the intrafirm understandings and practices needed to get the desired compliance. The result is often regulatory failure: inadequate performance standards, cumbersome reporting requirements on matters of uncertain relevance, inflexibility in adjusting standards to varied or changed circumstance, and weak enforcement.

As countless European examples attest, using mandated in-plant committees to perform regulatory functions—in effect, deputizing workers as coadministrators of regulatory schemes—is one way to address these problems. In principle such an approach can offer a monitoring and enforcement capacity greater than that of any state inspectorate, a cheaper form of worker input into decisionmaking than that offered by lawyers, and a system of information exchange within the regulated site that yields earlier identification of problems and efficient solutions through the of local knowledge.

In North America, occupational safety and health regulation is the most prominent area in which this alternative approach is being tried. Several U.S. states have experimented with one or another form of mandated health and safety committees, with early evaluations suggesting some promise (Rees, 1988; GAO, 1992). By far the most advanced North American case, however, is that of Canada. Joint health and safety committees (JHSCs) were first mandated in Saskatchewan in 1972 and have since spread throughout Canada's highly federated polity.

JHSC powers, functions and incidence of formation vary across jurisdictions. Typically they are required in firms of twenty or more employees; they provide for workers' rights to information and consultation on health and safety matters, as well as their right to refuse hazardous work; they are required to meet a certain number of times per year or month; and they are deliberately constructed as "joint", with mandated equality of worker and management representatives and sharing of leadership responsibilities. The size of JHSCs varies, with some jurisdictions mandating proportionality to firm size and others not. Actions by worker members in pursuance of their responsibilities enjoy explicit protection from employer reprisal.

Representatives to JHSCs are chosen in different ways. Management selects its representatives. In unionized work sites in most jurisdictions, the local union selects worker representatives; where more than one union exists at a site, the unions are typically encouraged to work together to appoint representatives of overall employee interests. In nonunion worksites, employees typically select their own representatives, though their method of doing so is sometimes left to management, and in a substantial number of cases management picks the worker representatives. Ontario legislation provides that nonunion employers have a responsibility to "cause a joint committee to be established" and to ensure that "members of the committee who represent workers shall be selected by the workers they are to represent." Quebec legislation declares that "the workers' representative on a committee shall be designated from among the workers of the establishment."

In most provincial legislation, committees function as advisory bodies; they do not hold formal codetermination powers, and there are no formalized mechanisms for resolving worker-management disputes in cases of deadlock. Typical is the language of the British Columbia law, which states that the JHSC "shall assist in creating a safe place of work, shall recommend actions which will improve the effectiveness of the industrial health and safety program, and shall promote compliance with these regulations," but provides no mechanism for handling disputes. An exception is Quebec, where legislation permits either party to appeal to an oversight body for binding resolution of impasse disputes; in Ontario, the law requires timely management response to committee recommendations.

The costs of JHSC operation are borne chiefly by employers. Under Ontario law, for example, they must pay for training, instructional material, and salaries for at least one worker as well as one management member of their firm's JHSC; the legislation also provides for some compensated preparation time for committee members; in general, across provinces, any time spent directly in committee meetings is compensated. Direct government support for the JHSCs has been uneven, but the need for it is recognized, particularly in the area of training worker members. In Quebec and Ontario, provincial governments have established provincewide bipartite bodies with responsibility for overall promotion and direction of the JHSCs. These bodies, which receive substantial funding, are chartered to do research, promote public awareness of JHSC functions and conduct training of JHSC members and others. Ontario has moved to a credentialing program for JHSC members, administered through this bipartite committee. The net effect will be some professionalization and convergence in JHSC operations across the approximately 55,000 committees in that province's jurisdiction.

Despite tensions—over representation, funding, the threat of management domination of committees in nonunion settings, and the terms of bipartite control over the training provided for JHSC members—management and labor, as well as the government, appear broadly satisfied with JHSC operation. As Table 4.4 indicates, committee members themselves, from both management and labor, offer strongly positive assessments. In combination, the reach of JHSC coverage and the general level of satisfaction with the committees suggest that they function adequately outside unionized contexts. At the same time, Canadian unions do not report the JHSCs as having any significant union-avoidance effect. They appear, then, neither to be merely auxiliary to unions nor a tool of management. Instead, inside labor-management circles and out, they are increasingly described as a vehicle by which a traditional source of labor-management conflict has been domesticated, to mutual gain, and as a welcome complement to state inspectorates in health and safety.

CONCLUSIONS ABOUT WORKS COUNCILS

Our general discussion, and the review of specific country experiences, can be summarized in four simple claims.

First, works councils in general perform useful functions, at tolerable cost, and make an important net contribution to democracy and economic welfare. They facilitate representation and the achievement of public regulatory goals, and help underwrite a variety of desired economic practices. The latter include better intrafirm communication and the diffusion (across as well as within firms) of advanced practices with regard to training, technology, compensation, and other ingredients in industrial upgrading. Works councils are a means to greater social consensus and a greater

Table 4.4 Committee-Member Assessments of the Impact of the Joint Health and Safety Committee

Survey Question/ Response Choices	Management Members (%)	Worker Members (%)
Overall Record in Improving Safety and Reducing Accidents		
Poor to less than adequate	9.2	11.0
Adequate	34.7	29.6
More than adequate to excellent	56.2	59.4
Overall Record in Reducing Potential Health Hazards		
Poor to less than adequate	5.4	12.6
Adequate	34.2	28.8
More than adequate to excellent	60.3	58.9

Ability to Obtain Necessary Changes in
   Equipment, Materials, and Work
   Practices to Improve Health and Safety		

Poor to less than adequate	5.3	16.0
Adequate	26.1	24.3
More than adequate to excellent	68.6	59.6
Ability to Improve Health and Safety Knowledge and Concern Among Workers		
Poor to less than adequate	14.8	21.1
Adequate	28.4	30.9
More than adequate to excellent	56.8	47.9

Ability to Improve Health and Safety
   Knowledge and Concern Among
   Management, Including Supervisory Staff		

Poor to less than adequate	10.7	24.9
Adequate	30.1	28.8
More than adequate to excellent	59.2	46.2
Rating of Success of Inspection		
Poor to less than adequate	7.1	7.9
Adequate	26.4	24.5
More than adequate to excellent	66.5	67.6

Rating of Danger from Accidents
   in the Workplace (now as compared to
   5 years ago)		

Worse now	1.4	4.8
Unchanged	16.6	17.5
Better now	81.9	77.6

Rating of Danger from Health Hazards
   in the Workplace (now as compared to
   5 years ago)		

Worse now	0.9	5.4
Unchanged	19.9	19.9
Better now	79.9	81.2

Rating of Management and Worker
   Understanding of, and Concern for, Health
   and Safety (now as compared to 5 years ago)		

Worse now	0.7	2.6
Unchanged	9.9	16.1
Better now	89.3	81.2

SOURCE: ACOHOS, 1986, 97–98.

capacity to respond to changed economic circumstances in broadly beneficial ways.

Second, there is striking convergence among developed nations, *with the sole exceptions of the United States and Great Britain*, that works councils or similar institutions, intermediate between managerial discretion and collective bargaining, are part of a well-functioning labor relations system. In most of Europe, the past decade witnessed both an expansion of the collective participation rights of workers and more extensive production-related communication and cooperation between managements and work forces. As union rejection of workplace participation as paternalistic and detrimental to worker solidarity has receded, so have management fears that collective participation will interfere with managerial prerogative. As a result, the consultative councils that were set up in all European countries to promote labor-management cooperation after World War II, and that later fell into disuse due to union opposition and lack of employer interest, came back in modified form in the 1970s and 1980s. They were enriched with participation rights to supplement their communication functions, and more closely linked to union movements—themselves exhibiting increased interest in and presence at the workplace.

Third, despite their usefulness and the support they eventually receive from labor and management, councils are as a rule initially resisted by managers, unions, or both. Their emergence and stable performance therefore normally require legal-institutional supports. In Sweden, exceptionally strong unions live with, and indeed prefer, council-like structures based on collective bargaining or employer initiative, operating under no more than a general legal charter for industrial democracy. In Italy, unions and employers were able to agree on a largely voluntary council system, drawing for limited legal support on the statutory rights of union workplace organizations. But these are exceptions, reflecting the extraordinary strength and centralization of unions in Sweden, and union centralization and political multiunionism in Italy. Elsewhere, councils need specific juridical guarantees of their powers.

Fourth, at least in Europe, the union-substitution effect of councils seems small. In France and, to an extent, Spain their introduction coincided with a sharp decline in unionism; the primary causes of this decline, however, appear not to have been the introduction of councils, but the inability of political unionism to adjust to the decline of communist parties. In the Netherlands, union decline in the 1980s is primarily attributed to fast economic and social-structural change. Elsewhere, in countries as diverse as Germany and Italy, councils have helped preserve or increase union strength, by safeguarding the presence of unions in the workplace and enabling unions to represent their members on "qualitative" nonwage matters. And in all European countries— except perhaps Spain, where the distinction between unions and councils is least developed—councils preserve some measure of worker influence in the governance of the workplace even as unions experience difficulty. Under more heavily decentralized and adversarial bargaining systems, like those of Canada and the United States, these results may not hold for general-purpose councils. The Canadian example of limited-purpose committees, however, appears to show little substitution even under "Wagner Act" conditions.

NOTES

1. This chapter summarizes the results of a cross-national study of works councils (the Works Councils Project) that we directed as part of NBER's broader research project, *Working under Different Rules.* For purposes of the study, works councils were defined as any legally based and union-independent (not necessarily nonunion, let alone anti-union) institutions for the collective representation and participation of employees at the workplace. Countries surveyed included Canada, France, Germany, Italy, the Netherlands, Poland, Spain, Sweden, and the United States; in addition, one subproject investigated current efforts in the European Economic Community to institute "European Works Councils," while another sought to build a general model of works councils' economic effects. Research for the project was carried out in 1991 and 1992. The financial support of the NBER, the International Labor Organization in Geneva, the Washington bureau of the Friedrich-Ebert-Stiftung, the German Marshall Fund of the United States, the Hans-Böckler-Stiftung, and the Research Committee of the University of Wisconsin—Madison is gratefully acknowledged.

2. Even in systems classed as "mandate" systems, some expression of employee interest is typically required for their formation.

3. As used here, in reference to the structure of systems with works councils, "information" denotes rights to receive information and obligations to inform. "Consultation" involves obligations, usually for management, to inform before a decision is taken, to wait for a considered response or counterproposal, and to take such a proposal into consid-

eration when deciding the issue. Under joint decision making ("codetermination"), decisions can be made only if they are agreed to by both sides in advance.

4. This claim relies on various polls, including those reported in Gallup (1988), Fingerhut/Powers (1991), Quinn and Staines (1979), Louis Harris and Associates (1984), Davis and Smith (1991), and Farber and Kreuger (1992). See the review in Freeman and Rogers (1993).

5. See the review in Freeman and Rogers (1993).

6. In the case of Denmark and Italy, labor and management are permitted to establish such institutions at their discretion, with a strong presumption against their discontinuance once established.

7. In these areas, councils may refuse consent to an employer action:

   if there is factual reason to assume that the staff movement is likely to result in the dismissal of or other prejudice to employees of the establishment not warranted by operational or personal reasons; [or] if the employee concerned suffers prejudice through the staff movement although this is not warranted by operational or personal reasons (Section 99, Works Constitution Act).

8. Union fears of councils have been strong where unions or collective bargaining are not highly centralized, such as in the United States. Where all or most union functions are performed at the workplace, being crowded out by councils is more of a threat to unions than it is when they have a secure base outside the workplace, in strong territorial or sectoral organizations and in multiemployer bargaining. Also, the dangers of worker identification with the market interests of their employers must appear greater where *bona fide* unionism itself is traditionally workplace-based, making it difficult even for unions to mobilize solidarities that transcend the limits of individual firms.

9. The legislation is also as rarely changed, and practically as difficult to change, as a constitution. For example, the Kohl government, which succeeded the Social-Liberal coalition in 1982, has let its predecessor's entire body of codetermination legislation stand.

10. For a review of the reasons that such an extension might be thought reasonable, see Freeman and Rogers (1993).

11. Some of course would argue that unions should only advance the interests of "vanguard" workers. That councils force unions to make wider policy appeals is one traditional reason radical and communist unions have often opposed them.

12. Typically, the German Works Constitution Act, while guaranteeing the existence of councils by "constitutionalizing" them, also obliges councils and employers to seek and maintain "trustful cooperation."

13. The German Works Constitution Act explicitly makes the state of ergonomic knowledge the criterion for what works councils may demand in job design and work organization.

14. Collusion between employer and works council against government agencies is possible and does occur. But this does not render obsolete the principle that partly opposed interests, if properly mobilized for the purpose, will often serve as checks and balances for each other, enhancing the ability of the third-party state to "make them behave" and act as more perfect agents of the sovereign people.

15. The country summaries and the review of the U.S. and Canadian experiences in North America draw on the following sources: Germany, Müller-Jentsch (1994); Netherlands, Visser (1994); France, Tchobanian (1994); Spain, Escobar (1994); Sweden, Brulin (1994); Italy, Regalia (1994); United States, Rogers and Wootton (1992), Rogers (1994), Freeman and Rogers (1993); Canada, Bernard (1994).

16. There are some analogies here to the present situation in Poland (and perhaps more broadly in Eastern Europe), where councils are performing much the same role, filling a power vacuum left by discredited state managers and weakened unions. See Federowicz and Levitas (1994).

17. This refers to private sector manufacturing and services. There is a parallel system of council representation in the public sector that is not discussed here.

18. Both sides are obliged to consult with each other before they make a decision on labor issues or make their views public. While the law provides mechanisms for outside arbitration of disagreements, all possibilities for a consensual internal solution must be exhausted before matters go to a court.

19. Dutch law is highly flexible with respect to the demarcation of council "bargaining units" in multiplant firms. Whatever solution is adopted, consensus between the work force—represented *de facto* by the unions—and the employer is required.

20. This includes the so-called competitive public sector, that is, the nationalized firms. There are special laws on work force representation in the "noncompetitive" public sector. A little less than one-half of the private and competitive public-sector workforce in France is employed in firms with fifty or more employees.

21. Also because the 1982 laws had made local working time regimes a required subject of collective bargaining. Before that, working time had often been informally negotiated with the works councils.

22. Among unions, support for the Communist CGT (Confédération Générale du Travail) has steadily declined from 40 percent in 1976–77 to 22 percent in 1990–91. Support for the other unions has re-

mained by and large the same, accounting for the fast growth of the nonunion vote.

23. So named after Frederick Taylor, the father of scientific management. Taylorist work organizations typically feature large supervisory forces overseeing a mass of isolated workers performing·repetitive and narrowly defined tasks. See Taylor (1911).

24. One recent reform proposal focuses on firms with fewer than 200 employees. It suggests merging the functions of works councils, employee delegates, and union delegates into one body, a so-called "enterprise council," which would combine consultative and bargaining tasks. This would compensate for the absence of unions and, subsequently, joint regulation in such firms, and would help avoid a dualism in industrial relations under which institutionalized dialogue between employers and workers would be confined to large and unionized firms.

25. Because the Communist union, the CCOO, controlled the councils and its Socialist rival, the UGT, was strong politically but weak at the workplace, setting up union workplace organizations with legal rights and formally centralizing collective bargaining at the multiemployer level would have been a twofold attack on the CCOO—something for which the Socialists and their union allies at the time did not have sufficient clout.

26. Pay bargaining in Sweden was traditionally centralized at the national level. This led to progressive erosion of wage differentials between sectors, firms, and occupational categories—an effect intended by a union movement that has historically emphasized egalitarian values. The egalitarian values, in turn, were seen as incompatible with close attachment of workers to the specific economic fortunes of individual employers.

27. A council is formally certified as a union branch when a "representative" union sends a list of its designated council representatives to the employers' association, which then forwards the list to the employer.

28. However, drawing on the experience of the past decade, the powerful metalworkers union, affiliated with the largest, formerly Communist union federation, CGIL (Confederazione Generale Italiana del Lavoro), is asking that formal codetermination rights for councils be recognized by employers under a national agreement.

29. Section 8(a)(2) of the Labor-Management Relations Act makes it unlawful for an employer to "dominate or interfere with the formation or administration of any labor organization or contribute financial or other support to it." Deliberately, "labor organization" is elsewhere defined broadly to include not only labor unions, but also "any organization of any kind or any agency or employee representa-

tion committee or plan" that features employee participation, or the representation of some employees by others, in dealings with the employer regarding one or more of six traditional subjects of collective bargaining: grievances, labor disputes, wages, rates of pay, hours of employment, and conditions of work.

30. Harris (1982, 138–139) also describes efforts at "progressive" firms—notably U.S. Rubber and General Electric—that were allied with the Committee for Economic Development and the National Planning Association, two industry associations that encouraged labor-management cooperation, to raise productivity through labor-management cooperation.

REFERENCES

Advisory Council on Occupational Health and Occupational Safety (ACOHOS). 1986. *Eighth Annual Report*, April 1, 1985, to March 31, 1986. Vol. 2. Toronto: ACOHOS.

Bagnara, Sabastiano, Raffaello Misiti, and Helmut Wintersberger, eds. 1985. *Work and Health in the 1980s: Experiences of Direct Workers' Participation in Occupational Health*. Berlin: Edition Sigma.

Bernard, Elaine. 1994. "Canada: Joint Committees on Occupational Health and Safety." In J. Rogers and W. Streeck, eds., *Works Councils: Consultation, Representation, Cooperation*. Chicago: University of Chicago Press for NBER. Forthcoming.

Bernstein, Harry. 1991. "Southern California Job Market: Worker Participation Survives Early Woes." *Los Angeles Times*, September 16, p. 15.

Bernstein, Irving. 1970. *The Turbulent Years: A History of the American Worker, 1933–1945*. Boston: Houghton Mifflin.

Blinder, Alan S., ed. 1990. *Paying for Productivity: A Look at the Evidence*. Washington, D.C.: Brookings Institution.

Bok, Derek C., and John T. Dunlop. 1970. *Labor and the American Community*. New York: Simon & Schuster.

Brandes, Stuart. 1976. *American Welfare Capitalism*. Chicago: University of Chicago Press.

Brulin, Göran. 1994. "Sweden: Joint Councils Under Strong Unionism." In J. Rogers and W. Streeck, eds., *Works Councils: Consultation, Representation, Cooperation*. Chicago: University of Chicago Press for NBER. Forthcoming.

Cutcher-Gershenfeld, Joel. 1987. "Collective Governance of Industrial Relations." *Proceedings of the 40th Annual Meeting, Industrial Relations Research Association*. Madison, Wis.: Industrial Relations Research Association. Pp. 533–543.

Cooke, William N. 1990. *Labor-Management Cooperation: New Partnerships or Going in Circles?* Kalamazoo, Mich.: Upjohn Institute for Employment Research.

Davis, James Allan, and Tom W. Smith. 1991. *General Social Surveys, 1972–1991* Machine-readable data file. Chicago: National Opinion Research Center.

de Schweinitz, Dorothea. 1949. *Labor and Management in Common Enterprise.* Cambridge, Mass.: Harvard University Press.

Delaney, John Thomas, David Lewin, and Casey Ichniowski. 1989. *Human Resource Policies and Practices of American Firms.* U.S. Department of Labor, Bureau of Labor-Management Relations and Cooperative Programs, BLMR 137.

Derber, Milton. 1970. *The American Idea of Industrial Democracy, 1865–1965.* Urbana: University of Illinois Press.

Eaton, Adrienne E., and Paula B. Voos. 1992. "Unions and Contemporary Innovations in Work Organization, Compensation, and Employee Participation." In L. Mishel and P. Voos, eds., *Unions and Economic Competitiveness.* Armonk, N.Y.: M. E. Sharpe. Pp. 173-215.

Escobar, Modesto. 1994. "Spain: Works Councils or Unions?" In J. Rogers and W. Streeck, eds., *Works Councils: Consultation, Representation, Cooperation.* Chicago: University of Chicago Press for NBER. Forthcoming.

Farber, Henry, and Alan B. Krueger. 1993. "Union Membership in the United States: The Decline Continues." In M. Kleiner and B. Kaufman, eds., *Employee Representation: Alternatives and Future Directions.* Madison, Wis.: Industrial Relations Research Association.

Federowicz, Michal, and Anthony Levitas. 1994. "Poland: Councils Under Communism and Neo-Liberalism." In J. Rogers and W. Streeck, eds., *Works Councils: Consultation, Representation, Cooperation.* Chicago: University of Chicago Press for NBER. Forthcoming.

Fingerhut/Powers. 1991. "National Labor Poll." Washington, D.C.: Fingerhut/Granados.

Freeman, Richard B., and Edward P. Lazear. 1994. "An Economic Analysis of Works Councils." In J. Rogers and W. Streeck, eds., *Works Councils: Consultation, Representation, Cooperation.* Chicago: University of Chicago Press for NBER. Forthcoming.

Freeman, Richard B., and Joel Rogers. 1993. "Who Speaks for Us? Employee Relations in a Non-Union Labor Market." In M. Kleiner and B. Kaufman, eds., *Employee Representation: Alternatives and Future Directions.* Madison, Wis.: Industrial Relations Research Association.

Gallup Organization (Gallup) 1988. "Public Knowledge and Opinion Concerning the Labor Movement". Princeton: Gallup Organization.

General Accounting Office (GAO). 1992. *Occupational Safety and Health: Worksite Safety and Health Programs Show Promise.* GAO/T-HRD-92-15.

Gustavsen, Bjørn, and Gerry Hunnius. 1981. *New Patterns of Work Reform: The Case of Norway.* Oslo: Universitetsforlaget.

Harris, Howell John. 1982. *The Right to Manage: Industrial Relations Policies of American Business in the 1940s.* Madison, Wis.: University of Wisconsin Press.

Hogler, Raymond L., and Guillermo J. Grenier. 1992. *Employee Participation and Labor Law in the American Workplace.* Westport, Conn.: Quorum Books.

Jacoby, Sanford M. 1989. "Reckoning with Company Unions: The Case of Thornton Products, 1934–1964." *Industrial and Labor Relations Review* 43, no. 1: 19–40.

Jacoby, Sanford M., and Anil Verma. 1992. "Enterprise Unions in the U.S." *Industrial Relations* 31, no. 1: 137–158

Katz, Diane. 1992. "Unions, Employers Watch Case on Labor Management Teams." *Detroit News*, September 1.

Kelley, Maryellen R., and Bennett Harrison. 1992. "Unions, Technology, and Labor Management Cooperation." In L. Mishel and P. Voos, eds., *Unions and Economic Competitiveness.* Armonk, N.Y.: M. E. Sharpe.

Kochan, Thomas A., Harry C. Katz, and Nancy R. Mower. 1984. *Worker Participation and American Unions: Threat or Opportunity?* Kalamazoo, Mich.: Upjohn Institute for Employment Research.

Louis Harris and Associates. 1984. *A Study on the Outlook for Trade Union Organizing.* New York: Louis Harris and Associates.

Millis, Harry, and Royal Montgomery. 1945. *Organized Labor.* New York: McGraw-Hill.

Montgomery, David. 1987. *The Fall of the House of Labor.* Cambridge: Cambridge University Press.

Müller-Jentsch, Walther. 1994. "Germany: From Collective Voice to Co-Management." In J. Rogers and W. Streeck, eds., *Works Councils: Consultation, Representation, Cooperation.* Chicago: University of Chicago Press for NBER. Forthcoming.

National Industrial Conference Board (NICB). 1919. *Works Councils in the United States.* Boston: NICB.

―――. 1922. *Experience with Works Councils in the United States.* New York: Century.

Nelson, Daniel. 1989. "Managers and Unions in the Rubber Industry: Union Avoidance Strategies in the 1930s." *Industrial Relations Research Review* 43, no. 1: 41–52.

————. 1993. "Employee Representation in Historical Perspective." In M. Kleiner and B. Kaufman, eds., *Employee Representation: Alternatives and Future Directions*. Madison, Wis.: Industrial Relations Research Association.

Quinn, Robert P., and Graham L. Staines. 1979. *The 1977 Quality of Employment Survey: Descriptive Statistics with Comparison Data from the 1969–70 and 1972–73 Surveys*. Ann Arbor, Mich.: Institute for Social Research.

Rees, Joseph. 1988. *Reforming the Workplace: A Study of Self-Regulation in Occupational Safety*. Philadelphia: Temple University Press.

Regalia, Ida. 1994. "Italy: The Costs and Benefits of Informality." In J. Rogers and W. Streeck, eds., *Works Councils: Consultation, Representation, Cooperation*. Chicago: University of Chicago Press for NBER. Forthcoming.

Regalia, Ida, and R. Ronchi. 1988, 1992. "Le relazioni industriali nelle imprese lombarde." *Annual Report*. Milan: IRES Papers.

Rogers, Joel. 1994. "The United States: Lessons from Abroad and Home." In J. Rogers and W. Streeck, eds., *Works Councils: Consultation, Representation, Cooperation*. Chicago: University of Chicago Press for NBER. Forthcoming.

Rogers, Joel, and Barbara Wootton. 1992. "Works Councils in the United States: Could We Get There from Here?" Paper delivered to the Works Councils Project summary conference. Geneva, May.

Taylor, Frederick W. 1911. *The Principles of Scientific Management*. NY: Harper and Bros.

Tchobanian, Robert. 1994. "France: From Conflict to Social Dialogue?" In J. Rogers and W. Streeck, eds., *Works Councils: Consultation, Representation, Cooperation*. Chicago: University of Chicago Press for NBER. Forthcoming.

Visser, Jelle. 1991. "Trends in Trade Union Membership," *OECD Employment Outlook* (July): 97-134.

————. 1994. "The Netherlands: From Paternalism to Representation." In J. Rogers and W. Streeck, eds., *Works Councils: Consultation, Representation, Cooperation*. Chicago: University of Chicago Press for NBER. Forthcoming.

Weiler, Paul C. 1990. *Governing the Workplace: The Future of Labor and Employment Law*. Cambridge, Mass.: Harvard University Press.

Wilcock, Richard C. 1957. "Industrial Management's Policies toward Unionism," In M. Derber and E. Young, eds., *Labor and the New Deal*. Madison, Wis.: University of Wisconsin Press. Pp. 275–315.

Williams, Karen. 1988. *Industrial Relations and the German Model*. Avebury, England: Aldershot.

5

DOES A LARGER
SOCIAL SAFETY NET MEAN
LESS ECONOMIC FLEXIBILITY?

Rebecca Blank

H igher employment growth and lower unemployment in the
United States than in Western Europe in the 1980s generated
widespread discussion of the employment problems potentially
caused by government social protection programs. The U.S.
economy has long been characterized by limited state welfare
programs and a relatively unregulated labor market, while Western European countries have had extensive social protection programs for workers and a highly regulated labor market. Following
the recession in 1981 and 1982, the United States experienced
strong job growth, while Western Europe's record of job growth
was poor (see Chapter 1, this volume). Many analysts and policymakers interpreted these patterns to mean that Europe's labor
market regulations and income support programs were harmful to
job growth. This chapter investigates the argument that social
protection programs have sizable adverse effects on labor market
flexibility. Is there evidence of a trade-off between social protection
and employment flexibility?

This chapter uses the results of new NBER-sponsored research on social programs in seven advanced economies to
assess the protection-flexibility trade-off. All of the studies take
the United States as a benchmark and thus examine overseas
programs relative to American programs.[1] The primary con-

clusion from these studies and related work is that while the design of social programs affects employer and worker behavior, these programs do not create major inflexibilities in the labor market. Whether social programs are judged as successful or unsuccessful should depend on how effectively they deal with the problems they are designed to address, not on their seemingly modest effects on labor market flexibility and long-run unemployment.

SOCIAL PROTECTION VERSUS ECONOMIC FLEXIBILITY

The terms *social protection* and *economic flexibility* are often used loosely in discourse. One person's social protection is another's giveaway or poverty trap. One person's economic flexibility is another's loss of livelihood.

By social protection programs I refer broadly to government-sponsored programs to protect individual workers or families from significant income declines or job loss. These include income transfer programs that lift families out of poverty and in-kind programs such as housing and health insurance that assure access to particular goods or services, as well as social insurance programs that cushion workers against unemployment, disability, and old age. These programs also include employment regulations that provide job security or that mandate employer payments toward fringe benefits, such as social security and health care. In general, the United States has fewer such programs and regulations, and those that it does have are more limited than similar programs in Western Europe.

Employment flexibility is harder to define, because of the many margins along which economic agents can be flexible. The most common usage refers to the speed of labor market adjustment in a changing economic environment. The flexible market is one in which firms adjust wages rapidly to accomodate price changes or unemployment; firms alter employment or work hours quickly when labor demand changes; and workers move smoothly from unemployment to employment and across sectors or geographic areas as labor demands shift. The employment growth in the United States over the past decade is cited by many observers as an indication that the United States has a flexible economy that adjusts quickly to economic change.

Employment flexibility is also used, however, to refer to workplace programs and institutions that promote the long-term productivity growth of the workforce, such as worker training, even though these programs may keep workers from making short-term adjustments, such as changing jobs or moving in or out of the labor force. The success of Japan, in particular, has been ascribed to this type of flexibility—what Ronald Dore described as the Japanese pattern of "flexible rigidities" (Dore, 1986). In comparison with the United States, Japanese employers and workers are inflexible along some dimensions—labor turnover, for instance, is extraordinarily low—but are more flexible along other dimensions such as wage determination.

Initially those claiming that social protection adversely affected employment in Western Europe argued that protective programs limited short-run wage and employment adjustments in the face of macroeconomic shocks. As high unemployment persisted, however, the argument changed. Labor market flexibility was said to determine not just the speed of recovery from recession but also to be necessary for reducing long-term unemployment and restoring growth (Lawrence and Schultze, 1987; Boyer, 1988; Dréze and Bean, 1990; OECD, 1990). From this perspective, social protection programs that created inflexibility had long-run and persistent harmful effects on the economy.

DEBATING THE TRADE-OFF

The claim that protective government regulations reduce flexibility derives from the fear that they induce people to engage in economically inefficient behavior. The following are some illustrative types of social programs that might create "inflexibility" in the labor market and unintentionally promote high unemployment.[2]

1. *Legislation that limits employers' ability to hire or fire workers in the face of short-run shocks.* Employment protection laws presumably make it more expensive to hire new workers, since firms cannot easily dismiss them later. Firms may therefore limit employment growth during economic expansions.

2. *Income protection, such as unemployment insurance payments or welfare programs, that provides workers with income support.* Paying support to people when they don't work may reduce the intensity of their job search and lead them to remain jobless longer than they would have been otherwise.[3]

3. *A minimum wage or centralized wage setting that raises the wage of the less skilled.* When less skilled workers become more expensive, employers may be unwilling to hire them or to invest in sectors or technologies that employ them.

4. *Mandated social security taxes or household leave policies that raise the cost of labor.* Forcing employers to pay for mandated fringe benefits increases compensation costs and reduces the demand for labor.

5. *Housing support or employer-based health insurance that ties people to a given area or job.* If workers lose subsidies or benefits when they move, this will reduce their willingness to respond to changing market opportunities.

In addition to these program-induced inefficiencies, social protection programs can also have sizable opportunity costs in the form of taxes to fund the programs and public-sector personnel to implement them. Most government programs create some "excess burden" through the tax system or budget deficits. In addition, most social programs expand public-sector employment. If the public-sector labor market is less responsive to changes in economic conditions than the private sector, its expansion will further add to economic rigidities.

There is also the possibility that income support programs may change individual preferences by creating "dependency." If attitudes toward work and work habits are malleable, programs that induce people to remain out of the labor market may permanently shift their preferences toward greater leisure and away from work, resulting in lower labor market involvement even after the transfer program comes to an end. In a worst-case scenario, income protection programs that enable people to remain jobless for an extended period might permanently raise long-term unemployment. This would occur if workers' skills deteriorated, if they took underground-economy jobs in conjunction with unemployment benefits, or if their work discipline declined as the duration of joblessness increased.

The argument that social protection programs reduce market flexibility and contribute to unemployment is a plausible one, but many are not convinced that this argument is sufficient or even that it is correct. Defenders of social protection programs respond to these criticisms in several ways. Some admit that social programs might affect behavior in costly ways but assert that the benefits of the programs exceed the costs. To judge a social program one must, after all, measure benefits as well as costs, which critics almost never do. Social programs are designed to increase social well-being by increasing worker's security in the face of economic change, unemployment, sickness, and aging. Many supporters of the welfare state argue that the inefficiency costs of these programs are well worth the substantial gains in well-being among citizens that these programs provide.

Other supporters of social programs point out that even if the programs create one-time efficiency losses, these need not reduce growth rates. In other words, programs may reduce the pie available for investment but leave unaltered the share of savings and investment in national output, and thus the rate of economic growth as well.

Supporters of social programs often note that many critics posit a "counterfactual" world for assessing program inefficiencies in which, absent social protection, the economy would operate as an ideal, perfectly competitive system. This may be a questionable assumption, given the many overlapping constraints from tax laws, trade and legal regulations, and complex institutional structures. Some social programs may offset the inefficiencies and distortions caused by other political or economic constraints. For instance, if collective bargaining requires firms to lay off younger workers before older workers, employment protection laws that mandate four months' notification before a layoff may bring the employment outcome for younger workers closer to the competitive outcome. The effects of any program must be analyzed in the context of the economic system in which it fits rather than as an isolated change in an otherwise ideal competitive world.

Finally, many proponents of social protection programs stress that these programs enhance human capital and productivity in the labor market and that their net effect is to increase the potential for economic growth, not to decrease it. Programs that make it difficult for firms to fire workers create incentives for employers to invest in training. Maternity leave programs that allow women to keep their job while away from the labor market for child rearing might increase the long-term self-efficacy of the child, give those women a chance to acquire additional training, or induce firms to maintain a flexible employment structure that allows women to leave and return. Social assistance programs aimed at children and teenagers, such as health care programs, child allowances, or educational assistance, may improve the health or emotional well-being of those children, resulting in lower future social expenditures and higher future productivity.

SO WHO IS RIGHT?

Following the recession in 1981 and 1982, as the U.S. economy grew and European economies seemed to lag, criticism swelled against the more extended European social protection programs. The claim that flexibility is necessary for employment creation led the Organization for Economic Cooperation and Development (OECD) and many governments to endorse policies to increase flexibility and reform social insurance programs and labor market regulations (see Table 5.1). France decentralized collective bargaining, as did the Netherlands and Spain. Italy eliminated automatic wage indexing. Virtually all European countries expanded training targeted at unemployed workers. France tried work sharing. Germany and Spain introduced short-term employment contracts as an alternative to "standard" employment contracts that made it costly for firms to displace workers once hired. A wave of privatization reduced governments' share of employment throughout Europe, led by the United Kingdom's efforts to weaken trade unions and deregulate the economy. Some countries cut unemployment benefits and social protection expenditures. By the end of the 1980s, most Western European countries had less state involvement in labor market outcomes, less centralized labor relations, and more limited transfer programs than a decade earlier.

If cutting back labor market regulations and social protection programs were enough to restore full employment, by the early 1990s Europe should have shown much better job growth than a decade earlier. For a brief period, efforts to increase flexibility seemed to move some economies in the right direction. Unemployment fell in Spain as fixed-term contracts replaced permanent employment. Prime Minister Thatcher bragged that Britain was developing an economic model for the world. But the reduction in social protection did not prevent the recession of the early 1990s. Spanish and British unemployment rose sharply. The claim that labor regulations and social insurance programs were the root of Europe's problems could no longer be as easily made.[4]

Table 5.1 Sample Policy Changes Implemented Over the 1980s to Increase Labor Market Flexibility in Europe

Belgium
  Expanded short-time unemployment benefits
  Created programs to assist temporary work placements
  Weakened dismissal laws
France
  Increased decentralization in bargaining
  Weakened dismissal laws
  Increased training for long-term unemployed
  Decreased work week
Germany
  Weakened dismissal laws
  Increased incentives for early retirement
  Made changes in unemployment benefit laws
  Increased training for long-term unemployed
  Decreased work week
Italy
  Eliminated automatic wage indexation
Netherlands
  Decentralized wage agreements
  Lowered relative minimum wage
  Created programs to assist temporary work placements
  Tightened limits on unemployment benefit receipt
  Increased training for long-term unemployed
Spain
  Decentralized wage agreements
  Decreased work week
  Increased training and job creation for long-term unemployed
  Increased availability of part-time and short-term work
Sweden
  Increased training and job search requirements for those receiving
  unemployment benefits
United Kingdom
  Implemented privatization of major government-owned industries
  Decentralized wage agreements
  Weakened dismissal laws
  Tightened limits on unemployment benefit receipt
  Increased training for long-term unemployed

SOURCE: OECD, 1990.

At the same time, the U.S. model began to seem less attractive. Accumulating evidence indicated that the rapid job growth of the 1980s had occurred along with rapidly widening wage inequality (see Chapter 2, this volume). The recession of the early 1990s led to higher U.S. unemployment and a sluggish U.S. economy that did not seem to recover any more rapidly than the European economies.

Assessing the magnitude of the social protection-flexibility trade-off and its contribution to the different employment growth records of Europe and the United States in the 1980s requires more thoughtful analysis, not just sweeping interpretations of aggregate economic outcomes. Studies of particular social protection programs are needed that estimate the magnitude of undesirable responses to social programs, the cost of those responses in terms of efficiency and employment generation, and the social cost of the resources needed for the programs to operate.

The new NBER-sponsored research mentioned at the beginning of this chapter focuses largely on the first two issues.[5] The studies contrast specific social protection programs in European countries and Japan with programs in the United States and examine the effect of weakening social protection in Europe in the 1980s on the flexibility of European labor markets. For clarity, I will group this research into three categories: studies of programs affecting employer flexibility, studies of programs affecting worker mobility, and studies of programs affecting labor market participation. The results of these studies are summarized in Table 5.5.

LABOR REGULATIONS AND EMPLOYER FLEXIBILITY

Social programs that provide employment protection may reduce the ability of employers to respond to a changing economic environment. In this section I will discuss three studies that look at employment protection laws; mandated employer taxes to support health benefits; and institutions that govern wage setting and hiring and firing within the public sector.

Do Employment Protection Laws Limit Employer Flexibility?

In the early 1970s many European countries strengthened their requirements for advance notice and negotiated compensation packages to protect workers suddenly threatened by mass layoffs and plant closings.[6] These programs were intended to slow the employment decline that occurs during an economic downturn, but they should also limit employment growth in a boom, as firms will be reluctant to hire workers who will be costly to fire. As a result, countries with strong job security legislation should have less cyclical employment than the United States, which had no advance notice or severance pay requirements during this period.[7]

Often countries that adopt strong employment protection policies adopt other policies that encourage firms to make adjustments in hours of work. Germany and France, for instance, which have particularly strong employment protection policies, provide partial wage replacement to workers whose hours have been reduced because of slack demand. The United States, in contrast, does not assure short-time benefits to workers whose hours are reduced, although some states allow short-time benefits as part of their state unemployment insurance system. If European firms are restricted in their employment adjustments but encouraged to make greater adjustments in work hours, the result might be that total labor adjustment in European countries is differently distributed between employment and hours than it is in the United States.

To determine the effects of employment policies, Katherine Abraham and Susan Houseman have compared the relationship between changes over time in output and employment in the United States and in three European countries with strong employment protection laws: France, Germany, and Belgium. These comparisons show that while both employment and hours are highly cyclical in the United States, in Belgium and Germany hours are more cyclical than employment.[8] They also show that employment in the United States adjusts more quickly when demand changes than does employment in Germany, France, or Belgium, but hours adjust at about the same speed in Germany, Belgium, and the United States. This indicates that hours adjustment is a more important component in aggregate labor adjustment (hours adjustment plus employment adjustment) in these European countries, but it also indicates that the aggregate labor market response to demand changes in these European countries is slower than in the United States.

If employment protection regulations were a major cause of slower labor market adjustments, loosening these regulations ought to produce greater employment responses to given shocks in output. As European unemployment remained high in the 1980s, several countries loosened their employment protection regulations. Germany, which had strict rules on advance notice and severance arrangements from 1972 through 1985, loosened them in 1985. France required authorization and consultation for mass dismissals between 1975 and 1986, but eased these rules in 1987. Belgium reduced its advanced notice and compensation rules in 1985. All of these countries also had short-time benefits available for workers whose work time was reduced.

Table 5.2 compares the speed of employment adjustments—measured by the lag, in months, of change in employment to a given change in output—in Germany, France, and Belgium before and after changes in the stringency of job protection laws. When employment responds quickly to a given change in output, the lag will be short; when it responds slowly the lag will be longer. The loosening of the employment security laws in the mid-1980s had no noticeable effect on the average monthly lag. If weakening employment security provisions had little effect on the speed of employment adjustment in Europe, it is hard to see how those provisions could be a prime cause of the slower employment adjustment in Europe than in the United States.

Why do employment protection laws not have the adverse effects that their critics expected? One possibility is that the laws were not binding for most firms: other constraints, such as collec-

Table 5.2   Mean Lag (in months) of Employment Adjustment to Output Change in Manufacturing

	Prior to Easing Severance Restrictions (in months)	After Easing Severance Restrictions (in months)
Germany	4.8	6.4
France	8.7	8.1
Belgium	4.9	6.5

SOURCE: Calculated from Abraham and Houseman, 1994 (Table 6A).
NOTES:
German data are quarterly from 72:1–90:4. Laws changed prior to 85:2.
French data are quarterly from 75:1–91:1. Laws changed prior to 87:1.
Belgian data are quarterly from 73:1–90:4. Laws changed prior to 85:1.

tive bargaining and works councils, have been more important in limiting employment adjustment than job security provisions have been.[9] Another possibility is that employers adapted their labor policies to the strong job security regimes by using hours adjustments rather than employment adjustments over the business cycle, and when those job security regimes were changed, employers saw no reason to change their behavior. A third explanation is that employers used side payments (in the form of agreed-upon training and social expenditures for laid-off workers) to gain the adjustments they desired even when the regulations were in place.[10]

Whichever explanation has more validity, strong job security provisions may be compatible with labor market flexibility. This is a different sort of flexibility than that in the United States, however, with more emphasis on hours adjustment and less on employment adjustment. One effect of adjusting through hours rather than employment is that the costs of an economic downturn are spread more broadly among workers.

Do Mandated Fringe Costs Limit Employer Flexibility?

Employers in the United States pay about 11 percent of wages toward required public benefit programs, such as social security and unemployment insurance; on average, they pay another 12 percent in "voluntary fringes" toward private health, disability, and pension benefits.[11] In contrast, employers in Europe have much higher rates of mandated employer spending for fringe benefits, due to more generous and extensive mandated benefits.

Spain is representative of Europe in this regard. In Spain fringe benefits, including health insurance, are publicly provided and supported through a mandatory social security tax per worker. Employers pay 29 percent of wages toward this tax. These high mandatory tax rates create incentives for workers and firms to strike deals that allow firms to hire the workers "off the books." Since enforcement of the payment for social security and related fringes is weak and fines for noncompliance are not punitive, Spain in effect "allows" many firms to evade these laws through the underground economy. If workers are hired off the books, they will not receive a social security card, which they need to gain access to the national health care system. But since care is provided to all members of a workers' family, those who have working spouses can receive insurance through their spouse. In 1985, 12 percent of all workers reported that they avoided social security taxes. Almost all of these workers reported themselves covered by health insurance through another worker.

Most criticisms of mandatory social protection legislation assume that enforcement is effective. But if noncompliance is possible, as in Spain, the workers and firms who find these mandates most costly will avoid government regulations, thereby creating greater economic flexibility. Research by Sara de la Rica and Thomas Lemieux indicates that workers and firms who evade the mandates in Spain are similar to the workers and firms in the United States who do not have employer-based health insurance; those for whom social security taxes are paid resemble Americans who obtain health insurance through their employers. In Spain, as in the United States, married men in full-time jobs, who have longer tenure, higher wages, and more education, and those working in industries with a high value added per worker and high unionization rates are more likely to get health insurance through their employer. Thus, although the institutional systems governing health care are different, similar groups of workers remain uncovered.

The implication is that the provision of health insurance by American firms and Spanish firms reflects similar labor demand and supply factors. The possibility of noncompliance in Spain produces a market outcome that resembles the outcome in the United States. The implications of these two systems for workers' well-being are very different, however. Virtually all uncovered Spanish workers have a working spouse who is covered by the system, which means that no one goes uninsured. This is not true for all uncovered American workers. For instance, 13 percent of employed married women in the United States do not get health insurance from either their own or their spouse's employer. The implication of these findings is not that the United States should be lax in enforcing compliance with mandatory laws, but rather that the operation of such mandatory laws may create much less employment inflexibility than initially appears to occur, depending on the way in which the laws are implemented and enforced.

Does Public Sector Employment Limit Labor Market Flexibility?

Expansions of social protection programs almost inevitably increase public-sector employment, as government workers are needed to implement and oversee the programs.[12] In the 1980s politicians in the United States and in several other countries launched strong attacks on public-sector bureaucracy. Many European countries privatized large sectors of their economies in the hope of increasing efficiency and flexibility; under Prime Minister Thatcher the United Kingdom was a world leader in the move to reduce public employment and privatize major industries (Kay et al., 1986). If employment and wages in the public sector were less responsive to changes in output, reducing the public share of employment would increase labor market flexibility. My own research on this issue, however, indicates that there appears to be only modest differences in responsiveness between the public and private sectors in the United Kingdom and in the United States, which has a much smaller public sector relative to its overall economy. In the United Kingdom, both the public and the private sectors are less responsive to economic growth than they are in the United States.

In the United States, public-sector workers have distinct characteristics. They are more likely to be female, well educated, older, and nonwhite, and to work in selected white-collar occupations that range from public schoolteacher, to clerical worker, to police officer, to judge and legislator. Federal employees in the United States earn, on average, more than private employees with similar background characteristics. The more numerous state and local public employees, however, are paid less than similar private employees. Public employees in Britain are also disproportionately female, well educated, nonwhite, and working in white-collar jobs. They are more likely to be part-time, as well. Compared with private employees with equivalent characteristics, British public employees earn more.

The structure of wages in the public sector differs from that in the private sector in similar ways in the United Kingdom and United States. In the late 1980s, senior managers and professionals earned less in the public sector than in the private sector in both countries, while manual workers earned more in the public sector, though their relative advantage over private-sector workers declined during the decade. Women have larger wage advantages in the public sector than men, although for them, too, the differences shrank over the 1980s.

Are employment and wages more rigid in the public sector than in the private sector, or do the two sectors show similar patterns of change in response to economic shocks? As chapter 2 of this volume documents, the wage distribution in both the United States and United Kingdom widened greatly in the 1980s. In the United Kingdom the distribution of public-sector wages widened as much as the distribution of private-sector wages. In the United States, however, the private-sector widening was greater. The British public sector was, by this metric, more "responsive" than the American public sector. In both countries in the 1980s, public-sector wages became more aligned with private-sector wages. In the United Kingdom, the difference in pay between the two groups shrank from 14 percent to 11 percent by 1987. In the United States, pay differentials between federal and private workers remained about constant, but state and local workers moved closer to parity with the private sector. Overall, U.S. public-sector workers were earning 3 percent more than private workers by 1989.

In both countries, public-sector employment and wages vary over time as much as private-sector employment and wages, although the timing of the changes differs between the sectors in both countries. Public-sector employment and wages move less with the business cycle than private-sector employment. If public-sector demand for labor does not move cyclically, however, there is no reason for public-sector employment or wages to move cyclically. In both the United States and the United Kingdom, changes in government output have little long-run effect on public-sector employment. But in the United States, increases in private gross national product (GNP) increase public- and private-sector employment, whereas in the United Kingdom increases in private GNP increase private employment but have few effects on public employment. Whether this indicates less flexibility in the United Kingdom is unclear.

In sum, changes in the size of the public sector will affect the level of demand for workers with particular characteristics and skills, but will have no major effect on the variability of changes in wages or employment. Public-sector employment and wages move differently than private-sector wages and employment, but they are not inflexible. The belief that public-sector employment is rigid and unresponsive to demand changes is not correct, or at least it was not correct in the United States and the United Kingdom in the 1980s.

SOCIAL PROTECTION PROGRAMS AND LABOR MOBILITY

Programs that give people benefits at their current residence or workplace can reduce labor mobility, whereas programs that decrease the cost of moving can increase mobility. This section covers three studies that look at rental and housing subsidies, employer health benefits, and worker relocation assistance.

Does Housing Policy Affect Worker Mobility?

Most governments intervene in housing markets through tax laws, building codes, rent subsidies, subsidized housing construction, and tenant protection.[13] These policies are designed to provide protection for and increase the well-being of renters and homeowners, but they may also limit labor mobility. Laws that protect tenants from large rent increases, for example, ought to produce a "discount" for sitting tenants compared with new tenants, reducing the incentive to move and thus decreasing residential and job mobility. Laws that encourage homeownership are also likely to lower mobility.

German housing policy provides a good example of strong tenant protection laws, as research by Axel Börsch-Supan indicates. Laws introduced in 1971 (and weakened in 1983 and 1987) make it difficult to increase rents on sitting tenants but do not regulate starting rents. As a result initial rents are high in Germany, and sitting tenants pay less than new tenants for equivalent housing: after fourteen years in a rental unit, for example, a tenant pays 19 to 29 percent less than a new tenant would pay for an equivalent unit. Such a discount provides a substantial incentive against mobility for long-term renters. In contrast, the United States has few cities with rent control or tenant protection legislation and thus ought to have lower discounts for sitting tenants and higher mobility. On average Germans do have lower mobility than Americans, and German renters have lower mobility than American renters. German tenant protection laws must, therefore, be a major deterrent to mobility.

Case closed? No. There are three problems with this argument. First, rental discounts for sitting tenants are as large in the United States as they are in Germany, and they are virtually the same in American cities without rent control as in cities with rent control. Discounts in the rental price for long-standing tenants primarily reflect the structure of the rental market, where sitting tenants are viewed more favorably by landlords, not rent control laws. Second, changes in German mobility do not match changes in German tenancy laws. Mobility declined in the early 1970s, when the rental protection law was first implemented, but declined even further in the 1980s, when the law was being weakened. Third, Japan has housing laws that are much stricter than Germany's, and yet residential mobility in Japan is greater than in Germany.

Homeowner subsidies are another major government intervention designed to improve households' well-being. The United States has historically had high homeowner subsidies imbedded in its tax system. In the 1980s Germany expanded its tax advantages for homeowners so that for some groups of families subsidies came to be larger than those in the United States. Japan's tax and loan programs also provide large subsidies homeowners.

Homeowner subsidies increase homeownership. The biggest increase in homeownership in Germany occurred among those families who had large increases in their homeowner subsidies. Similarly, simulations of the effects of the U.S. tax laws in Germany indicate that differences in homeowner taxes are a major reason for the differences in homeownership rates between the two countries.

Homeownership and labor market mobility correlate within countries. Homeowners have much lower rates of mobility than nonhomeowners in both the United States and Germany. For example, in Germany renters have an annual mobility rate of 9.0 percent, while homeowners have an annual mobility rate of 3.4 percent. To the extent that homeowner subsidies encourage more homeownership, this may decrease labor mobility. Cross-national mobility rates are not dominated by this effect, however (Table 5.3). Homeownership rates in the United States and Japan are 64 percent and 62 percent, while they are only 39 percent in Germany. Nevertheless, 18 percent of U.S. households move every year, while 10 percent of Japanese households move and only 7 percent of German households move. Thus, contrary to what one might predict, the country with the lowest homeownership level has the lowest

Table 5.3 Housing and Labor Market Indicators Across Countries

	Germany	Japan	United States
Tenant Protection Laws	Law restricts eviction and limits rent increases.	All changes in rent contracts subject to "just clause" claim in court.	Some local jurisdictions have limited laws.
Homeowner Subsidies	Depreciation and some mortgage interest deductible from income tax. (Subsidy small in past but growing.)	Mortgage interest subsidies plus small tax credit. (Subsidy quite large.)	Mortgage interest and property tax deductible from income tax. (Subsidy currently smaller than in Germany or Japan.)
Homeownership Rates (%)	39.3	62.1	64.0
Mobility Rates[a]			
Home owners	3.4	3.6	8.5
Renters	9.0	19.6	37.5
Total Population	6.6	9.6	17.6

SOURCE: Börsch-Supan, 1994 (Tables 5, 7, 16).

[a] Percent of households that have moved within past 12 months.

mobility rate, while the country with the highest homeownership has the highest mobility rate.

The bottom line is that housing market regulations have a substantial impact on the mode of housing (rental or ownership), but they have at most modest secondary effects on national labor mobility.

Does Employer-based Health Insurance Limit Worker Mobility?

The standard view of mandated workplace benefits is that they create rigidity, but this need not always be true.[14] Consider the different effects of health insurance mandated of all employers and health insurance that is voluntarily provided or negotiated by employers, as in the United States. Since the American system of employer-provided health care is employer-specific, it can interfere with the smooth functioning of the labor market by creating "job lock." Workers, who in an ideal world should shift employers, might be discouraged from changing jobs by the fear that such a change could interrupt or terminate health insurance.

At first blush, comparisons by Douglas Holtz-Eakin of job changes among American workers with and without health coverage show substantial job lock. Twenty-six percent of married workers who are insured on their job change jobs in three years, compared with 37 percent of those who are uninsured. But persons who are insured differ from the uninsured in important ways: the uninsured are more likely to be women, working for a lower wage, with less experience, and in occupations and industries where mobility is likely to be high. Taking account of these characteristics in fact eliminates the relationship between health insurance coverage and mobility. There is no evidence of significant job lock among married or single workers with comparable characteristics. Even workers in poorer health or with larger families are no less likely to change jobs if they are insured than if they are not insured.

Germany has a different health insurance system. All workers have health care through insurance funds, but some of these funds are localized. When German workers change jobs, about 50 percent must change insurance funds. Those who change funds can face a change in the price they pay and thus may be deterred from changing jobs. While job changes in Germany are quite infrequent compared with the United States, workers with local coverage who face potential insurance price changes are less likely to change jobs than those who are covered by one of the national insurance funds. Comparisons of workers with the same demographic and job characteristics show, in contrast to the United States, modestly lower job changes for workers who are likely to change insurance funds when they change jobs.

Looking across countries, the difference between the health insurance programs of the United States and Germany ought to produce lower mobility in the United States than in Germany, but this is not the case. These very different health insurance systems do not appear to have major effects on labor market mobility. This implies that the health care systems should be judged on their primary effects on access to health care and on the efficiency and quality of health care they provide, not on their secondary effects on labor mobility.

Is Regional Mobility Necessary for Economic Growth?

Many analysts believe that regional mobility within a country is an important ingredient in economic flexibility.[15] In a dynamic economy some regions invariably grow while others decline. This should induce interregional labor and capital flows, and these movements should help to maintain full employment and optimize resource allocation. Is interregional mobility high in Japan, the economy that has performed the best by many criteria since the 1973 oil shock?

Japan has a set of policies to enhance mobility. The Japanese public employment service runs an extensive job search assistance program. Relocation assistance is available to workers and to firms through the unemployment insurance system, and there are bonuses for unemployed workers who enter training or find jobs quickly. In contrast, the United States provides limited relocation assistance, and its system of state employment agencies does not coordinate across regions and is used relatively infrequently by firms seeking workers.

Regional migration rates in both countries respond to economic forces: migration into a region rises with high employment growth in that region; it declines when unemployment increases (in the United States) and when regional housing prices rise (in Japan). The overall level of migration is lower in Japan, however. Despite policies to increase regional mobility, migration across prefectures in Japan is less than half the 6.5 percent migration rate between counties in the United States.[16] There is a certain degree of interprefectural commuting that substitutes for migration; commuting patterns are affected by economic forces in the same way as mobility.

Unemployment rates and rates of economic growth by region show greater persistence across Japanese prefectures over time than across American states. A Japanese prefecture that has above-average unemployment in one year is more likely to have above-average unemployment in another year than is a U.S. state with above-average unemployment. While regional differences in wages are less persistent over time in Japan than in the United States, this is due more to demand-influenced wage setting than to the effect of regional flows of labor: in Japan regional employment growth is associated with higher prefectural wages, whereas in the United States employment growth is greater in states with lower wages. While there are similarities in the pattern of regional wages in Japan and the United States—high-unemployment regions have lower wages in both countries, as they do in other countries (Blanchflower and Oswald, 1993)—on net the Japanese labor market is less flexible across geographic regions than the American labor market. Yet Japan has an admirable economic record, with exceptionally low unemployment. High regional migration rates are clearly not a prerequisite for economic success, as this comparison indicates.

INCOME SUPPORT PROGRAMS AND LABOR PARTICIPATION

Programs that provide income support to nonworkers may reduce the supply of labor by increasing the length and frequency of either spells of unemployment or time out of the labor market. This section looks at three studies that investigate income support programs for women and children, maternity leave and childcare policies, and pension programs for elderly workers.

Do Time-Limited Welfare Payments Increase Labor Force Participation?

Income transfer programs for low-income single mothers exist in all industrialized countries, but the magnitude of support offered and the design of the programs differs.[17] In the United States a key issue is the extent to which welfare payments keep women out of the labor market by giving them income and benefits, including health care, that they would lose by working. Various reforms, including limiting the time over which welfare payments are made, have been proposed to encourage welfare mothers to work.

French income support programs offer a distinct "experiment" with which to evaluate time-limited welfare payments, as research by Maria Hanratty indicates. Single-parent families in France receive assistance in several ways. For women with children under the age of three, benefits are between $1,300 and $4,700 greater than what similar women in the United States could receive in public support. After the youngest child reaches age three, however, French mothers' benefits become less generous than those in the United States. Married mothers with three or more children who quit work for the birth of a child also receive a special allowance until their youngest child turns three (or until they reenter the labor force, whichever occurs first). In addition, public nursery school is available in France. Virtually 100 percent of children age three and older attend public nursery school. This substantially decreases the cost of childcare for mothers with preschoolers.

The reduction in welfare payments when children reach age three and the availability of subsidized daycare at that age are associated with increased work activity by single mothers in France. Employment of single mothers with preschoolers over age three is substantially greater than employment of those with preschoolers under age three, and more women with children three and older choose full-time work than choose part-time work.

Is this pattern due to time-limited welfare? One way to tell is to contrast the behavior of single mothers in France with single mothers in America, where welfare payments are not time limited. The increase in labor activity when children pass age three is greater among French single mothers than among single mothers in the United States. But American mothers do not have free public preschool available for their three-year-olds. A better comparison may be between French single mothers and French married mothers. Single mothers in France increase their labor force participation when their children reach age three more than married mothers do, largely because more single mothers move from part-time to full-time work. Married women with three or more children increase both their labor force participation and their rate of full-time work when their assistance is cut.

In France, limiting the duration of welfare payments seems to increase women's labor market involvement. But the availability of all-day public schooling for three-year-olds in France reinforces this policy and produces a much stronger effect than would occur in the United States, where free public daycare is not available.

Do Childcare and Maternal Leave Policies Affect Labor Market Participation?

The United States provides little public support for women who have children, except those with very low incomes.[18] It has no program for paid maternity leave and little publicly funded daycare. Many European countries have more extensive maternity leave policies and more publicly available childcare than the United States. For instance, Sweden has a set of universally available and generous childcare policies. A working parent who has a child can claim up to 30 months of maternity leave at 90 percent of her previous earnings, while publicly provided childcare is available after parental leave, on a needs-based payment scale. Support for nonworking parents in Sweden is much lower. The Netherlands, on the other hand, encourages women to stay home with their children. It provides little public daycare and offers few incentives for women to enter the labor force.

These differences in policy are associated with substantial differences in family behavior, as research by Siv Gustafsson and Frank Stafford demonstrates (see Table 5.4). In the United States, female labor-force participation is high. Many working mothers return to work almost immediately after a child is born. In Sweden more than 75 percent of the mothers of older preschool children work and they make heavy use of the public daycare system, but labor force participation among mothers with children under age one is lower, as these women take advantage of the extensive maternity leave provisions. The Netherlands has relatively low labor-force participation rates among all young mothers. In the United States, where wages among young women are much higher for those with more experience, the high returns on labor market experience encourage mothers to return to work quickly and to remain in the labor market over their lifetime. Similarly, other

Table 5.4   Employment of Mothers, by Age of Youngest Child

Age of Youngest Child (yr)	Mothers Not in Labor Force (%)	Mothers Working Part-time (%)	Mothers Working Full-time (%)
Sweden			
< 1	58.8	19.2	22.1
1 – 1.99	20.4	69.4	10.2
2 – 3.99	23.9	59.4	16.8
Netherlands			
< 1	74.4	22.2	3.5
1 – 1.99	78.0	20.4	1.7
2 – 3.99	73.2	22.6	4.2
United States			
< 1	57.6	17.0	25.4
1 – 1.99	45.1	21.5	33.3
2 – 3.99	44.5	17.0	38.6

SOURCE: Data from Gustafsson and Stafford, 1994 (Tables 3, 5, 6).

research finds that the structure of maternity leave laws in the United Kingdom leads relatively more British women to return to their same employer, and the law maintains their pay (Waldfogel, 1993).

While childcare and maternity leave policies are not the prime factors determining women's work and wages, they influence these outcomes. The labor market participation patterns among young mothers are quite different among countries, in ways that reflect institutional differences in the labor market policy that affects them. The effect of higher or lower levels of labor force participation on market flexibility and family well-being may be mixed. On the one hand, women with more labor market experience should have higher skills, which raises short-term labor market productivity. On the other hand, time spent in nurturing children may also have positive effects on the productivity of future generations.

Do Public Pension Plans Affect Work of the Elderly?

Publicly supported pension and early retirement plans exist in all industrialized countries.[19] They were implemented to improve the well-being of the elderly and to open job opportunities for younger workers. They are also an important factor in the huge reductions in elderly poverty rates and in the decreased labor participation of older men found in most countries.

Public pension plans and retirement patterns differ among the United States, Japan, and Sweden, as research by Marcus Rebick demonstrates. In the United States, workers are eligible for social security at age sixty-five and can take early retirement with reduced benefits at sixty-two. In Sweden, full public pensions are available at sixty-five and various partial pensions are available after age sixty, even if workers continue part-time employment. Relatively liberal unemployment benefits are also available to older workers who leave or lose their jobs. In Japan, full public pensions start at age sixty. Older workers in Japan can collect both unemployment and pension income when they leave their job.

In all three countries, the share of older men who are employed decreases when unemployment rises. The response among Japanese and Swedish men is larger than among American men, in large measure because the Japanese and the Swedes have a larger propensity to drop out of the labor market when the unemployment rate rises. Thus Japan and Sweden, two of the countries with the lowest unemployment rates in the world, maintain this in part by relying on their older workers to leave the labor force in times of economic downturn.

Japan and the United States expanded the generosity of their public pension systems in the 1970s. These changes have affected the timing of retirement decisions in both countries, making early retirement easier, but they are not associated with any consistent pattern of increased or reduced responsiveness to unemployment. The primary effects of these changes have been seen in the level of labor participation and the economic well-being of the elderly, not in their responsiveness to business cycle fluctuations.

PULLING IT ALL TOGETHER

The studies reviewed in this chapter cover a potpourri of programs and countries. There is clear evidence here that these diverse programs influence behavior. Faced with employment protection laws, German, French and Belgian firms adjust employment less than American employers. Rising public retirement benefits produce a downward trend in the labor market participation of older men. Cutting off income transfers to young mothers increases their propensity to spend more time in the labor market.

Remarkably, however, there is little evidence that labor market flexibility is substantially affected by the presence of these social protection programs, nor is there strong evidence that the speed of labor market adjustment can be increased by limiting these programs (see Table 5.5).[20] Japan's greater economic growth does not appear related to greater interregional mobility. Housing market regulations do not strongly affect country-specific mobility rates. Tying health insurance to jobs does not appear to prevent interjob mobility. Mandated fringe benefit packages in Spain have less impact on the labor market than expected, because of noncompliance. Growth in public-sector payrolls may not cause substantially greater labor market rigidity.

One reason that the flexibility costs of social protection are smaller than alleged is that employers, workers, and governments have many ways to adjust to a changing economy. Social protection legislation that limits individuals from adjusting to changing conditions in one direction often leads them to find other ways to respond. For example, in comparison with the United States, Germany and Belgium rely more heavily on adjustment of work hours rather than employment adjustment when faced with an economic downturn. Japan has less interregional mobility than the United States but high rates of interregional commuting. Sweden and Japan rely on older workers leaving the labor market in an economic downturn to keep unemployment rates low. The implication is that single measures of economic flexibility may say little about the overall adaptability of an economy.

The conclusion that European social welfare programs have only modest effects on employment flexibility is consistent with the results of studies of welfare programs within the United States. In a major review of this literature, Robert Moffitt notes that there is "considerable uncertainty regarding the magnitude of the effects" on labor supply, and that the effects of the welfare system on the growth of single-parent families and children born out of wedlock are "generally small in magnitude" (Moffitt, 1992, 16 and 31).

Given the modest effects of social welfare programs on economic adjustment, it is not surprising that the changes in these programs enacted by European countries in the 1980s had only a

Table 5.5 Scorecard of Effects of Social Protection Programs on Labor Market Flexibility

Program	Countries	Results vs. United States
Programs Affecting Employer Flexibility		
Employment protection laws Advance notice and severance pay	Belgium, France, Germany	Hours adjustment more important than employment adjustment No effect of easing laws on adjustment speed
Mandated payroll tax for health benefits	Spain	Extensive noncompliance among those covered by other family members
Public sector employment	United Kingdom	Public sector as flexible in wages and employment as private. Both public and private sectors less flexible in U.K. than U.S.
Programs Affecting Worker Mobility		
Tenant protection laws and homeownership subsidies	Germany, Japan	Little evidence of effects on aggregate mobility rates
Health insurance plans that are not entirely portable across jobs	Germany	Little evidence of effects on aggregate mobility rates
Regional mobility policies	Japan	Less interregional mobility in Japan, despite greater policy efforts to promote mobility
Programs Affecting Labor Market Participation		
Public pension benefits	Japan, Sweden	Reduced labor participation among elderly. More generous benefits don't affect responsiveness to unemployment
Time-limited welfare Public daycare	France	Increased labor force participation by single mothers
Maternity leave Public daycare	Sweden, Netherlands	Affects patterns of labor force participation among women

SOURCE: Rebecca M. Blank, 1994.

limited impact on labor market flexibility. The interlocking systems of social protection and labor market regulations in European countries, while different from those in the United States and Japan, had their own internal logic in that workers and employers adopted modes of behavior that minimized any distortionary effects (such as the government's tacit acceptance of some tax avoidance in Spain or the more extensive use of hours adjustment in Germany). To be sure, most of the changes in the 1980s involved the expansion or contraction of existing programs. Perhaps a major economic restructuring in European economies that involved the complete abolishment of labor regulations or the welfare state would produce noticeable increases in the speed of labor market adjustment. But no country, not even Margaret Thatcher's United Kingdom nor Ronald Reagan's United States, has had the interest or political will to conduct such an experiment.

Even if the efficiency costs of these programs were substantial, moreover, the evidence linking such costs to the poorer labor market performance of Europe versus the United States over the 1980s is weak. Burtless (1987) indicates that the more extensive unemployment benefits in European countries did not cause the relative rise in European versus U.S. unemployment rates over the 1970s and 1980s, because the estimated effects are far too small to generate the huge observed unemployment changes. Blanchflower and Freeman (1993) find that even the most liberal estimates of the effects of Prime Minister Thatcher's programs on labor market flexibility were dwarfed by aggregate economic conditions. Buechtemann (1993) argues that mechanisms to limit labor market adjustment and protect workers arise due to failures in the labor market, and that these "inflexibilities" would exist even in the absence of strong employment protection laws.

One additional finding emerges from comparative studies of U.S., European, and Japanese social programs: different countries have structured their labor market and income maintenance systems quite differently. Individual programs that might appear problematic by themselves, may fit coherently into a web of country-specific institutions. For example, time-limited income support payments to young single mothers in France have strong labor market effects partly because free public childcare is available at just the point when transfer payments drop. Higher homeowner subsidies in the United States than in Germany do not produce lower mobility rates in the United States, since many other factors raise mobility in this country. High and mandatory per-employee taxes to pay for public health and pension plans in Spain do not produce major unemployment of low-skilled workers, because of the prevalence of tax avoidance.

If, then, critics have exaggerated the flexibility costs of social protection programs, does this mean that these programs are desirable? This remains an open question, not proved or disproved by the evidence in these studies. Certainly there is evidence here that some programs seem to accomplish their desired ends. Homeowner subsidies in Germany, Japan, and the United States increase homeownership. Higher public retirement benefits allow the elderly to retire without falling into poverty. The Spanish health insurance system imposes high mandated employer costs but provides health insurance to virtually 100 percent of Spanish workers. Extensive maternity leave programs in Sweden result in more time out of the labor market for mothers with young children. The desirability of these programs should be judged by whether their benefits to individuals and society outweigh the direct and indirect costs of the programs. To judge the overall effectiveness of social welfare programs, we need more and better evidence on their long-term benefits.[21]

The research reviewed here shows that the differences between the U.S. economy and other developed economies over the 1980s cannot be easily ascribed to the relatively low level of social protection programs in the United States. International comparisons indicate that the high worker mobility and faster employment adjustment in the United States are not strongly correlated with the presence or absence of social protection programs. Greater flexibility—as measured by a variety of "speed of adjustment" measures—is not necessarily the best or the only way to produce an adaptable and responsive labor market.

NOTES

1. These papers will be published in Rebecca M. Blank, ed., *Social Protection vs. Economic Flexibility: Is There a Tradeoff?* (Chicago: University of Chicago Press and NBER, 1994).

2. This section is derived from Blank and Freeman (1994).

3. Katz and Meyer (1990), for instance, estimate that two months of additional unemployment benefits increase the average time a per-

son is unemployed by one to two weeks. Some may regard this in horror while others may find it an acceptable cost of assisting the unemployed.

4. For a series of papers that review this claim with some skepticism, see *Labour and Society* (1987).

5. These studies have not tried to estimate the excess burden of funding programs, a task best left to public finance experts.

6. This section is based largely on Abraham and Houseman (1994).

7. The United States did enact legislation in 1988 to provide workers with early warning of plant closings, but this did not require any severance pay and has not been particularly effective (U.S. Government Accounting Office, 1993).

8. France is excluded from the analysis of hours adjustments because the French do not have equivalent data on hours.

9. Buechtemann (1993) makes this argument for Germany. See also Chapter 4, this volume.

10. This is an example of the Coase theorem, which states that under certain circumstances, laws that change property rights (including the right to a job) affect the distribution of economic outcomes but not economic efficiency.

11. This section is derived from de la Rica and Lemieux (1994).

12. This section is derived from Blank (1994).

13. This section is derived from Börsch-Supan (1994).

14. This section is derived from Holtz-Eakin (1994).

15. This section is derived from Montgomery (1994).

16. Prefectures and counties are better comparisons than prefectures and states in analyzing geographic mobility, because the former are closer in geographic size.

17. This section is derived from Hanratty (1994).

18. This section is derived from Gustafsson and Stafford (1994).

19. This section is derived from Rebick (1994).

20. These conclusions are consistent with those of Buechtemann (1993), who focuses only on employment protection programs.

21. Blank and Freeman (1994) argue that the best attitude toward the "trade-off" hypothesis should be one of open-minded skepticism. But they also note the limited research available on the full effects of social protection programs. There are almost no studies that effectively estimate the magnitude of the purported benefits of social protection programs in terms of worker well-being, security, or

investment. Thus it is difficult to make full cost-benefit judgments that weigh the efficiency costs of social support programs against their personal and social benefits.

REFERENCES

Abraham, Katharine G., and Susan N. Houseman. 1994. "Does Employment Protection Inhibit Labor Market Flexibility? Lessons from Germany, France, and Belgium." In R. Blank, ed. *Social Protection vs. Economic Flexibility: Is There a Tradeoff?* Chicago: University of Chicago Press for NBER.

Blanchflower, David G., and Richard B. Freeman. 1993. "Did the Thatcher Reforms Change British Labour Performance?" NBER Working Paper no. 4384. Cambridge, Mass.: NBER.

Blanchflower, David G., and Andrew J. Oswald. 1994. "International Wage Curves." In R. Freeman and L. Katz, eds., *Differences and Changes in Wage Structures*. Chicago: University of Chicago Press for NBER.

Blank, Rebecca M. 1994. "Public Sector Growth and Labor Market Flexibility: The U.S. vs. the U.K." In R. Blank, ed., *Social Protection vs. Economic Flexibility: Is There a Tradeoff?* Chicago: University of Chicago Press for NBER.

Blank, Rebecca M., and Richard B. Freeman. 1994. "Evaluating the Connection Between Social Protection and Economic Flexibility." In R. Blank, ed., *Social Protection vs. Economic Flexibility: Is There a Tradeoff?* Chicago: University of Chicago Press for NBER.

Börsch-Supan, Axel. 1994. "Housing Market Regulations and Housing Market Performance in the U.S., Germany and Japan." In R. Blank, ed., *Social Protection vs. Economic Flexibility: Is There a Tradeoff?* Chicago: University of Chicago Press for NBER.

Boyer, Robert. 1988. *The Search for Labour Market Flexibility*. Oxford: Clarendon Press.

Buechtemann, Christoph F. 1993. *Employment Security and Labor Market Behavior*. Ithaca, N.Y.: ILR Press.

Burtless, Gary. 1987. "Jobless Pay and High European Unemployment." In R. Lawrence and C. Schultze, eds., *Barriers to European Growth: A Transatlantic View*. Washington, D.C.: Brookings Institution.

de la Rica, Sara, and Thomas Lemieux. 1994. "Does Public Health Insurance Reduce Labor Market Flexibility or Encourage the Underground Economy: Evidence from Spain and the U.S." In R. Blank, ed., *Social Protection vs. Economic Flexibility: Is There a Tradeoff?* Chicago: University of Chicago Press for NBER.

Dore, Ronald P. 1986. *Flexibility Rigidities: Industrial Policy and Structural Adjustment in the Japanese Economy*. Stanford, Calif.: Stanford University Press.

Dréze, Jacques H., and Charles R. Bean. 1990. *Europe's Unemployment Problem*. Cambridge, Mass.: MIT Press.

Gustafsson, Siv, and Frank P. Stafford. 1994. "Three Regimes of Childcare: The U.S., the Netherlands, and Sweden." In R. Blank, ed., *Social Protection vs. Economic Flexibility: Is There a Tradeoff?* Chicago: University of Chicago Press for NBER.

Hanratty, Maria J. 1994. "Social Welfare Programs for Women and Children: The U.S. vs. France." In R. Blank, ed., *Social Protection vs. Economic Flexibility: Is There a Tradeoff?* Chicago: University of Chicago Press for NBER.

Holtz-Eakin, Douglas. 1994. "Health Insurance Provision and Labor Market Efficiency in the United States and Germany." In R. Blank, ed., *Social Protection vs. Economic Flexibility: Is There a Tradeoff?* Chicago: University of Chicago Press for NBER.

Labour and Society. 1987. Vol.12, no.1. Special volume on labour market flexibility.

Lawrence, Robert Z., and Charles L. Schultze. 1987. *Barriers to European Growth: A Transatlantic View*. Washington, D.C.: Brookings Institution.

Katz, Lawrence F., and Bruce D. Meyer. 1990. "The Impact of the Potential Duration of Unemployment Benefits on the Duration of Unemployment." *Journal of Public Economics* 41: 45–72.

Kay, John, Colin Mayer, and David Thompson. 1986. *Privatisation and Regulation: The UK Experience*. Oxford: Clarendon Press.

Moffitt, Robert. 1992. "Incentive Effects of the U.S. Welfare System: A Review." *Journal of Economic Literature* 30:1–16.

Montgomery, Edward B. 1994. "Patterns in Regional Labor Market Adjustment: The U.S. vs. Japan." In R. Blank, ed., *Social Protection vs. Economic Flexibility: Is There a Tradeoff?* Chicago: University of Chicago Press for NBER.

Organization for Economic Cooperation and Development (OECD). 1990. *Labor Market Policies for the 1990s*. Paris: OECD.

Rebick, Marcus. 1994. "Social Security and Older Workers' Labor Market Responsiveness: The U.S., Japan and Sweden. In R. Blank, ed., *Social Protection vs. Economic Flexibility: Is There a Tradeoff?* Chicago: University of Chicago Press for NBER.

U.S. Government Accounting Office. 1993. "Dislocated Workers: Worker Adjustment and Training Notification Not Meeting Its Goals." Report to Congressional Committees. Washington, D.C.: GAO.

Waldfogel, Jane. 1993. "Women Working for Less: A Longitudinal Analysis of the Family Gap." STICKERED Discussion Paper no. 93. London, England: Suntory-Toyota International Centre for Economics and Related Disciplines.

6

SMALL DIFFERENCES THAT MATTER: CANADA VS. THE UNITED STATES

David Card and Richard B. Freeman

To outsiders Canada and the United States often look like two sides of the same coin. The two countries have a closely intertwined history; they share similar cultures, similar economic institutions, and similar standards of living. The U.S. and Canadian economies are linked by massive trade flows, by the interlocking ownership of multinational firms, and by a steady stream of cross-border migration. Canada and the United States are each others' largest trading partners. Americans control 30 percent of business assets in Canada; Canadians are the fourth largest group of foreign investors in the United States. Eight percent of immigrants in Canada were born in the United States and 6 percent of U.S. immigrants were born in Canada.

Labor market institutions in Canada and the United States have more in common with each other than with institutions in other developed economies. The highly decentralized system of collective bargaining in the two countries is a case in point. Virtually identical labor agreements between the same firms and the same international unions[1] have historically applied to large sectors of the United States and Canadian economies. Programs such as unemployment insurance are similar in the United States and Canada and much different from programs in Western Europe and elsewhere.

Against this backdrop of broad similarity, however, are "small differences" in policies and institutions that distinguish Canada from the United States. Although the United States initially led Canada in the adoption of universal social insurance in the 1930s, Canadian income maintenance programs gradually expanded to surpass the generosity of comparable U.S. programs. The burst of industrial unionism in the United States during the 1930s preceded similar developments in Canada by almost a decade. Since the 1970s, however, union membership rates have fallen in the United States while holding steady in Canada. Canada and the United States accommodated huge waves of European immigrants during the late nineteenth and early twentieth centuries. These flows essentially stopped during the Depression and resumed at a slower pace after World War II. In the 1960s, policy reforms on both sides of the border led to changes in the size and composition of immigrant flows and a widening gap in the economic performance of immigrants compared with natives in the two countries.

If employment, unemployment, incomes, and poverty rates were nearly identical in the two countries, the differences in institutions and policies just noted would be matters of style rather than substance—small differences that don't matter, contrary to the title of this chapter. But labor market and poverty outcomes did *not* follow the same path in United States and Canada during the 1980s. Unemployment rates were much higher in Canada in the 1980s. Wage differentials between more and less educated workers expanded massively in the United States but hardly at all in Canada (see Chapter 2, this volume). And while income inequality increased during the 1980s in the United States it was stable or even decreased in Canada.

The mixture of similarities and differences in institutions and policies between Canada and the United States provides a series of "experiments" for studying how policies and institutional developments affect the labor market and economy. The presence of a distinct institution or policy in one of the countries can be seen as a "treatment," while its absence in the other country provides a natural "control" for determining what would have happened without that institution or policy. The basic similarity of the two economies and their comparable social patterns make it easier to attribute differences in outcomes to differences in specific institutions or policies in Canada and the United States than is possible between countries with very different labor market systems and social patterns, such as Japan and the United States.

By the same token any divergence in outcomes between the United States and Canada, such as the widening differential in unemployment or unionization, automatically draws attention. Since so much is the same in the United States and Canada, sustained differences cry out for a explanation in terms of different policies and institutions.

Recognizing the potential for learning from each other, policy advocates in Canada and the United States routinely refer to the experiences of the other country in arguing for or against a particular initiative. Voters and decision makers recognize that what works in one country has a good chance of working in the other. Indeed, few countries offer a more natural pairing for evaluating policies and institutions or for uncovering the reasons for differences in outcomes than the United States and Canada.

What can we learn about the rising inequality and poverty in the United States from the experiences of Canada? Would wage inequality and rates of child poverty have increased less in the United States if it had adopted Canadian social and economic policies? What does each country have to learn from the other's immigration policy or the divergence in trade union representation? Similarly, what are the lessons for Canada from American policies and institutions? Could Canada have lowered its unemployment rate by moving in the direction of American unemployment compensation and related social policy? Harking back to our title, do the small differences in policies and institutions between Canada and the United States help explain the observed differences in economic outcomes?

This chapter seeks answers to these questions. It relies extensively on an NBER research project that contrasts the overall economic record of Canada and the United States and the specific labor market performance of thousands of Canadian and American individuals and families.[2] The key to this research project is the set of household surveys used to measure such important concepts as unemployment, family income, and union membership in the two countries. These surveys provide an extraordinarily rich portrait of labor market participants on both sides of the border, permitting detailed comparisons of individuals with similar characteristics and simulations of how Americans would fare under Canadian working rules and how Canadians would fare under American working rules.

The major theme that emerges is that small differences *do* matter. Different institutional and policy choices in the United States and Canada lead to differences in economic outcomes. Similarly, differences in outcomes are due to differences in specific institutions and policies. Sometimes, as in the case of unemployment insurance, alternative policy choices seem to have produced unintended differences in outcomes. In other cases, such as income support programs, alternative policy choices have led to predictable differences, although the magnitude of the divergence may not have been fully anticipated by policymakers.

OVERVIEW OF THE U.S. AND CANADIAN
LABOR MARKETS

How similar are labor market outcomes in Canada and the United States? What were the major changes in both economies over the past decade? Table 6.1 gives a capsule summary of patterns in employment, income, and demography in the United States and Canada. Data are presented for each country at the beginning and end of the 1980s. The final column of the table shows the relative change in each outcome over the period from 1980 to 1989, measured as the change in Canada minus the change in the United States. A positive number implies that the change in Canada exceeded that in the United States, while a negative number means the opposite.

Which country did better in terms of employment generation? The labor market data in the first three rows of the table show that Canada and the United States had similar employment and unemployment patterns at the start of the 1980s. Of particular interest are the relatively high employment-to-population rates for women in both countries. By comparison, the 1980 employment-to-population rates for women in most other developed economies were lower.[3] From 1979 to 1989, the proportion of the working age population that was employed grew less rapidly in Canada than in the United States and unemployment in Canada rose compared with unemployment in the United States.

Comparisons of changes in country outcomes in two years, however, can be misleading. The countries may be at different points in their business cycle, or one of the years may be abnormal due to some economic peculiarity. For this reason, we present in

Table 6.1 Comparative Statistics on the United States and Canada

	United States		Canada		Relative Percentage Change Canada—U.S.
	1980	1989	1980	1989	
Labor Market					
1. Employment-Population Rate (All Civilians)	59.2	63.0	59.3	62.0	-1.1
2. Employment-Population Rate (Civilian Women)	47.7	54.3	46.2	53.3	0.5
3. Unemployment Rate (All Civilians)	7.1	5.3	7.5	7.5	1.8
Income					
4. Per Capita GNP (in 1989 U.S. Dollars)	$17,670	$19,100	$16,540	$18,140	1.6
5. Median Family Income (in 1989 U.S. Dollars)	$31,637	$34,213	$35,568	$37,603	-2.4
6. Gini Coefficient of Family Income (×100)[a]	39.8	41.1	37.3	37.1	-1.5
Demography					
7. Percent Female-Headed Families[b]	15.0	17.0	9.3	10.6	-0.7
8. Percent of Births to Unmarried Mothers	18.0	27.0	13.0	23.0	1.0
9. Immigrants Per Year Over Decade[c] (as a Percent of Total Population)	0.2	0.3	0.7	0.4	-0.5

SOURCES: U.S. Bureau of the Census *Statistical Abstact of United States* (Washington, D.C.: U.S. GPO, 1992) (Tables 1, 5, 56, 1359); Statistics Canada *Canada Year Book* (Ottawa: Statistics Canada, 1990) (Tables 2.2, 2.3, 2.24); Statistics Canada *Perspectives on Labour and Income* (Ottawa: Statistics Canada, Spring 1993); Blackburn and Bloom, 1993 (Table 7).

[a] Gini coefficients of family income are for 1979 and 1987.
[b] 1980 for Canada is 1981; 1989 for Canada is 1987.
[c] 1980 for U.S. is 1971–1980 change; 1989 for U.S. is 1981–1990 change; 1980 for Canada is 1971–1980 change; 1989 for Canada is 1981–1986 change.

Figure 6.1 the pattern of unemployment rates (on the left) and employment-population rates (on the right) for a longer time period, 1966 to 1990. Consistent with the 1980 to 1989 data in Table 6.1, the graph shows that a significant "unemployment gap" emerged between Canada and the United States in the early 1980s. On the *employment* side, however, there is less evidence of a newly emergent gap. Between 1980 and 1989 Canadian employment grew by 1 percent less than American employment (relative to the population at working age). But 1980 was not a normal year in which to compare American and Canadian employment rates. From the mid-1960s to the early 1970s Canada had a smaller employment-population ratio than the United States. Canada attained a higher or similar ratio in the mid 1970s and in 1980–81, after which the U.S. employment-population rate rose above the Canadian rate. Comparisons of the trend in U.S. and Canadian employment rates using base years other than 1980 show little change in the gap between

Figure 6.1   Employment and Unemployment Rates in Canada and the United States, 1966–1990

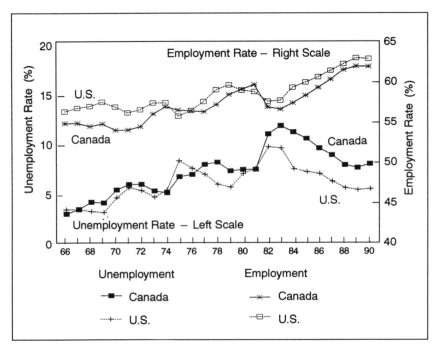

the countries, or even an *increase* in employment in Canada relative to the United States. Indeed, the figure shows that the gap in employment-population rates in 1989 was actually smaller than that in the late 1960s and early 1970s. The implication is that Canada had a higher rate of unemployment than the United States not because the Canadian economy failed to generate additional jobs but because the proportion of the population seeking work rose more in Canada than in the United States (for reasons we will explore later).[4]

Rows 4 and 5 of Table 6.1 contain measures of income—per capita GNP and median family income in 1989 U.S. dollars. There are two ways in which to transform Canadian dollars into U.S. dollars: by using exchange rates to convert Canadian currency into U.S. currency or by using purchasing-power parity rates that measure the equivalent cost of a basket of goods between countries. In this table we give the figures in terms of 1989 U.S. dollars using the 1989 exchange rate, but the results would be similar with purchasing power parity figures.[5] Using per capita GNP as a standard, income is slightly higher in the United States. Using (pretax) median family income as a standard, income is slightly higher in Canada. The reversal is attributable to higher taxes in Canada and the smaller frequency of single-person families in Canada. Family income growth was faster in Canada than the United States during the 1970s but slower in Canada during the 1980s. We emphasize the high degree of similarity in average living standards in the two countries.

Average or median incomes give only a partial description of economic well-being. Another important dimension is the *dispersion* of incomes across families or individuals. An increase in income dispersion, for example, implies that there are more families below any fixed low-income standard, leading to a higher poverty rate. One widely used measure of dispersion of incomes, the Gini coefficient, is shown in row 6 of Table 6.1. The Gini coefficient represents the fraction of total income that would have to be redistributed to give all families the same income, and varies from 1.00 (the highest possible inequality) to 0.00 (the lowest possible inequality). In 1979 the Gini coefficient was 2.5 percentage points lower in Canada, indicating that Canada had a more even distribution of family incomes than the United States. During the 1980s, family income inequality grew in the United States but fell in

Canada, leading to an even greater cross-country difference in inequality.

Poverty rates also diverged between the countries (see Figure 6.2).[6] From 1975 onward the Canadian poverty rate was lower than the U.S. rate, mainly as a result of the more generous Canadian transfer system. Even more significantly, although poverty rates in both countries rose during the 1982 recession, the Canadian rate eventually returned to its earlier level, whereas the U.S. rate did not. Among families headed by single women, the poverty rate rose during the 1980s from 34 percent to 41 percent in the United States, while it fell from 32 percent to 26 percent in Canada (Blank and Hanratty, 1993).

Since increased income inequality and poverty were two of the main features of the American economy in the 1980s, the fact that Canada did not experience trends of similar magnitude, or even similar direction, suggests that rising inequality and poverty were potentially avoidable in the United States. An explanation of why the Canadian income distribution did not widen, or widened only moderately, in the 1980s could direct attention to policies that might ameliorate or reduce inequality in the United States.

The last set of comparisons in Table 6.1 pertain to demographic developments. Row 7 shows that a higher proportion of families are headed by single women in the United States than in Canada, although the rate of growth in the proportion of single female

Figure 6.2   Poverty Rates of Families in the United States and Canada

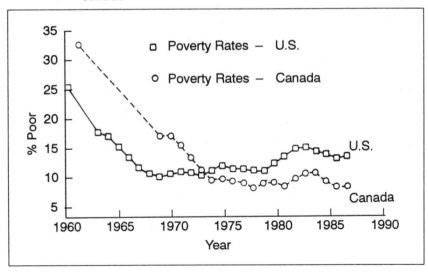

heads was about the same in the two countries. The data in row 8 show that the share of children born to unmarried mothers rose in a parallel fashion in both countries.

The final line in Table 6.1 presents average annual immigration rates in the 1970s and 1980s. Immigration is a major source of population growth for both countries, contributing 20 to 30 percent of net growth. During most of the postwar period, immigration rates were two to three times higher in Canada,[7] so that twice as large a proportion of the Canadian population was born abroad: 16 percent of Canadians as of 1986 compared with 8 percent of Americans as of 1990. However, in the 1980s immigration to the United States increased while immigration to Canada fell off.

INSTITUTIONS AND POLICIES

Do economic policies and institutions in the United States and Canada diverge in ways likely to explain the differing patterns of labor market outcomes and family incomes? At the outset it is important to recognize that Canada and the United States are large and geographically diverse countries that operate under relatively decentralized federal systems. Provinces and states play an important role in labor market regulations and income support policies, so that the level of social assistance payments available to a particular family, the laws governing collective bargaining, and other labor market institutions vary widely within each country. Furthermore, the specific policies that fall under federal as opposed to provincial or state control differ between the countries. For example, unemployment insurance is a federal program in Canada but a state program in the United States, whereas labor law is largely a provincial issue in Canada but mainly a federal issue in the United States. Contrasts of Canadian and American policies thus require sensitivity to within-country differences in the level of government that makes the policies.

One of the most important and volatile issues facing any country is its immigration policy. Both Canada and the United States amended immigration laws in the 1960s to allow greater inflows of non-European immigrants. The new U.S. policy stressed family reunification, although substantial inflows of refugees and illegal immigrants meant that immigrants admitted under the quota system made up less than one-half of total immigrants in the 1980s (see Borjas, Freeman, and Lang, 1991). Canada adopted a "point system" designed to produce a more skilled immigrant flow; we shall show that this choice had profound effects on immigrant characteristics.

Differences in the Canadian and American education systems affect the supply of highly educated labor in the two countries.[8] Many more Canadian than American students leave high school without completing the requirements to attend university, but many more Canadians also attend vocational and community college programs.[9] In the 1960s America expanded its higher education system more rapidly than Canada. By 1987, 18 percent of American adults had a college degree compared with only 12 percent of Canadian adults. In the 1980s Canada began to catch up. From 1979 to 1987 the ratio of the number of men with a college degree to the number with only a high school education climbed by 20 percent in Canada compared with only 5 percent in the United States. Among young men (age twenty-five to thirty-four) the ratio of college to high school graduates increased by 4 percent in Canada but *fell* by 18 percent in the United States. These trends contributed to the widening of earnings differentials by education between the two countries.

Social safety net programs also differ between Canada and the United States. Canada's unemployment insurance system offers a longer duration of benefits (up to fifty weeks) than the comparable U.S. program (twenty-six weeks). Less restrictive eligibility requirements imply that a far larger share of job losers are eligible for benefits in Canada. Benefits are also available for maternity leaves, sickness, and training in Canada. Finally, the take-up rate among those eligible for benefits is higher in Canada; for reasons that are poorly understood many American workers fail to receive the benefits available to them (Blank and Card, 1991). All of these differences add up to a remarkable gap in the ratio of unemployment insurance recipients to unemployed workers. In the United States only about one-third of the unemployed collect unemployment benefits; in Canada, more than 90 percent do.

Canada's income support system for nonelderly persons is also broader than the American system. Canada's means-tested transfer programs (programs limited to people below certain income levels) have wider eligibility and higher benefits than comparable U.S. programs. And until very recently Canada had an important non–means tested program, the Family Allowance program, unlike any program in the United States.[10] Canadian antipoverty transfer programs include child tax credits and social assistance to low-income families and individuals. Comparable U.S. programs (Aid to Families with Dependent Children, food stamps, school lunches, and earned income tax credits) are more narrowly targeted and provide less per program participant.

A final important difference is in the regulation of collective bargaining. Canadian labor laws were modified in the early 1940s along lines parallel to America's 1935 Wagner Act, which established the system of legal procedures for labor organization and collective bargaining. Despite this common heritage, Canadian laws have since become more favorable to unions while American laws have become less favorable. Under Canadian law it is easier to unionize: in most cases unions need only obtain the signatures of a majority of workers, and management has less scope for expressing opposition to unionism. Firms cannot permanently replace strikers, and legislation in some provinces makes even temporary strike replacements illegal. The province of Quebec has adopted the practice of many Western European countries of allowing the minister of labor to extend union contracts to nonunion workers.

Whether because of differences in labor laws or other factors, unionization rates in the two countries have diverged from the approximate equality reached in the 1950s to a substantial difference in the 1980s (see Figure 6.3). After 1975, union membership rates dropped precipitously in the United States, with the percentage organized in the private sector falling to a bare 11 percent in 1992. In contrast, membership rates in Canada expanded in the late 1970s (reflecting growing unionization in the public sector) and fell only slightly in the 1980s. Private-sector union rates in Canada averaged 30 percent in the 1980s.

POLICIES, INSTITUTIONS, AND OUTCOMES

The question that naturally arises next is: Are the differences in labor market outcomes and policies between the United States and Canada closely linked? Do the small differences in policies and institutions explain the differences in labor market outcomes? Our conclusion is that the differences in policies and institutions mattered in several important areas:

Figure 6.3 Union Membership Rates in the United States and Canada

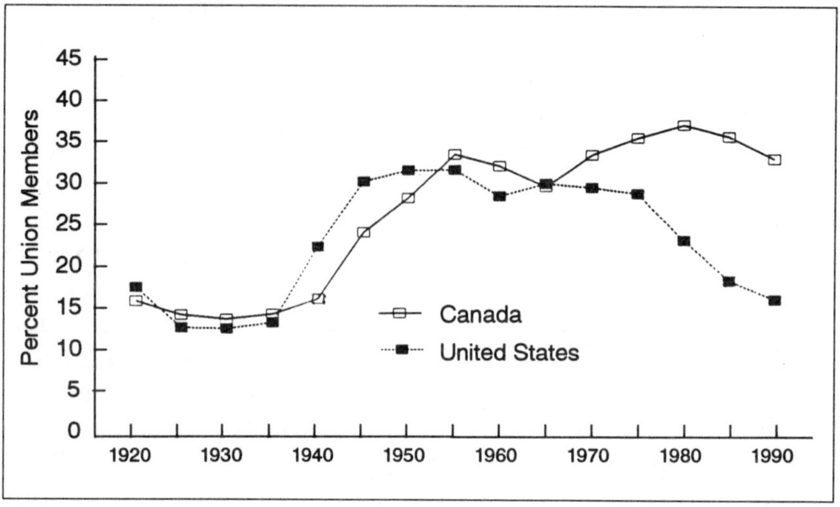

NOTES: Data for 1920 to 1980 are based on union records; 1985 and 1990 are based on microeconomic survey data.

1. in the number and types of immigrants who came to the two countries;

2. in the number of low-income workers who sought jobs, and thus in unemployment rates;

3. in the trends in income inequality and poverty; and

4. in the evolution of unionism.

These conclusions are based on studies that take one of two different approaches to assessing the link between policies, institutions, and outcomes. One set of studies begins with policy differences and asks, Does this difference in policy affect some outcome? The other set begins with outcome differences and asks, What factors might explain this difference in outcomes?[11] The fact that both approaches yield a similar conclusion—that small differences in policies and institutions matter—makes us reasonably confident of the validity of this conclusion. We turn next to the evidence and arguments that small differences matter.

Immigrant Policy

Did the changes in immigration laws that occurred in Canada and the United States in the mid-1960s affect the flow of immigrants?[12] An answer is provided by Table 6.2, which shows education levels and relative wages for immigrant cohorts (those who came in a particular time period) in the United States and Canada. Prior to the legislative reforms, immigrants to Canada had fewer years of schooling than immigrants to the United States: 11.2 years in Canada for the 1960 to 1964 cohort of immigrants versus 11.9 years in the United States. Relative to natives in the respective countries, however, immigrants to Canada looked slightly better. On average, immigrants from 1960 to 1964 had 0.1 fewer years of schooling than natives in Canada, versus 0.8 years' less schooling in the United States. In 1980–81, these immigrants actually earned slightly *more* than natives: 4.8 percent more in Canada; 0.1 percent more in the United States.

Starting with immigrants who arrived from 1965 to 1970, however, immigrants to Canada were substantially better educated than immigrants to the United States. For example, Canadian immigrants in the 1975 to 1980 cohort had 1.3 more years of education than natives, whereas U.S. immigrants had 0.9 years fewer of education than natives. And while immigrants in both countries made less than natives (in part because they lacked experience in the new setting), the immigrant-native earnings gap is also smaller in Canada than in the United States: immigrants who arrived in Canada from 1975 to 1980 earned 17 percent less than natives, whereas immigrants in the United States earned 30 percent less.[13]

Why were immigrants closer to natives in education and earnings in Canada than in the United States? A major reason is the difference in immigration policies described earlier. Canada's greater stress on occupational skills in admitting immigrants means that it admits relatively more immigrants from high-income European countries than the United States. Immigrants from the same source country have about the same education (and earnings) in the United States or Canada. Thus the key difference between the education (and earnings) of all immigrants in the two countries is due to differences in the mix of origins of immigrants. The fraction of immigrants from less developed Asia and Latin America in-

Table 6.2 Mean Education of Immigrants, and Education and Wage Differential Between Immigrants and Natives

Year of Immigration	Canada			United States		
	Mean Educ. of Immigrants (yr)	Immigrant Gap in Educ. (yr)	Log Wage (%)	Mean Educ. of Immigrants (yr)	Immigrant Gap in Educ. (yr)	Log Wage (%)
1960–1964	11.2	-0.1	4.8	11.9	-0.8	0.1
1965–1970	12.4	1.1	6.5	11.4	-1.3	-6.9
1970–1975	12.4	1.1	-8.4	11.1	-1.6	-20.0
1975–1980	12.6	1.3	-17.2	11.9	-0.9	-29.9

SOURCE: Borjas, 1993 (Table 3).

NOTES: Data for Canada and the United States from the 1980 or 1981 census. The immigrant gap is the difference in mean education (in years) or mean log wages (in percent) between immigrants and natives.

creased in both Canada and the United States, but Canada maintained a larger share of European immigrants, leading to a more highly skilled immigrant work force after 1965.

Labor Participation and Unemployment

The emergence of an unemployment gap between Canada and the United States in the 1980s was initially attributed to the more sluggish Canadian recovery from the 1982–83 recession.[14] However, Canadian unemployment rates were 2 to 3 percentage points higher than U.S. rates at the *end* of the 1980s—six years into a sustained recovery that saw vacancy rates and GNP growth rates converge in the two countries. Six years of comparable aggregate economic expansion rules out a cyclical explanation for higher unemployment rates.

What else might cause unemployment to be higher in Canada? It turns out that much of the rise in Canadian unemployment took the form of an increase in the fraction of persons without work reporting themselves seeking work. Labor force statistics classify people in three main categories: the employed, or jobholders; jobless persons who are looking for work and thus counted as unemployed; and jobless persons not looking for work and thus out of the labor force. In Canada the proportion of the working age population that was jobless changed little in the 1980s, but the fraction of the jobless counted as unemployed rose. In the United States, in contrast, there was little change in the proportion of jobless persons counted as unemployed. It is this difference that underlies most of the relative rise in Canadian unemployment.

To demonstrate this, in Figure 6.4, we have broken down the gap in the Canada-U.S. unemployment rates for men and women into: 1) the proportion of the population that is jobless, 2) the proportion of the jobless who are looking for work and counted as unemployed, and 3) the proportion of the population that is in the work force, either working or unemployed.[15] Among women, the proportion of the jobless who were unemployed jumps sharply in the mid-1980s in Canada relative to the United States. There is also a trend in female labor force participation rates in Canada compared with the United States—in the late 1960s Canadian women had 5 percent lower participation rates than U.S. women, but in

1989 Canadian women had *higher* participation rates—and a modest change in the proportion of the population that is jobless. It is the sharp jump in the proportion of the jobless looking for work in the 1980s that accounts for the increased unemployment rate among Canadian women compared with American women.[16]

Among men the pattern is similar. Male participation rates decline in the United States and Canada as more men retire earlier but show no great differential trend; and differences in the proportion of the population that is jobless also change only modestly. What stands out is that the proportion of the jobless who say they are seeking work rises in Canada relative to the United States, while also varying cyclically. About half of the relative rise in male unemployment in Canada is attributable to the increased proportion of nonworkers who say they are looking for work.

The finding that unemployment rose in Canada relative to the United States largely because jobless Canadians were increasingly likely to seek work compared with jobless Americans is not, of course, a full explanation. Why did jobless women and men increasingly look for work in Canada but not in the United States?

One reason is that unemployment insurance (UI) systems give different incentives for people to seek work in the two countries. In many parts of Canada individuals are eligible for unemployment benefits after working a minimum of ten or twelve weeks per year. In the United States individuals are typically eligible for UI only after they have worked a minimum of twenty weeks per year. Thus Canadians have a special incentive to work for ten to twelve weeks. Not only do they earn money, but they also gain eligibility for unemployment benefits. For comparable Americans the situation is different: if they are welfare recipients, for example, they typically lose welfare benefits, including health insurance, if they work for a short time. The fraction of workers with ten to twelve weeks of work in fact rose in Canada. One-quarter of the rise in Canadian unemployment relative to U.S. unemployment is attributable to the growth in the number of workers in this group and to their reporting that they were unemployed after their two-to-three-month work experience. Still, more generous unemployment benefits are not the only cause of the relative increase in Canadian unemployment. Among men, much of the relative increase in unemployment occurred among those with no weeks of work in the previous year—a group with declining UI recipiency rates in

**Figure 6.4 Differences in Labor Force Activity Rates,
Canada – United States**

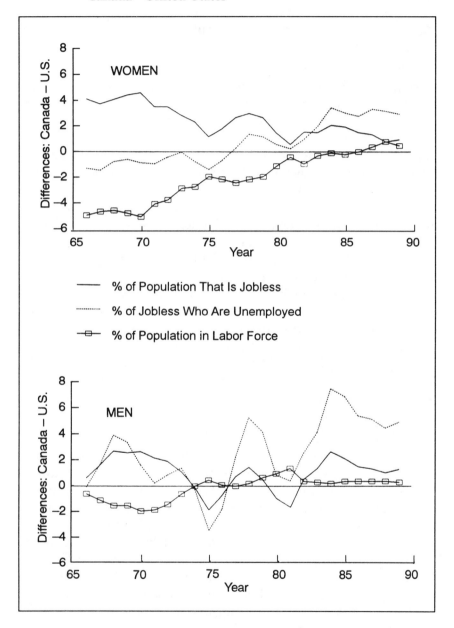

Canada. And reductions in the maximum duration of UI eligibility in the late 1980s failed to reduce the high levels of unemployment. Measured differences in unemployment benefits thus explain only part of the divergence in economic outcomes.

The Growth of Inequality

During the 1980s differences in earnings and employment rates between more educated and less educated workers widened exceptionally rapidly in the United States, and the pay gap between high- and low-paid workers increased, so that inequality rose to unprecedented levels (see Chapter 2, this volume). Explanations for increased inequality include reduced relative demand for less educated and lower paid Americans, due to increasing trade and competition from low-wage countries and to changes in technology; slower growth of the supply of college graduates in the United States; and the decline in American unionization.

Within the United States it is difficult to assess the importance of these competing explanations. A comparison between Canada and the United States can be more informative, since some of the potential explanations predict the *same* changes in Canada and the U.S. whereas others do not. Specifically, explanations based on trade or technology would seem to apply in both countries, leading to the prediction of parallel trends in the United States and Canada. Explanations based on institutions such as trade unionism would predict a divergence.

What Happened to Inequality in Canada?

Pay differentials based on education did not widen as much in Canada as in the United States.[17] One measure of these pay differentials is the percentage gap in average weekly earnings between college graduates and workers with only a high school education. From 1979 to 1987 the college–high school wage gap for young men (age twenty-five to thirty-four) expanded by 23 percent in the United States, compared with a rise of only 4 percent in Canada. The wage gap for young women similarly rose by 9 percent in the United States versus only 4 percent in Canada. Among all adult workers (that is, those age twenty-five to sixty-four) the college–high school wage gap increased by a modest 4 percent in Canada compared with an 18 percent rise for American men and an 11 percent rise for American women. Changes in ratios of average annual earnings may differ slightly from changes in ratios of average weekly wages, because of unemployment: many workers (especially less educated workers) lose some time each year to unemployment. While there was modestly greater growth of joblessness among less educated workers relative to more educated workers in Canada than in the United States, the college–high school difference in annual earnings, which measures both wages and the time people work over the year, increased less in Canada. Finally, from 1987 to the early 1990s even these modest rises began to reverse themselves in Canada.

Why were pay differentials by education more stable and the overall dispersion of earnings lower in Canada than in the United States? One reason for the smaller increase in pay differentials by education is that the college-educated work force grew more rapidly in Canada, dampening pressures for relative wage increases. About one-half of the divergence in education-based wage gaps over the 1980s is attributable to the greater expansion in the relative supply of college-educated workers in Canada than in the United States.

The decline in unionization in the United States relative to Canada explains another sizable chunk of the U.S.-Canada gap in overall dispersion of earnings.[18] It is well established that U.S. unions reduce wage inequality through standardization of wages within the organized sector and by raising blue-collar pay relative to white-collar pay (Freeman, 1980). Card (1992) and Freeman (1992) attribute about one-fifth of the rise in male wage inequality in the U.S. in the 1980s to the decline in unionization.

The effect of unions on the distribution of earnings depends on how much unions raise members' wages compared with those of otherwise similar nonunion workers; how much unions redistribute earnings from higher-paid to lower-paid workers in the organized sector; and whether unions organize high-paid, low-paid, or medium-paid workers. Canadian unions raise the average wages of union workers relative to nonunion workers by about as much (possibly a bit less) as American unions do; they reduce wage inequality in the union sector by about as much as American unions; and they are more likely to organize low-wage, less educated male workers than American unions. Thus Canadian unions are likely to reduce inequality by at least as much as American unions do, if not more.[19]

Table 6.3 shows how Canadian and U.S. levels of unionism affect one major measure of inequality, the variance of wages for men. Line 1 shows that among nonunion workers, men's wages are more unevenly distributed in the United States than in Canada, so differences in unionism cannot be the whole story behind different levels of inequality. But the gap in unionism in the 1980s did accentuate the greater earnings inequality in the United States. Thomas Lemieux estimates that about 40 percent of the lower wage inequality for men in Canada is attributable to the higher unionization rate in Canada, and that some 40 to 45 percent of the greater growth in the variance of earnings among men in the United States than in Canada in the 1980s is attributable to the approximate 7 point drop in union density in the United States relative to Canada. Among women, in contrast, unionization has little effect on inequality, largely because educated women, such as teachers and nurses, who are high in the earnings distribution of women are more unionized than less educated women.

Why Does Unionization Differ?

The finding that divergence in union rates accounts for a sizable chunk of the differential rise in labor market inequality between Canada and the United States directs attention to the reasons for that divergence.[20] Why did unionism decline greatly in the United States but not in Canada?

One possibility is that the structure of the two economies changed in different ways. Perhaps in the U.S. unionization fell because employment shifted to traditionally nonunion, private-sector industries and occupations, whereas greater governmental employment in Canada maintained the unionization rate. We reject this explanation. Canada and the United States had similar changes in the composition of the labor force and in the industrial and occupational mix of jobs. Union membership rates differ greatly among virtually all groups of workers, including those in the public sector: the proportion of workers who are unionized is one and a half to two and a half times greater in Canada than in the United States in almost all categories. Since unionization rates fell among all groups in the United States (Freeman, 1990) while changing only modestly in Canada, an explanation of the divergence in rates in terms of

Table 6.3   Estimated Effects of Unionization on Wage Inequality

	Canada	U.S.	Canada–U.S.
1. Actual variance of log hourly wages	0.23	0.28	−0.05
2. Estimated variance in the absence of all unions	0.27	0.30	−0.03
3. Estimated variance if U.S. pattern of union coverage existed in both countries	0.25	0.28	−0.03
4. Estimated variance if Canadian pattern of union coverage existed in both countries	0.23	0.26	−0.03

SOURCE: Lemieux, 1993 (Table 9).

NOTES: All calculations pertain to 1986. Calculations in rows 2–4 account for effects of unionization on average wages of union workers and on the variance of wages within the union sector for three skill groups (low, medium, and high).

changes in sectoral or occupational distribution does not hold water.

A second possible explanation for the diverging unionization rates is that Canadians like unions and Americans don't. We reject this, as well. Polls of the general public that ask whether people think unions are good or bad, or if they approve or disapprove of trade unions, show no difference in attitudes nor in trends in attitudes between the two countries. The attitudes of Canadians and Americans toward unions were no different in the 1980s, when Canadian unionization was double that in the United States, than in the 1950s, when the rates were roughly the same.

This leaves two contending explanations for the difference in unionization: that American workers want unions less than Canadian workers do; or that American employers and labor laws make it more difficult for workers to unionize than Canadian employers and laws. Actually both factors seem to play a part. To see if workers have different desires for unionization, researchers have examined surveys that ask nonunion workers if they would like to have a union represent them at their job.[21] If Americans and Canadians were equally able to obtain union representation when they wanted it, the proportion of nonunion workers who say they want unions (but can't get them at their workplace) should be the same in the two countries. Then we could attribute all of the difference in union density to differences in "tastes" for unionization. Comparable U.S. and Canadian surveys show, however, the contrary: a greater proportion of nonunion workers in the United States than in Canada say they want unions. In a 1984 U.S. survey, 36 percent of nonunion Americans said they wanted a union—a proportion comparable to those in other surveys of U.S. workers as well. This figure compares with 30 percent of nonunion Canadians in 1990 who said they wanted a union. Proportionately more nonunion Americans would like to have a union represent them at their workplace than nonunion Canadians, implying that it is more difficult to unionize in the United States.

But this does not mean that there are no differences in the desire for unionism between the countries. If we take the number of nonunion workers who want a union plus the number of unionized workers as a measure of workers' demand for unionism, 64 percent of Canadians would like to be represented by unions compared with 50 percent of Americans—a 14 percentage point difference. This contrasts with a gap in actual union representation between the countries that is nearly twice as great—26 percentage points.[22] The implication is that many more workers are frustrated in their efforts to unionize in the United States than in Canada. Indeed, only 44 percent of workers who want a union at their workplace have one in the United States compared with 76 percent in Canada. On the basis of these data, Craig Riddell estimates that 30 percent of the gap in actual unionization rates is due to a smaller desire by Americans for unions while 70 percent is due to the greater difficulty that Americans who want unions have in obtaining such representation.

Why do Americans have a harder time organizing unions? A likely reason is that differences in the labor laws between the two countries, described earlier, make it easier for workers to unionize and harder for employers to resist unionization in Canada than in the United States. Under Canadian laws a union is established once a majority of workers have signed a card indicating their support for the union. Under U.S. laws union representation is determined after a long and drawn out election campaign, often involving management consultants who are hired to convince workers that they don't want a union after all. Such campaigns make clear to workers that their employer is vehemently opposed to collective bargaining, and thus that choosing to unionize will create considerable employer animus in their enterprise.

Poverty and Income Maintenance

Poverty rates and inequality among families have been significantly lower in Canada than in the United States since the mid-1980s.[23] In 1986 the poverty rate in Canada was 10 percent compared with 15 percent in the United States (see Figure 6.2). The difference is not due to differences in the growth rate of the two economies. In the 1970s the Canadian economy grew more rapidly than the American economy, bringing Canadian poverty rates, which had been higher than American poverty rates, closer to U.S. levels (see Figure 6.2); but Canada did not grow more rapidly than the United States in the 1980s. Nor is the difference due to higher unemployment in the United States; unemployment was lower in the United States in the 1980s.

Surprisingly, the difference is also not due to the larger fraction of families headed by single women in the United States than in Canada. This is illustrated by the fact that "pretransfer" poverty rates, measured *before* the effects of government transfer payments, are actually higher in Canada than the United States, even though the United States has a higher fraction of families headed by single women (see Table 6.1, line 7). If differences in poverty arose from differences in family structure, one would expect a higher rate of pretransfer poverty in the United States. As shown in the top panel of Figure 6.5, however, pretransfer poverty rates are lower in the United States.

The implication is that Canada's income maintenance system raises more people out of poverty than does the American income maintenance system. Indeed, Canada provides greater income support for its poor citizens: transfers and tax credits are 7.3 percent of mean family earnings, compared with 2.7 percent in the United States, and Canada spends 60 percent more in transfers and tax credits to single-parent families than the United States. As Figure 6.5 shows, the Canadian transfer system reduces the poverty rate among all families by 5.7 percentage points, compared with the 1.9 percentage point reduction effected by U.S. transfers. Among single-parent families, the transfer system lowers poverty by 14.3 percentage points in Canada compared with 5.2 percentage points in the United States. Canada's income maintenance system reduces the poverty gap—the average income necessary to raise families below the poverty line up to the poverty threshold—by 48 percent, while America's income maintenance system reduces the poverty gap by just 30 percent.

What would happen to the American poverty rate if the United States had Canada's income maintenance system? Rebecca Blank and Maria Hanratty have simulated the income Americans would have if they faced the program rules and benefits of the Canadian transfer system in an "average" Canadian province. Since more generous income maintenance programs will induce some people to work less in order to qualify for program benefits, Blank and Hanratty also simulated how much potential welfare recipients might reduce their work effort to qualify for programs. This labor supply response would have the undesirable side effect of increasing pretransfer poverty. Their results are summarized in Table 6.4. Even with a generous allowance for people to shift from work to welfare, adoption of the Canadian welfare system would reduce poverty rates among all American families by 30 percent and would reduce poverty rates among single-parent families with children by 60 percent.[24]

Does the more generous social safety net in Canada also account for the fall in inequality of total family income (income from all sources, including transfers) in Canada compared with the United States (see Table 6.1)?[25] If it were the major cause for the differing trends in female income inequality, we might expect that inequality in the labor market earnings of family members, which excludes transfer payments, would show no marked difference. And that is precisely what the income statistics do show: inequality in family earnings from the labor market rose in Canada and the United States at about the same rate over the 1980s. In addition the family type that is least affected by transfers in either country, dual-headed families with no children, also had similar income inequality rises, whereas the family type most affected by transfers, fe-

Figure 6.5 Poverty Rates in the United States and Canada, Before and After Transfers

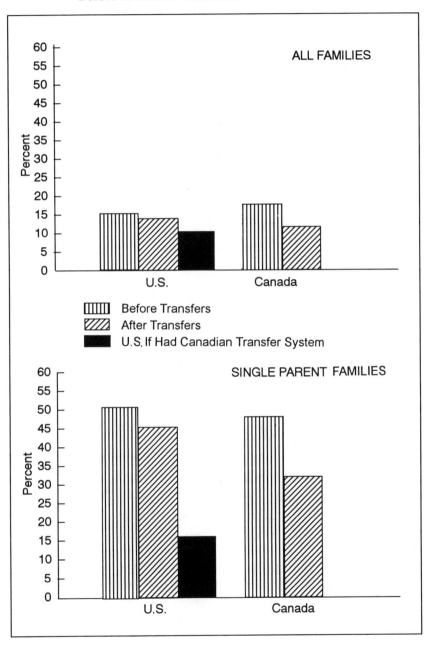

SOURCE: Blank and Hanratty, 1993 (Table 10).

213

Table 6.4   Estimated Effect of "Average" Canadian Transfer System on U.S. Poverty

	Poverty Rate (%)
All Families	
Actual	13.5
Simulated Under Average Canadian Transfer System	
Assuming least-elastic labor supply responses	9.4
Assuming most-elastic labor supply responses	9.5
Single-Head Families with Children	
Actual	45.3
Simulated Under Average Canadian Transfer System	
Assuming least-elastic labor supply responses	15.8
Assuming most-elastic labor supply responses	16.2

SOURCE: Blank and Hanratty, 1993 (Table 10).

NOTES: "Average" Canadian transfer system is a population-weighted average of systems in various Canadian provinces. Labor supply response parameters are taken from range of estimates obtained in the Seattle-Denver Income Maintenance Experiment. Estimates assume that program participation rates for eligible families equal actual participation rates among eligible Canadian families.

male-headed families, showed a greater increase in poverty in the United States relative to Canada.

COSTS OF TRANSFER POLICIES

The fact that Canada's income support programs reduced inequality and lowered poverty in the 1980s does not mean that these programs are better than comparable U.S. programs. Transfer programs, after all, are not costless manna from heaven. They require taxes, or deficit financing, that extracts a cost from the economy. The expansion of Canada's income maintenance system raised the share of GNP devoted to transfers and was accompanied by an even larger increase in the Canadian national debt than was seen in the American national debt.

Table 6.5 compares the costs of the Canadian and American transfer programs in terms of share of GNP for needs-based cash and in-kind (nonmonetary) transfers for the nonelderly[26]; unemployment insurance; and cash-based child support programs (Family Allowance and Child Tax Credit programs in Canada; Earned Income Tax Credit program in the United States). These programs account for virtually all of the measured transfer income in the two countries, although they ignore government spending on health care, housing, and education.

Spending on needs-based transfers (line 1) rose in both the United States and Canada during the 1960s and 1970s. Canadian spending was lower than American in 1960, reached equality with American spending by 1975, and then rose during the 1980s by 25 percent to 2.2 percent of GNP, while American spending fell by 25 percent to 1.3 percent of GNP. Spending on unemployment insurance programs (line 2) was higher in Canada than the United States throughout the 1960s and 1970s, and increased in the 1980s, while the U.S. unemployment insurance program contracted. By the close of the decade Canadian spending on unemployment compensation was five times greater as a fraction of national income. As for spending on children (line 3), while Canadian expenditures on child tax credits and family allowances declined from the 1960s through the 1980s, they remained considerably above the spending levels for comparable programs in the United States. Finally, the sum of the spending on all three programs (line 4) shows the extent to which the dollars spent on the income maintenance systems in Canada and the United States diverged after 1980. Canada did not reduce poverty in the 1980s relative to the United States by some miraculous sleight of hand. It did it the "old-fashioned way," by spending more than the United States.

CONCLUSION

The divergent policies and economic outcomes in Canada and the United States in the 1980s provide an insightful "natural experiment" for judging the effects of more or less activist policies on labor market outcomes. The two countries were buffeted by similar market forces—new technology, shifts in relative labor demands, world competition in traded goods—that made it difficult for less skilled workers throughout North America to prosper. Despite

Table 6.5 Transfer Program Expenditures in the United States and Canada, 1960–1990

		Program Expenditures as a Percentage of GNP						
		1960	1965	1970	1975	1980	1985	1990[a]
1. Needs-based Transfers Including for Disabilities[b]	Can.:	0.66	0.98	1.37	1.69	1.76	2.15	2.20
	U.S.:	0.80	0.89	1.10	1.72	1.70	1.40	1.30
2. Unemployment Insurance	Can.:	1.22	0.54	0.78	1.81	1.28	2.13	1.77
	U.S.:	0.59	0.44	0.38	0.87	0.68	0.46	0.32
3. Child Programs: Tax Credits and Family Allowance[c]	Can.:	1.36	1.05	0.63	1.06	0.86	0.82	0.77
	U.S.:	—	—	—	0.06	0.05	0.04	0.09
4. Sum of Three Programs	Can.:	3.24	2.57	2.78	4.56	3.90	5.10	4.74
	U.S.:	1.39	1.33	1.48	2.65	2.43	1.90	1.71

SOURCES: Statistics Canada *Canada Year Book* (Ottawa: Statistics Canada, 1980–81, 1991 editions); Social Security Administration *Social Security Bulletin Annual Statistical Supplement* (Washington, D.C.: GPO, 1991); Committee on Ways and Means, U.S. House of Representatives *1992 Green Book* (Washington, D.C.: GPO, 1992).

[a] 1990 data for Canada; 1989 data for U.S.
[b] Canadian data include expenditures under Canada Assistance Program and earlier programs for disabled people, as well as provincial and municipal welfare. U.S. data include Aid to Families with Dependent Children (AFDC), Supplemental Security Income (SSI), Food Stamps, general assistance and other categorical payments under the Social Security Act, *excluding* Medicaid expenditures.
[c] Canadian data include Family Allowance and Child Tax Credit. U.S. data include refunded portion of Earned Income Tax Credit.

these shared conditions, and despite the great overall similarity of the American and Canadian economies, the two countries had different labor market and poverty outcomes.

The United States gave relatively free play to market forces, allowing the incomes of less skilled workers to fall and poverty rates to rise. Canada chose a more activist strategy of providing a broad social safety net for the poor. American labor regulations permitted unionism and collective bargaining to wither away, while Canada's regulations grew more favorable to trade unionism. American policies generated substantial growth of low-wage jobs. Canadian policies generated nearly comparable employment growth while mitigating the forces that led to increased inequality and poverty in the United States. The experience of 1980s shows vividly that even the relatively small differences in policies and institutions between Canada and the United States affected economic outcomes. With a different set of policies, the United States could have had labor market and income outcomes comparable to those in Canada. With a different set of policies, Canada could have looked more like the United States. Yes, Virginia, the debates over policy and institutions in Ottawa and Washington matter.

NOTES

1. Many Canadian local unions are part of unions that have members on both sides of the border; they are called internationals.

2. The results of this project are contained in Card and Freeman, 1993.

3. See OECD, 1992 (Tables 2.8 and 2.17). In 1980 EEC countries had about a 10 percentage point lower participation rate in the workforce than the United Statesa and Canada, but comparable rates of unemployment.

4. The contrast with Western Europe is instructive here. The gap in employment between the United States and Western Europe is largely the result of falling employment-to-population rates in Europe compared with the United States rather than one of increasing labor participation rates.

5. We use the average 1989 exchange rate of 0.84 U.S. dollar per Canadian dollar to transform Canadian to U.S. currency, and national price indices to put all the figures on a 1989 price basis. Highlighting the basic similarity between the American and Canadian economies, purchasing-power parity figures yield a similar picture to that given with exchanges rates.

6. Blank and Hanratty (1993) constructed the poverty rates using Canadian poverty thresholds for cash income. The U.S. Bureau of the Census (1992) tabulates poverty rates using a variety of other income measures, including imputations for the value of noncash transfers, principally food stamps and school lunches. All of these measures show a rise in U.S. poverty rates between 1979 and 1991.

7. The immigration rates in Table 6.1 make no allowance for emigration, which is a significant factor in Canada. During the past three decades Canadian emigration rates, mainly to the U.S., have averaged about one-half of gross immigration rates; see Statistics Canada, 1990 (Table 2.3).

8. The Canadian system varies across provinces, with high school graduation after eleven years of schooling in some provinces and after twelve or thirteen in others. Different provinces also have different requirements for a university degree: a minimum of three years of university in Ontario; two years of junior college and three years of university in Quebec; four years of university elsewhere. In the United States all states have four years of high school and four-year university programs.

9. This can be seen in the educational distributions of the two countries; see Card and Riddell, 1993.

10. Until 1993 the Family Allowance program paid each family a monthly sum per child (based on the age of the child). The program became means-tested at the end of 1992.

11. In Card and Freeman, (1993), the studies that take a do-different-policies-matter approach are Borjas, and Blank and Hanratty. The studies that begin with an observed outcome difference are: Riddell, Card and Riddell, Freeman and Needels, Lemieux, and Blackburn and Bloom.

12. This section derives from Borjas, 1993.

13. The prime reason for this gap is the relatively higher level of schooling of Canadian immigrants. Given that a year of schooling raises earnings by about 6 percent, this relative education gap implies that immigrants in Canada would earn 13 percent more relative to natives than immigrants in the United States would earn relative to native-born Americans. In fact, the size of the actual relative gap differs by 13 percentage points for this group.

14. This section derives from Card and Riddell, 1993.

15. Let U = the number of unemployed, O = the number of people out of the labor force, and N = the population. Then the unemployment rate is U/(N-O); the proportion of not employed who are unemployed is U/O; and the labor force participation rate is (N-O)/N. The text says

that the unemployment rate equals the proportion of the population that is not working times the proportion of the not-employed who are unemployed, divided by the labor force participation rate: $U/(N-O) = [(O+U)/N)] \times [U/(O+U)]/[(N-O)/N]$.

16. Put differently, it is a relative change in the *behavior* of nonworkers, rather than a relative change in the *number* of nonworkers, that is the key to understanding the divergence in unemployment rates.

17. This section is derived largely from Freeman and Needels, 1993.

18. This section is derived largely from Lemieux, 1993.

19. See Lemieux, 1993.

20. This section is derived from Riddell, 1993.

21. The U.S. surveys were conducted in 1984 and, with a smaller sample, 1992. The Canadian survey was conducted in 1990. The survey questions that elicit union preferences from nonunion workers differ in the two countries, reflecting the different processes involved in unionization (winning a formal election in the United States; obtaining signed cards indicating a desire for union coverage in Canada). Farber and Krueger (1992) compared responses to the two questions among workers in the U.S. and concluded that they give very similar estimates of the desire for union coverage.

22. The actual figures in the two surveys for unionization were: U.S. 22 percent and Canada 48 percent. These are larger unionization rates than are generally reported for these countries. One reason is that these statistics exclude self-employed workers, managers, and those without jobs. The Canadian survey also classifies members of professional associations as union workers. The difference in unionization of 26 points compares to a 21 point difference in standard union densities and a 24 point difference in collective bargaining coverage between the countries and thus gives a correct picture of the differences. See Riddell (1993) for details.

23. This section is derived from Blank and Hanratty, 1993.

24. The efficacy of the Canadian program is not much different under the alternative labor supply assumptions. Given a realistic range of labor supply responses (calibrated from the experimental results of the Seattle-Denver Income Maintenance Experiments (SRI, 1983)), the move to a Canadian-style transfer program would not have large effects on the earnings of low-income families.

25. This section is derived from Blackburn and Bloom, 1993.

26. These include payments to blind and disabled individuals but exclude medical payments.

REFERENCES

Blackburn, McKinley L., and David E. Bloom. 1993. "The Distribution of Family Income: Measuring and Explaining Changes in the 1980s for Canada and the United States." In D. Card and R. Freeman, eds., *Small Differences That Matter: Labor Market and Income Maintainance in Canada and the United States.* Chicago: University of Chicago Press for NBER.

Blackburn, McKinley, David Bloom, and Richard B. Freeman. 1990. "The Declining Position of Less-Skilled American Males." In G. Burtless, ed., *A Future of Lousy Jobs?* Washington D.C.: Brookings Institution.

Blank, Rebecca, and David Card. 1991. "Recent Trends in Insured and Uninsured Unemployment: Is There An Explanation?" *Quarterly Journal of Economics* 106 (November): 1157–1190.

Blank, Rebecca and Maria Hanratty. 1992. "Down and Out in North America: Recent Trends in Poverty Rates in the United States and Canada." *Quarterly Journal of Economics* 107 (February): 233–254.

———. 1993 "Responding to Need: A Comparison of Social Safety Nets in the United States and Canada." In D. Card and R. Freeman, eds., *Small Differences That Matter: Labor Market and Income Maintainance in Canada and the United States.* Chicago: University of Chicago Press for NBER.

Borjas, George J. 1993. "Imigration Policy, National Origin, and Immigrant Skills: A Comparison of Canada and the United States." In D. Card and R. Freeman, eds., *Small Differences That Matter: Labor Market and Income Maintainance in Canada and the United States.* Chicago: University of Chicago Press for NBER.

Borjas, George J., Richard B. Freeman, and Kevin Lang. 1991. "Undocumented Mexican-Born Workers in the United States: How Many, How Permanent?" In Abowd and Freeman, eds., *Immigration, Trade, and the Labor Market.* Chicago: University of Chicago Press for NBER.

Bound, John, and George Johnson. 1992. "Changes in the Structure of Wages in the 1980s: An Evaluation of Alternative Explanations." *American Economic Review* 82 (June): 371–392.

Card, David. 1992. "The Effect of Unions on the Distribution of Wages: Redistribution or Relabelling?" NBER Working Paper no. 4195 (October).

Card, David, and Richard B. Freeman, eds. 1993. *Small Differences That Matter: Labor Market and Income Maintainance in Canada and the United States.* Chicago: University of Chicago Press for NBER.

Card, David, and W. Craig Riddell. 1993. "A Comparative Analysis of Unemployment in Canada and the United States." In D. Card and R. Freeman, eds., *Small Differences That Matter: Labor Market and Income Maintainance in Canada and the United States.* Chicago: University of Chicago Press for NBER.

Committee on Ways and Means, U.S. House of Representatives. 1992. *1992 Green Book.* Washington, D.C.: GPO.

Farber, Henry. 1983. "The Determination of the Union Status of Workers." *Econometrica* 51 (September): 1417–1437.

Farber, Henry, and Alan Krueger. 1992. "Union Membership in the United States: The Decline Continues." NBER Working Paper no. 4216, November.

Freeman, Richard B. 1976. *The Overeducated American.* New York: Academic Press.

———. 1980. "Unionism and the Dispersion of Wages." *Industrial and Labor Relations Review* 34: 3–23.

———. 1990. "On the Divergence of Unionism Among Developed Countries." In R. Brunetta and P. Dell'Aringa, eds., *Labour Relations and Economic Performance.* Hampshire, England: MacMillan.

———. 1992. "How Much has De-Unionization Contributed to the Rise in Male Earnings Inequality?" In S. Danziger and P. Gottschalk, eds., *Uneven Tides.* New York: Russell Sage Foundation.

Freeman, Richard B., and Karen Needels. 1993. "Skill Differentials In Canada in an Era of Rising Labor Market Inequality." In D. Card and R. Freeman, eds., *Small Differences That Matter: Labor Market and Income Maintainance in Canada and the United States.* Chicago: University of Chicago Press for NBER.

Katz, Lawrence F., and Kevin M. Murphy. 1992. "Changes in Relative Wages 1963–1987: Supply and Demand Factors." *Quarterly Journal of Economics* 107 (February): 35–78.

Lemieux, Thomas. 1993. "Unions and Wage Inequality in Canada and the United States." In D. Card and R. Freeman, eds., *Small Differences That Matter: Labor Market and Income Maintainance in Canada and the United States.* Chicago: University of Chicago Press for NBER.

Murphy, Kevin M., and Finis Welch. 1992. "The Structure of Wages." *Quarterly Journal of Economics* 107 (February): 285–326.

Organization for Economic Cooperation and Development (OECD). 1992. *Historical Statistics, 1960-1990.* Paris: OECD.

Riddell, W. Craig. 1993. "Unionization in Canada and the United States: A Tale of Two Countries." In D. Card and R. Freeman, eds., *Small Differences That Matter: Labor Market and Income Maintainance in Canada and the United States.* Chicago: University of Chicago Press for NBER.

Social Security Administration. 1991. *Social Security Bulletin Annual Statistical Supplement.* Washington, D.C.: GPO.

SRI International. 1983. *Final Report of the Seattle/Denver Income Maintenance Experiment: Volume 1, Design and Results.* Menlo Park, Calif.: SRI International.

Statistics Canada. 1980–81. *Canada Year Book*. Ottawa: Statistics Canada.

———. 1990. *Canada Year Book*. Ottawa: Statistics Canada.

———. 1991. *Canada Year Book*. Ottawa: Statistics Canada.

United States Department of Commerce, Bureau of the Census. 1992. *Measuring the Effect of Benefits and Taxes on Income and Poverty: 1979 to 1991*. Current Population Report Series P–60, no. 182–RD (August). Washington, DC: U.S. GPO.

7

LESSONS FOR
THE UNITED STATES

Richard B. Freeman

U nlike many investigations of foreign economic systems, the
Working under Different Rules project was motivated not by
intrinsic interest in Europe or Japan (fascinating though they
may be) but by concern about the specific problems that plague
the United States as we prepare to enter the twenty-first century:
rising wage and income inequality, low and falling real earnings
for less skilled workers, sluggish growth of productivity, loss of
employee representation, and so on. The goals of the project
were threefold: first, to determine whether other advanced countries have managed to avoid some of the problems that face
workers in the United States; second, to see if different institutions and social protection policies affect labor market performance in important ways; and third, to assess which, if any,
experiences in other countries offer lessons for the design of U.S.
policy and institutions. Underlying the entire project was the
premise that learning how workers fare in different advanced
countries would illuminate American problems and suggest
possible solutions to them.

In this concluding chapter I will provide a capsule "executive
summary" of the findings, occasionally drawing on related studies
to fill in some gaps in the picture, and try to derive some guide for
improving American labor outcomes.[1]

FINDINGS

Do Workers in Other Advanced Countries Face the Same Problems as American Workers?

The studies summarized in this volume provide a fairly conclusive answer to this question. They show that many of the problems of American workers in the late twentieth century were not endemic to advanced capitalist economies.

1. Other advanced countries did not experience either massive increases in wage differentials and wage inequality or drops in the real earnings of the less skilled.

Wage inequality increased in Canada, Japan, and in some continental European countries, as it did in the United States, but by much less than in the United States. Inequality barely changed in France and Italy, fell in the Netherlands, and rose less in Sweden and Germany than in the United States. The only country in which the relative position of less skilled male workers fell as much as it did in the United States was Great Britain, but because real earnings increased rapidly in Britain, low-paid British workers realized modest increases in earnings in the 1980s. Only low-paid American men had sizable decreases in real wages. Moreover, nowhere did the ratio of the earnings of college graduates to less educated workers rise as much as in the United States. Earnings differentials by education barely changed in the Netherlands, and they fell in the rapidly growing Korean economy.

2. Loss of collective representation or employee voice was most severe in the United States.

The huge drop in union representation of workers in the United States, combined with a labor law that treats company-sponsored committees of workers as illegal antiunion devices, has meant that most Americans lack any form of collective voice at the workplace. The American move toward a union-free private sector contrasts with the continued large role of collective bargaining in the country most similar to ours, Canada. Whereas most workers who want unions are so represented in Canada, a large proportion of those who want unions in the United States are not organized. The loss of employee representation in the United States contrasts also with the situation in continental Europe where, even in the face of falling union membership in several countries, workers have maintained a collective voice within firms through legally mandated works councils. Works councils have legal rights to information about the performance of the firm as it relates to labor issues. They also have rights to "consultation" on changes in labor and personnel policies. In Germany, the councils have codetermination rights over certain decisions, and arbitration is used to settle disputes with management. In all countries except Spain, councils cannot strike and do not negotiate wages. In countries with different union and labor systems, works councils seem to provide a forum for cooperative labor-management relations and a place for workers to voice concerns and influence management decisions. Councils operate successfully in France, where unions are weak and management has an extensive influence on councils; they succeed in Germany and Belgium, where unions are strong. The growing role of councils in Europe in a period when collective bargaining became increasingly decentralized suggests that councils are a "robust" institutional form for labor-management relations, well suited for building worker voice and participation within enterprises. The successful operation of works councils limited to occupational health and safety issues in Canada shows that this institution can work even in a decentralized U.S.-style labor market.

3. American workers get less training within firms than workers do in several other countries, even though such training appears to have a good payoff.

Worker training differs across countries in many ways. Some countries base their training systems largely on the firm. Other countries rely more on government training programs, or on school-based or individual training decisions. Evidence of the returns on training for individuals (in the form of wages) and for firms (in the form of productivity) suggests that company-based training has a high payoff. Presumably this is because it is linked directly to the skills needed at the particular workplace. In contrast, informal "learning by doing" raises worker productivity in the short run but not in the long run. Government-led and school-based job training systems have only marginal effects on wages.

The United States offers less within-firm training to workers than do several countries, notably Germany and Japan. In the United States, most firm training programs are for white-collar and educated workers. The limited training provided for blue-collar workers is more remedial than in other countries, covering basic literacy and mathematical skills rather than building technical skills. Measures of the proportion of labor costs going to training are, moreover, potentially misleading and likely to provide a poor guide to policy. The issue is not so much the amount spent on training as it is the actual training workers get, and the distribution of that training among them. Some American firms spend as much on training as firms in other countries do, but they get less "bang for the buck" because American high school dropouts and even graduates have weaker basic skills than comparable young workers overseas.

4. Persons at the bottom of the income or earnings distribution have lower standards of living in the United States than in most other advanced countries.

The combination of rising inequality in earnings and slow growth of real earnings and productivity meant that low-wage Americans in the early 1990s had lower living standards (using purchasing power parity to measure the value of foreign currencies) than low-wage workers in virtually all other advanced countries. The differences were, moreover, large ones that will not disappear if one measures wages or purchasing power slightly differently. The social safety net is also much lower in the United States than in other countries. Thus, despite America's overall high standard of living, the poor are worse off in absolute terms in the United States than in other countries. The contrast with Canada is particularly striking. From the 1970s to the mid-1980s the poverty rate in Canada went from above the American rate of poverty to substantially below the American rate. Homelessness was hard to find in Canada while it pervaded all major U.S. cities. Comparisons with European countries and Japan tell a similar story.[2]

The broad findings that other advanced countries have avoided massive increases in wage inequality and declining real earnings for low-paid workers, reduced poverty more than the United States, and provided mechanisms for employee representation and cooperation with employers, and that some have also provided better within-firm training for less educated workers is both bad news and good news for the United States. The bad news is that they suggest that American labor institutions and social protection policies may be ill-suited for improving the productivity and earnings of lower skilled workers into the twenty-first century. The good news is that the outcomes on which the United States did poorly are not inexorable or irremediable. If every country had the same outcomes, we would be pessimistic about finding ways to improve results. There is no point in trying to accomplish the impossible, however desirable it might be. Because other countries have done better along some dimensions for their work forces, it is realistic to believe that the United States can do better also.

Do Different Rules of Work and Social Protection Policies Affect Labor Outcomes in Important Ways?

The *Working under Different Rules* project highlighted the great variation in institutions that govern the labor market in otherwise comparable advanced economies. People do indeed work under different rules, with different modes of compensation, forms of representation, and levels of job security. The American way of determining labor outcomes differs from that in most other advanced countries in that greater reliance is placed on the decentralized labor market and the social safety net for citizens is correspondingly low. As noted in Chapter 1, the result is that market forces are more critical for determining Americans' economic well-being than they are for the citizens of other advanced countries.

The extent to which specific rules of work or labor and social policies explain specific differences in labor outcomes between the United States and other countries is, of course, difficult to determine. When the rules and institutions governing the labor market differ greatly between economies, there are many possible causes of differences in outcomes. And rules and institutions often fit together in systemic ways that produce "labor relations systems," which may make it unrealistic to attribute causality to single differences between countries (see point 15). Still, our analyses have found several important areas where particular labor market rules and social protection policies contributed substantially to differences in outcomes. We also found some areas in which differences in rules and policies had smaller effects than is often alleged.

5. Institutional differences are important determinants of the change in wage inequality and in the real earnings of low-paid workers.

Three things differentiate the countries that had smaller increases in wage differentials than the United States. First, those countries placed more emphasis on wage-setting institutions in determining pay and less on pure market forces than the United States did. The particular institutions that influenced wages in these countries—centralized collective bargaining of widely differing forms, as in Sweden or Italy; national minimum wages, as in France; the extension of collective bargaining, as in Germany—seem less important than the fact that the institutions universally intervened in favor of low-paid workers. Second, these countries maintained the strength of unions or had smaller declines in unionization than the United States. The United States (and the United Kingdom) had large declines in union penetration and large increases in wage inequality during the 1980s, whereas Canada and Germany maintained union strength and had smaller rises in inequality. Third, those countries with more extensive training systems than the United States, notably Japan and Germany, had smaller increases in inequality of earnings than the United States and also did reasonably well in employment growth, although the unification of Germany created a major economic shock for that economy. When less educated workers are better trained, they are more competitive with highly educated workers and are thus better able to adjust to shifts in labor demand that favor more skilled workers.

6. Institutional support is necessary for a successful firm-based training system.

The experiences of Germany and Japan, widely viewed as exemplary in their within-firm training, show that considerable institutional structure is needed to induce firms to provide training for workers. In Germany, unions and works councils help to determine the content of training in apprenticeship programs. Upon completion of a program, trainees receive national certificates of skills. In addition to certification, the government provides schooling that complements the workplace training, and government regulations make it costly to hire young people from outside of the apprenticeship system. In Japan, there is little mobility of labor in and out of large firms, but workers rotate between jobs within firms. Thus, workers acquire skills in a variety of broadly defined jobs at a company. Furthermore, all high school graduates in Japan have mastered similar skills, and there are strong links between firms and schools. A worker's performance in high school is the key to obtaining a job with a good firm that provides workplace training. The lesson is that developing a good workplace-based training system requires a range of institutional support, from schools, government, and so on.

7. Labor laws and regulations substantially affect modes of employee representation and participation in enterprises.

The development of works councils in Europe and Canada shows the importance of labor laws in the creation of institutions for employee representation within firms. Employers (and unions in organized workplaces) might create council-type organizations without legal mandate in those countries, but they did not do so, as both parties often opposed councils as possible threats to their position in the work place. American employers introduced councils in the early part of the century, partly as antiunion devices, partly to induce participation in the enterprise, but those institutions were short-lived, largely because they lacked independent power.

Legal regulations also determine the ways councils operate: whether they include management or consist solely of worker representatives; whether different groups of workers have their own representatives; how much power is given councils to affect outcomes. Canadian councils differ substantively from European councils, because Canadian law limits them to health and safety issues and allows the enterprise to choose its mode of selecting councilors, so long as that selection is "representative."

Even the relatively modest differences in labor law between the United States and Canada—the United States requires secret-ballot elections in campaigns for representation, and management is free to devote considerable resources to opposing unionization; whereas Canada relies extensively on workers' checking off their desire for a union on special cards, a system that limits management's role and otherwise leaves the decision to unionize more to workers—appear to have influenced the differing pattern of union strength between the two countries.

The lesson is that a system of employee representation within firms must be grounded in labor laws that provide legal support and that gives real responsibilities to the representational institutions, if not actually mandating them.

8. Greater social protection policies reduce poverty rates, though at a major tax or budget cost.

The higher earnings of low-wage workers in Europe compared with the United States contributes to higher rates of poverty in the United States. But so, too, does the lower level of the American social safety net. Indeed, comparisons of the distributions of income or disposable income, which includes taxes and transfers as well as labor market earnings, interest, dividends, and rent, shows that much of the higher rate of poverty found in the United States is attributable to differences in social protection policies, particularly for children (Smeeding, Torrey and Rein (1988); Smeeding and Torrey (1988).[3]

The contrast between social protection programs and poverty rates in Canada and the United States is a striking case in point. Canada has a modestly more equal distribution of earnings than the United States, but its distribution is extremely unequal by European standards. Canadian income per head is marginally below American income per head. As a result, measured by incomes before taxes and transfers, Canada had a higher rate of poverty than the United States in the mid-1980s. But Canadian unemployment benefits, family income maintenance programs, and other welfare state programs are so much stronger than comparable American programs that measured by incomes after taxes and transfers, Canada has a much lower poverty rate than the United States. The Canadian experience shows that an effective safety net can greatly reduce poverty even when wage inequality is relatively great. However, effective social safety nets do not come free: a larger share of national output is devoted to income transfers in Europe and Canada than in the United States, which in turn requires greater rates of taxation and/or budget deficits.

9. Most social protection programs have modest side effects on the labor market.

Many economists and social observers, unfamiliar with the equivocal evidence on the widely studied American welfare system (Moffitt, 1992), have blamed the more extensive income maintenance systems and employment regulations of Western Europe for the high unemployment in those countries. There are examples of poorly constructed programs, such as the sick leave system in Sweden, that adversely affect working time, and examples of unemployment insurance programs that extend periods of joblessness. But our study of a host of different programs in different countries shows that, in general, these programs do not have major efficiency costs.

One reason for this is that many European programs require people to work in order to receive benefits. In France, for instance, the combination of time limits on welfare payments and the availability of public daycare leads many single women to leave the welfare system and go to work when their child reaches age three. In Sweden, employer benefits such as maternity leave are generous, so single mothers are more likely to have worked before they have a child. Other European programs, such as tenant protections or subsidies for homeowners, primarily affect residence decisions and have only a minor impact on labor mobility.

Another reason that social programs do not necessarily have a negative effect is that firms or individuals find ways around them. For instance, when market conditions change in European countries such as Germany, France, and Belgium, employment security laws force firms to adjust their number of employees more slowly than they might like to. But instead, firms in these countries simply adjust the hours each employee works. In Spain, there is considerable noncompliance with high payroll taxes mandated to pay for health care, as small firms tend to evade those social security taxes. Since most Spanish workers have a family member in a firm that does pays the social security taxes, however, virtually all Spaniards are covered by the health care system.

The bottom line is that the primary effects of well-constructed social safety net programs fall on the well-being of the people they were designed to help, with only modest costs in terms of economic efficiency.

10. Changes in the relative supply of educated workers, due partly to differences in educational policies and partly to individual responses to the returns on education, contribute to differing trends in wage inequality.

In the United States, growth of the college-educated work force decelerated greatly in the 1980s—a direct response to the falling return on a college degree that was seen in the 1970s. In contrast, Canada and the Netherlands continued to expand their number of college graduates relative to high school graduates in the 1980s. As a consequence Canada had only modest increases in the college–high school wage differential, and the Netherlands had a modestly declining wage differential. In general, the change in the relative supplies of workers with given levels of education in a country greatly influences relative wages: a faster increase in the propor-tion of workers with college degrees resulted in a smaller increase in earnings differentials by education in the 1980s (or a large decrease, in the case of Korea). On the other hand, shifts in the industry or occupation mix in a country's demand for labor, in favor of more skilled workers, were too similar among countries to explain much of the different trends in earnings inequality. Only in Japan and Korea do shifts in industry structure—notably the con-tinued strength of manufacturing employment—help to account for their distinct change in relative wages. This finding suggest that policies to increase the supply of educated workers can effectively reduce inequality and that, by themselves, the normal response of individuals to obtain greater education when the return to educa-tion rises can be a powerful force toward reducing inequality.

The analyses in this project also found that market forces present economies with apparent "trade-offs" between some outcomes.

11. The experience of the 1980s is consistent with two potential, market-driven trade-offs: one between employment and real wages, and the second between employment and wage inequality.

Countries like the United States, with poor growth of productiv-ity and real wages, had better employment performance than countries with greater productivity and real wage growth; Euro-pean countries with strong real wage growth had relatively poor employment performances. Except for Japan, no country managed to do well on both of these levels, and even Japan had economic problems in the early 1990s. Within countries, also, there is a substantial labor demand-type "trade-off": high or increasing wages are associated with high or rising unemployment or slower growth of employment in a given period.[4] At any given time, the broader economy seems to offer labor markets the choice between jobs and high real wages/productivity—a choice which translates over time into a choice between growth of employment and growth of wages or productivity.

In addition, countries that maintained stable wage distributions had worse employment records than the United States (again excluding Japan).[5] This suggests that in an era when market forces favored workers with better education and skills, there was a second possible trade-off—between income inequality and employment of low-skill workers. Put differently, countries that maintained the earnings of the less skilled seem to have "paid" in terms of high unemployment of these workers; the United States paid for its growth of employment through the falling real earnings of less skilled workers. But the fact that less skilled and low-paid American men had relatively poor employment prospects despite falling real wages shows that the American problem goes beyond a simple trade-off analysis.

GUIDES TO IMPROVING U.S. LABOR OUTCOMES

What Implications Do the Experiences of Other Countries Have for Designing Policies to Overcome the Problems Facing American Workers?

This is the hardest question to answer. It requires that we establish not only that particular practices or policies helped a foreign country to overcome a problem plaguing the United States but also that those practices and policies or, more realistically, some U.S. variant thereof would "work" in the different economic environment of the United States. Unfortunately, neither economic theory nor evidence provides much guidance about the transferability of institutions or policies from one setting to another. Most economic theory assumes a given set of institutions, usually "pure" markets in which governments, unions, or business federations play only minor roles. Analyses that examine how particular institutions work invariably consider those institutions in isolation, rather than as part of broader labor relations and economic systems.

History presents a mixed record of success in transferring labor practices across country lines. Despite American efforts after World War II to introduce U.S.-style labor relations in Japan and Germany, both countries developed their own distinct workplace rules and labor institutions. Canadian labor legislation partially copied the American Wagner Act, but with small differences that have produced different levels of unionization in the two countries half a century later. Japanese transplants to the United States have imported some Japanese personnel practices but not others.

Given the problem of transferability, the lessons I draw from foreign labor practices for the United States are necessarily judgmental and provisional. I wish to lay out broad lessons for the design or direction of possible public and private policy to improve the condition of American labor, not to examine the pros and cons of particular policies. (And even at this level of generality, the reader may disagree with my assessment without necessarily contradicting the facts.) I draw three general lessons from the comparative analyses in this volume; they are described in the following points.

12. Reversing the decline in the living standards of less skilled workers and reducing poverty rates will require the United States to supplement market forces in wage determination and training as it has not done in the past.

The competitive labor market on which our country relies so intensely for pay determination has set in place forces to improve the well-being of lower paid and less skilled workers. For instance, the rise in educational earnings differentials in the 1980s led more Americans to enroll in college, reducing the future supply of low-skill workers, which will raise their earnings. But the 1980s showed that market forces are insufficient to give low-paid American workers living standards that are comparable to those of low-paid workers in other advanced countries which maintain the real earnings of the low paid through better training, some form of institutional setting of wages, or both.

While a "better training" solution would be more consonant with America's reliance on the market than interventions in pay setting or income determination would be, the training systems that are exemplary in the world, those that encourage training within firms, require considerable institutional support themselves, as was noted in point 6. Plus, training is only part of the reason for the narrower earnings distributions and higher real earnings of low-skill workers in Europe. By itself, training is no panacea to low and falling wages. Wage-setting institutions such as collective bargaining and national minimum wages (far above U.S. levels) were also important in maintaining the labor market position of the less skilled in other countries, albeit at the cost of some employment.

Some of the ways other countries raise the real earnings of their workers are alien to our decentralized labor market. I find it inconceivable that European-style national collective bargaining or government extension of labor contracts from some employers to their competitors would work in the United States. But the United States has its own set of policies that intervene in market wage setting and income determination. For example, the Earned Income Tax Credit supplements the pay of low-wage workers with a negative income tax, in keeping with our decentralized wage-setting system. Creation of additional social benefits attached to work, such as health insurance paid partly by general tax funds, would be another way to buttress the living standards of low-paid workers. Raising the minimum wage could also be a tool for intervention and would fit U.S. wage-setting practices.[6]

13. It is possible to reduce poverty through social safety nets that are largely complementary with work.

Other countries have more extensive social protection systems than the United States does, and these greatly reduce their poverty rates. In contrast to the American welfare system, however, many systems of social protection complement work, and these programs can serve as guides for designing policies to remove the welfare trap that reduces the work incentive for many Americans. When few mothers worked, many Americans viewed "workfare" as inequitable, but in fact workfare is the essence of the best state welfare and social protection programs in Europe. Programs that provide benefits for workers, such as the state-provided daycare for children of working mothers in France, or Sweden's diverse benefits that accrue largely to those with a work history, show that it is possible to design social protection programs that redistribute income and make work more attractive. As with training and wage setting, however, these programs require greater social intervention in the market's determination of outcomes than has been the practice in the United States. Even a welfare system that complements work would be expensive: no country provides an extensive social safety net without allocating a larger share of national output to that system than is allotted in the United States. If we want to improve the situation of the poor, we will have to pay.

14. Providing collective representation and venues for participation for American workers will require new labor institutions and changes in labor law.

European and Canadian experiences show that legal protection for the establishment of modes of worker representation is necessary to ensure that employees have a collective voice in firms, and that once in place, such institutions can create cooperative and productive labor relations. Canadian labor laws limit management pressures in union organizing efforts, and some labor relations experts suggest that those practices be adopted in the United States (Weiler, 1990). But Canada has also moved, in the health and safety area, toward European-style works councils that cover nonunion workers as well as union workers. One lesson from the European experience is that any such intrafirm organization should include all employees, not just the blue-collar workers that are normally unionizable in the United States.

Both Europe and Canada mandate councils, which suggests that legal mandating may be necessary for such organizations to be viable. A more conservative reading of the evidence indicates that voluntarily established councils or committees that have some legal standing could also work and might better fit the American labor scene. Such councils or commitees would need real power in some areas, say for regulating occupational health and safety, dealing with grievances, obtaining information about company plans, or for joint consultation in decision-making on training. The European experience further suggests that such institutions should not have rights to engage in wage bargaining or to call strikes.[7]

In addition to these guidelines for improving the situation for American labor, I offer one additional observation drawn from the comparative analysis.

15. Labor institutions and rules fit together in systemic ways that make the impact of any single labor policy or social program depend on the environment of other institutions and rules in which it operates.

This observation underscores the problem of transferring labor practices across countries, and also draws attention to the need for institutions to adapt to their economic environment. It has two implications for efforts to improve American labor practices. First, since the decentralized labor market of the United States differs greatly from the European and Japanese labor markets, we can be almost certain that what works in those countries will work somewhat differently in the United States. Even within Europe, there are striking cases in which the same policy has had different effects in different settings. For instance both Spain and Germany weakened their employment protection laws in the 1980s, but whereas in Spain the legal change led to a situation in which most new employees were hired under temporary contracts, there was very little change in German employment practices. The greater strength of German unions and works councils and the importance of apprenticeship in Germany meant that firms continued to hire people under permanent contracts. This in turn indicates that reforms are more likely to succeed when they are attuned to the overall labor system in which they operate. In an attempt to create U.S.-style labor market flexibility, several European countries sought to change their income maintenance and employment regulations in the 1980s. Their success was marginal at best, and did not "cure" the European unemployment problem. Even in Great Britain, which went the furthest with its efforts, unemployment was as high after Prime Minister Thatcher's reforms as before.

Second, the interaction of programs and policies suggests that a set of interrelated programs has a greater chance of succeeding than a single program designed to resolve a given problem. Multiple programs can reinforce each other in ways that make the effect of several programs together differ from that of any program alone. The coexistence of public daycare centers, time-limited welfare benefits, and general family child allowances in France, for example, creates a much greater chance for moving single parents from welfare to work than would otherwise exist.

Although the United States (and any country) has distinct features that make it infeasible to copy others' practices, the information in this volume about experiences of other countries provides insights for the design of institutions or programs that might improve our situation; it suggests directions in which we might go to alleviate our problems, and highlights the pitfalls in alternative ways of organizing the world of work. No country has a "lock" on the right institutions or policies; what works in some periods or settings may not work in others. Whether the reader agrees or disagrees with the lessons I have drawn, the declining position of American workers relative to those in other advanced countries shows clearly that it is appropriate to reconsider our labor institutions in light of experiences elsewhere. Unlike Samuel Gompers in the early 1900s, we cannot readily dismiss foreign labor practices as obviously inferior to our own.

NOTES

1. In particular, I refer to results from a study of extreme poverty across countries, that was part of this overall project, but that at this writing was in a preliminary working stage.

2. Comparisons of extreme poverty rates between the United States and Europe and Japan are part of the ongoing extreme poverty study, mentioned in note 1. In addition, I rely on the work of Timothy M. Smeeding and others. See Smeeding (1992); Smeeding, et al. (1990); and Smeeding, Torrey, and Rein (1988).

3. These studies compare "relative poverty" measured by the fraction of the population with incomes below 40 percent of the median. I prefer measures of absolute poverty that contrast persons with similar purchasing power across countries. As the per capita gross domestic product (GDP) of European countries has moved closer to that of the United States, the difference between absolute and relative poverty measures has diminished.

4. The evidence for within-country trade-offs between the level of earnings and unemployment is presented in Blanchflower and Oswald (1994a) and in their paper for our project, Blanchflower and Oswald (1994b).

5. It is important to recognize that while Japan has had an enviable growth record and export performance, Japan is not a world leader in GDP per capita or living standards and thus "benefits" from still being in a catch-up phase of economic development.

6. For a discussion of the relative benefits and costs of income tax credits and minimum wage in aiding lower paid workers, see Freeman (1993).

7. For a more detailed discussion of the implications of foreign experience with works councils for the United States, see Freeman and Rogers (1993).

REFERENCES

Blanchflower, David G., and Andrew J. Oswald. 1994. *The Wage Curve.* Cambridge, Mass.: MIT Press.

Blanchflower, David G., and Andrew J. Oswald. 1994. "International

Wage Curves." In Richard B. Freeman and Lawrence F. Katz, eds., *Differences and Changes in Wage Structures*. Chicago: University of Chicago Press for NBER.

Freeman, Richard B. 1994. "Minimum Wages—Again!" *International Journal of Manpower*, Special Issue (Spring).

Freeman, Richard B. and Joel Rogers. 1993. "Who Speaks for Us? Employee Representation in a Non-union Labor Market." In M. Kleiner and B. Kaufman, eds., *Employee Representation: Alternatives and New Directions*. Madison, Wisc.: Industrial Relations Research Association.

Gompers, Samuel. 1910. *Labor in Europe and America*. New York and London: Harper and Brothers Publishers.

Moffitt, Robert A. 1992. "Incentive Effects of the U.S. Welfare System: A Review." *Journal of Economic Perspectives* 30, no. 1 (March): 1–61.

Smeeding, Timothy M. 1992. "Why the U.S. Antipoverty System Doesn't Work Very Well." *Challenge* (January–February).

Smeeding, Timothy M., and Barbara Boyle Torrey. 1988. "Poor Children in Rich Countries." *Science* 242 (November).

Smeeding, Timothy M., Michael O'Higgins, and Lee Rainwater, eds. 1990. *Poverty, Income Inequality and Income Distribution in Comparative Perspective: the Luxembourg Income Study (LIS)*. Washington, D.C.: Urban Institute Press.

Smeeding, Timothy M., Barbara Boyle Torrey, and Martin Rein. 1988. "Patterns of Income and Poverty: The Economic Status of Children and the Elderly in Eight Countries." In J. L. Palmer, T. Smeeding, and B. Boyle Torrey, eds., *The Vulnerable*. Washington, D.C. Urban Institute Press.

Weiler, Paul C. 1990. *Governing the Workplace: The Future of Labor and Employment Law*. Cambridge: Harvard University Press.

APPENDIX

Books in the NBER Series on *Comparative Labor Markets*

The National Bureau of Economic Research *Working under Different Rules* project included five research teams. The technical papers for these projects are being published in the following volumes:

Rebecca Blank, editor. 1994. *Social Protection Vs. Economic Flexibility: Is There a Tradeoff?* University of Chicago Press for NBER.

> Abraham, Katharine G., and Susan N. Houseman. "Does Employment Protection Inhibit Labor Market Flexibility? Lessons from Germany, France, and Belgium."

> Blank, Rebecca M. "Public Sector Growth and Labor Market Flexibility: The U.S. Vs. the U.K."

> Blank, Rebecca M., and Richard B. Freeman. "Evaluating the Connection Between Social Protection and Economic Flexibility."

> Börsch-Supan, Axel. "Housing Market Regulations and Housing Market Performance in the U.S., Germany and Japan."

> de la Rica, Sara, and Thomas Lemieux. "Does Public Health Insurance Reduce Labor Market Flexibility or Encourage the Underground Economy: Evidence from Spain and the U.S."

> Gustafsson, Siv, and Frank P. Stafford. "Three Regimes of Childcare: The U.S., the Netherlands, and Sweden."

> Hanratty, Maria J. "Social Welfare Programs for Women and Children: The U.S. Vs. France."

> Holtz-Eakin, Douglas. "Health Insurance Provision and Labor Market Efficiency in the United States and Germany."

> Montgomery, Edward B. "Patterns in Regional Labor Market Adjustment: The U.S. Vs. Japan."

> Rebick, Marcus. "Social Security and Older Workers' Labor Market Responsiveness: The U.S., Japan, and Sweden."

> Scherer, Peter. "Trends in Social Protection Programs and Expenditures in the 1980s."

David Card and Richard B. Freeman, editors. 1993. *Small Differences That Matter: Labor Markets and Income Maintenance in Canada and the United States.* Chicago: University of Chicago Press for NBER.

Blackburn, McKinley L., and David E. Bloom. "The Distribution of Family Income: Measuring and Explaining Changes in the 1980s for Canada and the United States."

Blank, Rebecca M., and Maria J. Hanratty. "Responding to Need: A Comparison of Social Safety Nets in the United States and Canada."

Borjas, George, J. "Immigration Policy, National Origin, and Immigrant Skills: A Comparison of Canada and the United States."

Card, David, and W. Craig Riddell. "A Comparative Analysis of Unemployment in Canada and the United States."

Freeman, Richard B., and Karen Needels. "Skill Differentials in Canada in an Era of Rising Labor Market Inequality."

Lemieux, Thomas. "Unions and Wage Inequality in Canada and in the United States."

Riddell, W. Craig. "Unionization in Canada and the United States: A Tale of Two Countries."

Richard B. Freeman and Lawrence F. Katz, editors. 1994. *Differences and Changes in Wage Structures.* Chicago: University of Chicago Press for NBER.

Abowd, John, and Michael Bognanno. "International Differences in Executive and Managerial Compensation."

Abraham, Katherine G., and Susan Houseman. "Earnings Inequality in Germany."

Blanchflower, David, and Andrew Oswald. "International Wage Curves."

Blau, Francine, and Lawrence Kahn. "The Gender Earnings Gap: Some International Evidence."

Edin, Per-Anders, and Bertil Holmlund. "The Swedish Wage Structure: The Rise and Fall of Solidarity Wage Policy."

Erickson, Christopher, and Andrea Ichino. "Wage Differentials in Italy: Market Forces, Institutions, and Inflation."

Freeman, Richard B., and Robert Gibbons. "Getting Together and Breaking Apart: The Decline of Centralized Collective Bargaining."

Gregory, Robert, and Frank Vella. "Aspects of Real Wage and Employment Changes in the Australian Male Labour Market."

Katz, Lawrence F., Gary Loveman, and David Blanchflower. "A Comparison of Changes in the Structure of Wages in Four OECD Countries."

Kim, Dae-Il, and Robert Topel. "Labor Markets and Economic Growth: Lessons from Korea's Industrialization, 1970-1990.

Kreuger, Alan, and Jorn-Steffen Pischke. "A Comparative Analysis of East and West German Labor Markets Before and After Unification."

Schmitt, John. "The Changing Structure of Male Earnings in Britain, 1974-88."

Lisa Lynch, editor. 1994. *Training and the Private Sector: International Comparisons,* Chicago: University of Chicago Press and NBER.

Berg, Peter. "Strategic Adjustments in Training: A Comparative Analysis of the U.S. and German Automobile Industries."

Bishop, John. "Formal Training and its Impact on Productivity, Wages, and Innovation."

Blanchflower, David, and Lisa M. Lynch. "Training at Work: A Comparison of U.S. and British Youths."

Cameron, Stephen V., and James J. Heckman. "Determinants of Young Male Schooling and Training Choices."

Dolton, Peter, Gerald Makepeace, and John Treble. "Public and Private Sector Training of Youths in Britain."

Elias, Peter, Erik Hernaes, and Meredith Baker. "Vocational Education and Training in Britain and Norway."

Groot, W., J. Hartog, and H. Oosterbeek. "Returns to Within Company Schooling of Employees: The Case of the Netherlands."

Hashimoto, Masanori. "Employment Based Training in Japanese Firms in Japan and the U.S.: The Experience of Automobile Industries,"

Oulton, Nicholas, and Hilary Steedman. "A Comparison of the British, German and French Systems of Youth Training."

Soskice, David. "Reconciling Markets and Institutions: The German Apprenticeship System."

Weiss, Andrew. "Productivity Changes Associated with Learning by Doing."

Joel Rogers and Wolfgang Streeck, editors. 1994. *Works Councils: Consultation, Representation, Cooperation.* University of Chicago Press for NBER, forthcoming.

Bernard, Elaine. "Canada: Joint Committees on Occupational Health and Safety."

Brulin, Göran. "Sweden: Joint Councils Under Strong Unionism."

Escobar, Modesto. "Spain: Works Councils or Unions?"

Federowicz, Michal, and Anthony Levitas. "Poland: Councils Under Communism and Neo-Liberalism."

Freeman, Richard B., and Edward P. Lazear. "An Economic Analysis of Works Councils."

Müller-Jentsch, Walther. "Germany: From Collective Voice to Co-Management."

Regalia, Ida. "Italy: The Costs and Benefits of Informality."

Rogers, Joel. "The United States: Lessons from Abroad and Home."

Rogers, Joel, and Wolfgang Streeck. "The Study of Works Councils: Concepts and Problems."

Streeck, Wolfgang. "Works Councils in Europe: Combining Consultation and Representation."

Streeck, Wolfgang, and Sigurt Vitols. "The European Community: Between Mandatory Consultation and Voluntary Information."

Tchobanian, Robert. "France: From Conflict to Social Dialogue?"

Visser, Jelle. "The Netherlands: From Paternalism to Representation."

INDEX

230–231; and poverty, 230, 235–236; in U.S., vs. Canada, 198–199, 212–214; in U.S., vs. others, 226, 227; *see also* welfare benefits; welfare system; *and specific programs and types of programs*
social security programs, 158, 180; benefits, European, 21, 23; taxes, 160, 167–168; in U.S., 25
social wage, 23, 24
social welfare funds, and works councils, 122, 129
Soskice, D., 52, 91*n*13
South Korea: and education differential, 51, 224, 232; and inequality, 36, 58*n*13, 232
Spain: and employment protection, 237; mandated fringe benefits, 167–168, 181, 183, 184, 231; and social programs vs. flexibility, 162, **163**, **182**, 183, 231; and statutory regulations, **22**; and unions, 126–127, **128**, 237; and works councils, 97, 100, 102, 112, 126–130, **128**, 148, 149, 149*n*1, 151*n*15, 225
Stafford, Frank, 178, 185*n*18
Staines, Graham L., 150*n*4
Statistical Abstract of the United States, 26
Steedman, Hilary, 91*nn*
Streeck, Wolfgang, 97–153
strikes: in Italy, 136; in U.S., vs. Canada, 199; and works councils, 100, 108, 116, 117, 119, 129, 130, 131, 140, 225, 236
supervisors, 73, 98, 129
supply-demand-institutional (SDI) explanation, 44–49
Survey of Consumer Finances, 36
Swaim, Paul, 65
Sweden: and childcare and maternity policies, 178, **179**, 184, 231, 235; and female-to-male earnings ratios, **42**; and inequality, 36, **38**, **40**, 54, 58*n*13, 224, 228; and job turnover, 25*n*9; and pay, 9, 27*n*15; and pension plans, 180; and sick

leave program, 231; social programs vs. flexibility in, **163**, **182**; and training, 66, 67, 69, **70**, **71**; and unemployment, 181; and unions 16, **17**; and wage setting, 20, 51, 52, 53, 54, 58*n*14; and welfare benefits, 23, 24; and works councils, 102, 112, 130–135, 148, 149*n*1, 151*n*15, 152*n*26
Swedish Act on Board Representation for Employees in Joint Stock Companies and Cooperative Associations (1972), 132
Swedish Act on Codetermination at Work (1976), 130, 131–135
Swedish Shop Stewards Act (1974), 132
Swedish Work Environment Act, 132
Switzerland: 8, 10, 27*nn*, 52; and female-to-male earnings ratios, **42**; and unions, **17**

T

Tan, Hong, 91*n*22
tax credits, 211–212
taxes, 161; earnings before, 36; and housing policy, 172; and inequality, 58*n*11; for mandated fringe benefits, 167–168; and poverty rates, 230; and social programs, 160; training, on employers, 68–69, **89**, 90, 91*n*4; in U.S., vs. Canada, 195; and welfare benefits, 23
tax-transfer systems, 37
Taylorism, 126, 134, 135, 152*n*23
Tchobanian, Robert, 151*n*15
teamwork training, 74, 80
technical training, 74–75, 78, 226
technological change: and educated workers, 31, 46–47, 50, 55, 206; and training, 63–64, 67; and works councils, 100, 103, 109–110, 121, 126, 138
temporary workers, 118
tenant protection laws, 171–174, 231
Teulings, Coen N., 50, 57*n*8, 58*n*13